A Cure for the Common Company

Richard Safeer, MD

A Cure for the Common Company

A Well-Being Prescription for a Happier, Healthier, and More Resilient Workforce

WILEY

For general information on our other products and services or for technical support, please contact our Customer Care Department within the United States at (800) 762-2974, outside the United States at (317) 572-3993 or fax (317) 572-4002.

Wiley also publishes its books in a variety of electronic formats. Some content that appears in print may not be available in electronic formats. For more information about Wiley products, visit our web site at www.wiley.com.

Library of Congress Cataloging-in-Publication Data is Available:

ISBN 9781119899969 (Hardback)
ISBN 9781119899976 (ePDF)
ISBN 9781119899983 (ePub)

Cover Design: Wiley
Cover Image: © Calvindexter/Getty Images

SKY10038996_112922

———

To my wife, who was patient with me for years when my work–life balance wasn't balanced. For helping me lower my stress with her beautiful smile and joyful laughter.

To my parents, for creating a loving culture in our family (and driving us to Brooklyn).

To my children, for giving me pause to think about how their well-being impacts mine and how my well-being supports theirs.

To my siblings, cousins, nieces, and nephews, as well as the relatives who've since passed. Thanks for all the great Thanksgiving memories.

CONTENTS

A NOTE TO THE READER

THIS BOOK IS NOT INTENDED as a substitute for the medical advice of your own physician. The reader should regularly consult a physician in matters relating to their health.

This book is for educational purposes only and is not intended as specific professional advice for any organization.

Although the author has made every effort to ensure that the information in this book was correct at press time, the author does not assume and hereby disclaims any liability to any part for any loss, damage, or disruption caused by errors or omissions, whether such errors or omissions result from negligence, accident, or any other cause.

The author disclaims any liability whatsoever with respect to any loss, injury, or damage arising, directly or indirectly, from the use of this book.

The ideas expressed in this book are those of the author alone, and not those of Johns Hopkins Health System or Johns Hopkins Medicine.

ACKNOWLEDGMENTS

MY JOURNEY TO ARRIVING AT this book has been shaped by hundreds (possibly thousands) of peers, mentors, co-workers, authors, friends, researchers, speakers, leaders, and, of course, my family. Although I can't list everyone, I'd like to extend my appreciation to the following:

Meg Lucik, who has shared many years of my professional journey, and made many of the well-being culture building blocks come to life. My other colleagues in the Office of Well-Being at Johns Hopkins Medicine: Nicolette Amato, Tara Butler, Debi Celnik, Jennifer Salaverri, Carolyn Fowler, Lee Biddison, Suzanne Brockman, Julie Lavoie, and Daria McClamb. Former team members Wendy Bowen and Debbie Dang.

My manager, Inez Stewart, for advocating for the well-being of the Johns Hopkins Medicine workforce. My human resource colleagues who have worked alongside us for years: Jennifer Alexander, John Bowe, Lee-Ann Brazelton, Paul Brewer, Jennifer Clarke, Robyn Crowder, Mario Delgado, Theresa Forget, Jamestina Diop, Allisson Fritz, Laura Fricker, Mara Garcia, Sherita Golden, Jeff Goldman, Beth Gotjen, Kelly Greene, Nicki Hancock, Brentina Horshaw, Yariella Kerr-Donovan, Nancy Kinker, Elizabeth Edsall Kromm, Susan Kulik, Darlene Kurek, Denise Lannon, Stella Lee, Sharon Leitner, Destiny Lowery, Kris Lukish,

Maryalice Meister, Irish McClung, Yvonne Mitchell, Tim Moore, Tehani Mundy, Frederick Owusu, Essence Pierce, Dione Powell, Joe Ramacca, Leslie Rohde, Monica Sandoval, Michele Sedney, Jennifer Smith, David Strapelli, Beth Thierer, Julie Thomas, Misty Turner, Gaelle Valburn, Maura Walden, Beth Wilson, Michael Wittstadt, Carol Woodward, Aliyah Young, and those who have retired during my tenure.

The hundreds of Healthy at Hopkins champions supporting their peers.

My friends in finance: Jack Brossart, Keith Hall, Mike Larson, and Suzy Gerlak. Thanks for making sure we have a budget!

My colleagues in the legal department: Annette Fries and Neil Duke.

My colleagues in marketing and communications: Janet Anderson, Hope Byers, Mariann Calloway, Carla Chase, Kate Morrison, and Mia Scharper.

My faculty colleagues for your collaboration to bring world-class information to our well-being strategies and for serving as guests on our Ask the Expert program.

Cheryl Connors, Albert Wu, and members of the RISE teams. Matt Norvell, Paula Teague, and the rest of our chaplains. Karen Swartz and the department of psychiatry. Meghan Davis for leading our Total Worker Health effort. Beth Thierer, Kimberly Claiborne, and the EAP team.

My occupational health colleagues who contributed to work represented in this book: Amy Alfriend, Ed Bernacki, and Nimisha Kalia. The entire occupational health team for their challenging work with COVID-19 and contribution to navigating us through turbulent waters.

My colleague Angelo Mojica and his food service team, including the numerous dieticians who make it easier to choose healthy foods at Johns Hopkins Medicine every day.

The facilities, security, and environmental services teams for keeping our workplace safe and clean.

Every Hopkins leader who does their part to foster a well-being culture and every employee of Johns Hopkins Medicine. You make world-class healthcare possible.

Thank you, Judd Allen, for enhancing my understanding of workplace culture and its impact on employee health. I appreciate your peer support and encouragement of doing more celebrating!

My professional colleagues in the American College of Lifestyle Medicine: Susan Benigas, Noel Boyland, Cate Collings, Beth Frates, George Guthrie, Tyler Hemmingon, Julie Holtgrave, David Katz,

Kristen Collins, Padmaja Patel, Kaitlyn Pauly, Tom Rifai, Dexter Shurney, Ron Stout, Jean Tips, and Martin Tull.

My colleagues from other professional fields: Susan Brady, Bonnie Davis, Kerry Evers, Ron Goetzel, Susan Johnson, Al Lewis, Johns Harris, Michael O'Donnell, Janice and Jim Prochaska, Stacey Snelling, and Paul Terry. There are many more not listed here. You know who you are. Your collegiality and wisdom have helped me grow.

My colleagues from CareFirst BlueCross BlueShield: Dann Winn, Carrie Greene, Nancy Lesch, Jody Young, and Glenn Leary.

Fiona Shields and Emily Roberts, for joining Hopkins early on our journey to a well-being culture. Wellness Corporate Solutions made it possible for us to get off to a good start. Our Labcorp Employer Services team members: Shavise Glascoe, Lindsey Laborwit, Ann Namabiro, Emmaline Olson, Celeste Rose, and Laura Tringali.

Books aren't shaped alone, either. My book agent, Doug Hardy, for recognizing the importance of this work and finding a partner in Wiley. Lari Bishop for articulating the case for the book so that it made it an easy choice for Doug to snatch. Thanks for your patience, Zachary Schisgal and Jozette Moses, while I learned to navigate publishing my first book. Thanks to Russ Hall for guiding me through the writing process, researching examples, and shaping the book. My cousin Debbie Feit for her creative mind and giving the book some sparkle so that you don't fall asleep while reading (no money-back guarantee). Adaobi Obi Tulton for providing developmental editing services. Michelle Hacker for pulling it all together. Tim Moore and Gary June for helping me find people to read the book. Becky Robinson, Kelly Edmiston, Elizabeth Mars and the Weaving Influence team for helping me "Reach" a bigger audience.

Bonnie Maschinsky, for supporting our family while I continued my job and wrote at night and on weekends. My ninth-grade English teacher who said my writing wasn't good enough to be in the advanced group. I appreciate the lifetime of motivation to be a better writer.

Introduction

PAUL'S BEEN WORKING AT A large professional services company for more than 25 years. As technology accelerated to warp speed, the challenge of keeping a sane work practice became more difficult. Balancing his busy work schedule with his other commitments became increasingly challenging and finally caused him to focus on his well-being. Not only did he improve his diet and start running, but he also developed a meditation practice. The new habits improved his physical health, and being out in nature allowed him to decompress.

Kerry works at the same company. She recognizes that her well-being affects her performance and admits striving for balance in her personal and professional life is challenging. Like Paul, she is conscious of eating healthy foods, exercising, and the need for getting time away from work.

What makes Paul and Kerry different from many other employees at Accenture is that they are also managers. What makes Paul and Kerry different from most managers at all companies is that they are not only trying to keep themselves healthy and well, they are also making physical and mental health part of the normal conversation with their teams.[1] They even discuss mindfulness, a skill only recently, but

I

quickly, starting to seep into the vernacular of leadership. Paul goes as far as developing a team wellness plan and designating a team member for keeping well-being on the team agenda. Kerry's a trained mental health ally, there to help her colleagues when they are going through a tough time.

"A great place to work starts with a culture that enables all people to have the opportunity to reach their potential," says Ellyn Shook, Accenture's chief leadership and human resources officer. "Our cultural building blocks have served as our foundation for years—our behaviors, our beliefs, how we develop people and how we do business."

It's this philosophy that has contributed to Accenture's recognition as one of *Fortune*'s 100 Best Companies to Work For. And it's leaders like Paul and Kerry who have helped the company achieve 14 consecutive years as a great place to work.

Shook is one of many executives who recognize the impact of workplace culture on employee well-being. But how do we build a well-being culture and what are culture building blocks? When you type "workplace culture" into the Google search bar, you'll find more than 9 million results. However, when you enter "workplace-culture building blocks," you get one: an article on how to recruit physical therapists more effectively.[2] But have no fear—there's a prescription for a happier, healthier, and more resilient team and organization through building a well-being culture, and you can find it in these pages.

Contrast Accenture with a company across the street (figuratively speaking). Sam pulled himself out of bed after another restless night of sleep; count him among the majority of employees complaining of work-related insomnia.[3] Despite being tired and not feeling well, he drags himself to Toxic, Inc. Sam is not alone. Six out of 10 employees say they've gone to work sick (thank goodness this survey was before COVID-19),[4] many out of concern their employment status would otherwise be in jeopardy. Sam will eventually quit his job to escape the stress, joining many other Americans who've done the same to save their health and well-being.

How can you achieve the same success as Paul, Kerry, and Accenture and avoid being on the path of Toxic, Inc.? Every day, leaders in organizations small, large, private, and public are struggling to reconcile their own well-being with their work and figuring out how to support the health of their teams. Leaders and employees alike are struggling to overcome the pervasive and sometimes invisible workplace influences on their behaviors and mood. Many companies offer programs, a wellness portal and health-promoting policies, but the environment, the people, and the business priorities aren't always aligned. Employees need more—a lot more—for their well-being.

When the global pandemic hit in 2020, employee health and well-being became an urgent issue. Everyone faced new stressors, inside and outside of work. Isolation compounded the problem. Many families, communities, and organizations lost people they cared about. Some employees learned to work remotely, while others lost their jobs as employers struggled to get their footing.

Yet there were other companies like Accenture that stood out in this time of crisis. Organizations in which employees worked together, helped each other, and were recognized as places where people were glad they worked. Their cultures are a large part of why their employees are happy and resilient.

For some employers, it took a pandemic to realize the value of their employees' health and well-being. However, the fracturing of the workforce along the fault lines of well-being started long before. In the United States, employer-sponsored health insurance costs almost $8,000 for single coverage and more than $22,000 for family coverage and there is no end to the increases in sight.[5] That's a lot of donuts.

Employers have the real challenge of recruiting and retaining employees. In unhealthy workplace cultures, there is higher turnover. In addition to recruitment costs, vacancies take a toll on well-being. There are often overt or subtle messages that the work still needs to get done, albeit with fewer people.

Americans, as a group, aren't getting younger or healthier. The opposite is true. We have a nationwide culture of poor health and well-being. Chronic conditions are on the rise and we're one of the most stressed-out countries in the world.[6] And that was before the global pandemic. The leading causes of premature death in America are generally preventable. Now, pair that information with an aging workforce, a falling birth rate, a tighter labor market, and people needing to work longer than expected because they aren't financially prepared for retirement. We've been waiting for the tide to turn, for community leaders and politicians to make real change happen, but we're approaching the edge of the cliff. If companies and organizations want to be successful, which means having a viable and dependable workforce, they have no choice but to act now.

For decades, employers have recognized the role they could play and the importance of acting. A lot of companies have been trying. Consider the title of a recent *Forbes* column: "The Rise of the Chief Wellbeing Officer."[7] Count the number of articles on culture of health issues published in one week by the Society for Human Resource Management. Look at the growing number of universities offering degrees in health and wellness promotion to feed the demand from public and private organizations.

Leaders know the outcomes they would like to see and they're willing to make them a priority, but the wellness programs they offer—lunch and learns, biggest-loser contests, health-risk assessments, and the like—just aren't delivering. The real issue is that changing human behavior is too complicated to be shifted by transactional wellness tactics alone. If you are trying to live a healthy and well life, it's much easier to swim with the current of a workplace well-being culture.

In 2018, the majority of leaders from organizations representing more than 5.2 million employees around the globe conceded that they had not yet achieved a culture of well-being.[8] However, more than 80 percent of these employers without a culture of well-being aspired to create one. One challenge is that culture is a loose concept. They often don't know where to start and how to build a workplace well-being culture. Consequently, they throw money at it and are disappointed when not much changes.

What you'll discover in this book is that creating a culture of well-being doesn't take much money. It may only take you (well, maybe invite a few friends to help). Leaders who take a systematic approach by using the six building blocks of a well-being culture described in this book can impact their team's well-being and even the whole company, depending on your role in the organization. By building a more positive well-being culture, you'll be able to unlock employee engagement, morale, and productivity while improving the health and resiliency of your team.[9] When you act, you'll be able to compete for top talent. Frankly, a well workplace can make every leader's job more satisfying and enjoyable.

WHY CULTURE IS THE SOLUTION

We know, and research proves, that a key factor in anybody's ability to achieve their health goals is whether those goals are supported by the people they're closest to—at home and at work. We've all had the experience of working toward a goal with a buddy or family member, but we don't always recognize the more subtle influences of the other people around us and our work environment. But can organizations leverage these forces to support employees?

Compared to pervasive and often subtle cultural influences, employer-driven health and wellness tactics can feel transactional—or worse, hypocritical or manipulative. In one survey, 75 percent of respondents said their companies offered "wellness programs" strictly out of self-interest.[10] That means that three out of four employees on your team potentially feel coerced rather than supported in achieving their personal health goals. And just because resources are available doesn't mean people can or will take advantage of them, especially the people who need them most. The biggest reason these programs are only partially successful, though, is that *they expect the individuals to bear the full responsibility of changing their behavior despite the influence of their environment, rather than in conjunction with a supportive environment.*

Most people want to be challenged at work, but not to the point of causing excess stress. Unfortunately, work is a primary stressor in most people's lives, regardless of age or life stage. A culture that supports a well workforce can have a profound effect on avoiding anxiety, burnout, disengagement, and poor mental health. Companies that have a genuine caring culture have happier and healthier employees who experience a higher sense of well-being.[11]

I've been in this line of work for over 25 years. I have built strategies, executed plans, trained leaders, and measured results. I've explored research on individual and organizational change and the influence of companies on employee well-being. I've been a change agent. I've succeeded and I've fallen short. What I hear repeatedly is that most leaders genuinely care about the people on their teams: they want them to have lower stress levels, they want them to feel healthy and happy, and they want them to be excited to come to work! But they don't know how to make that happen. Culture is complicated and cultural change is not something you necessarily learn in college or when you're promoted to a leadership position . . . or ever! It's especially hard when it comes to health. It's a challenging and potentially uncomfortable topic, and leaders may project their own experiences onto others, which may get these leaders and organizations into trouble.

Leaders need guidance in their efforts to help employees, and that is the practical promise of this book. The missing piece for most leaders and companies is *a method and framework for influencing and shaping a culture of health. A Cure for the Common Company* offers practical steps for putting each well-being culture building block in place, avoiding the things that can derail your effort, and then providing specific ways to measure whether your plan is working.

That is my big goal, my big passion. I want more people to be happy, healthy, and resilient. I want more leaders to feel joy in their work with their teams, and I want more organizations to be successful and feel proud of their support for employee health and well-being.

1

Inspiration from a Fire Truck

The Case for Building a Workplace Well-Being Culture

ONE DAY, JUST A FEW months after starting my job at Johns Hopkins, I was walking on the hospital campus when I saw a big red truck parked in front of one of our buildings. I was deep in thought, and my brain registered it as a fire truck. As I passed by, though, something prompted me to take a second look. Turned out it wasn't a fire truck at all. It was a soda truck.

This sugar dispensary was parked under an old sign—a capital "E" on a round board—telling anyone needing help that this was the entrance to the emergency room of the hospital, or it had been at one time. Inside that building, some of the brightest minds and best caregivers in the world were treating people with diabetes, heart disease, and other increasingly common chronic illnesses that are partly caused by sugar or made worse by it. Outside the building . . . well, there was no escaping the irony.

For me, the irony was especially meaningful, because supporting the health and well-being of the employees in that hospital was my responsibility. I was certain some of the soda going through the delivery dock was going into the mouths of my colleagues shortly thereafter. When I arrived at Johns Hopkins, the dedication and commitment of the workforce toward taking care of our patients became quite apparent — even if it came at the cost of our own health. The same painstaking steps implemented to optimize the care of our patients were not being taken for our own workforce.

My story, of course, began much earlier than my employment at Hopkins. I grew up in a time when riding my bike and playing hide-and-seek in the neighborhood was a regular part of the day, sometimes well into sunset. Physical activity was a part of my fabric, my social circles, and my neighborhood culture. Finding time to play in the neighborhood got a little more difficult for me when I entered the workforce. However, at the outset of my career as a physician, movement at work was part of the job. I don't know how many steps I walked in the halls of the hospital during residency or between patient rooms during my first three jobs after finishing training. Moving from patient to patient is part of my professional culture.

My career trajectory had changed by the time I was 40. I became the Medical Director for Prevention at a large and prominent regional health insurance company. I found myself sitting in front of a computer more often and in meetings. When my wife identified "love handles," I realized that I spent most of my waking hours sitting in a workplace that wasn't supporting my health. I had been more than happy to partake in whatever snacks and treats my co-workers brought to share. To make matters worse, insomnia had started to creep into my nights. There it was, folks. I was married, with three kids and a house in suburbia. I had hit middle age and my health and well-being were deteriorating. I should have known better — and done better. I studied nutrition in college, and I had strayed from the fundamentals.

Along my career and health journey, I discovered that we don't need to choose one or the other. It started while working at George Washington University. While pursuing some academic work related to cholesterol, I stumbled upon an article about an employer helping its employees lower their cholesterol, then another company successfully supporting employee well-being, and so on.

Happiness, health, and work may exist together. In fact, when they do, it makes for a more resilient organization. Of course, our home and our community play a big role in our happiness and health as well. Yet because we spend most of our waking hours working, our thoughts and behaviors during these hours strongly influence our well-being. As a leader, manager, health promotion specialist, human resource professional, life-style medicine clinician, or any other professional influencing employees, you have a unique opportunity to create a happier, healthier, and more resilient team and workforce. You might even like the way it feels yourself!

WILLPOWER IS A FAILED STRATEGY (FOR MOST OF US)

Albert Einstein famously stated that insanity is "doing the same thing over and over again and expecting different results." Yet, every New Year's Eve, millions of people make one or more New Year's resolutions or goals. It may only be weeks or perhaps a month or two before our best intentions start to lie in the corner like a heap of dirty laundry. A year later we do it again; rinse and repeat.

Fewer than 10 percent of Americans feel they are successful keeping their New Year's resolutions, and yet we keep trying, year after year.[1] I don't know how many times I've stopped eating chocolate. While choosing a date to start a healthy habit or quit an unhealthy one can be an important part of achieving a healthier lifestyle, we've all come to understand there must be a better, more successful approach.[2]

There are plenty of reasons to have health and well-being goals. Foremost, in the wake of a global pandemic, there is an epidemic of mental health challenges. Our stress levels and feelings of happiness (or sadness) impact many, if not most of our other health choices. Who hasn't sat down in front of the TV with a bowl of ice cream or a bag of potato chips after a stressful day at work? When I am stressed, I forage the kitchen for a hidden piece of chocolate. The same health challenges that plagued us before the arrival of COVID-19, such as two-thirds of us being overweight or obese, millions still smoking, and fewer than 25 percent getting the recommended amount of exercise, still exist—possibly worse than before.[3]

All too often, our society praises individual achievement, while under-appreciating collective efforts. This starts early with elementary school report cards, art projects, and athletic performance. Don't forget those 100 percent attendance awards! Yes, sometimes teams are recognized, but this is America, the land of "rugged individualism," and by and large, the expectation is that we make advances on our own, including with our well-being. Even workplaces have traditionally focused on the individual's role in his or her own happiness and health rather than the collective well-being of the organization.[4] Hats off to those who can improve their health and well-being without anyone's help.

However, for most of us, we continue to learn and understand that it is communities that have the bigger and more lasting influence on our behaviors, beliefs, and thoughts. Dan Buettner traveled the world to better understand how pockets of centenarians reached their ripe ages. His work, articulated in *The Blue Zones*, highlighted shared aspects of these communities that contribute to their longevity, including the strength of their relationships and the like-mindedness of their health practices.

In the same context, through their book *Connected,* Nicholas Christakis and James Fowler decoded the science behind our strong propensity for sharing the same behaviors and emotions as those with whom we keep company. Not only do our family members, friends, and co-workers influence our choices and thoughts, but so do more distant relatives and friends of friends—for example, when my wife's hair salon keeps the bowl of chocolate on the front desk full so she can grab a piece before heading home. I sniff it out on days of distress. Without having ever met my wife's hairdresser, she influences my behavior every six weeks.

So why aren't organizations taking advantage of what we know to be true? We are more likely to be healthy and well when we are in a supportive group, team, and community that has aligned behaviors, beliefs, and attitudes around well-being (aka, well-being culture). Perhaps it's because we haven't previously clearly articulated the importance of organizational well-being culture and how to shape it. Our co-workers shouldn't approach a New Year's resolution alone when we know they are much more likely to be successful in a workplace well-being culture. This is not such an insane idea.

A WELL-BEING CULTURE IS A COMPETITIVE ADVANTAGE

Most people want to work in an environment in which they feel valued and supported. People generally know what is healthy, but they face challenges adopting healthy behaviors and getting rid of unhealthy ones. Consequently, many people in the workforce seek employers that support health and happiness, and those who already work for these employers tend to stay longer at their jobs.[5] It's often said that people don't leave their jobs—they leave their managers.[6] Being a manager who creates a well-being culture supportive of happiness and health guarantees a more satisfied, appreciative, and engaged employee as well as a more resilient team.

In addition to improving recruitment and retention, a well-being culture also results in improved team performance and decreased absenteeism.[7] These benefits alone lead to a positive financial picture. Yes, creating a well-being culture at work can even make it easier to create healthy habits. [8] These healthier lifestyle choices lead to lower medication needs and fewer physician visits and hospitalizations. Better health makes it easier to be happy.

Granted, there is skepticism that workplace wellness creates savings.[9] However, as you'll come to learn by reading this book, creating a well-being culture is a much more comprehensive approach and addresses concerns about a lot more than money itself. A well-being culture is nothing short of an essential element of a successful organization.

THE FOUNDATION OF EMPLOYEE HEALTH AND WELL-BEING

The culture-based approach is markedly different from most tools available in the workplace wellness industry. The "culture" piece is almost always missing. Historically, employers have focused on individual motivation and effort. Typically, the employee is encouraged to complete a health survey, seek coaching where needed, and read a health newsletter. Annual events such as health fairs and contests are sometimes thrown into the mix. They have a feel-good quality that fits with a culture preoccupied with self-determination and can be helpful to a small number of people. While inexpensive and easy to deliver, such efforts rarely address the underlying conditions that lead people toward unhealthy practices. Fortunately, some employers have progressed beyond this one-dimensional approach, but only to a limited degree. The elements of workplace culture that work against happiness, health, and resiliency are typically ignored.

The wellness industry's playbook offers excellent self-help tools that would be much more beneficial if delivered in a well-being culture. It's helpful and often necessary to partner with a wellness vendor to bring many aspects of culture building to the table. However, culture building has many more ingredients, and many key elements can only be pursued effectively internally. To make matters more complicated, "culture of health" is becoming a buzz phrase driven by clever workplace wellness marketing departments seeking to make their products more appealing. I hope you will not be distracted by shiny new packaging and instead, create the well-being culture you want and need.

Defining a Culture of Health

Excerpts within this box are from R. Safeer and J. Allen, "Defining a Culture of Health in the Workplace," *JOEM* 61, no. 11 (2019): 863–867.

Webster's defines "culture" as the "behaviors and beliefs characteristic of a particular social, ethnic, or age group." While well-intentioned, the same organizations, researchers and thought leaders that promoted wellness as a product, have rebranded under the buzz phrase, "culture of health." Unfortunately, the meaning behind "culture of health" has been hijacked from the social sciences, and what is being promoted in the commercial space often lacks any reference to key culture frameworks and concepts that are shared in this book. Your organization will be better served to appreciate that a culture of health is a web of social influences that manifests itself in shared healthy beliefs and behaviors.

The analogy to a web is fitting for several reasons. Webs are complicated and intricate works that connect a common structure in multiple ways. When pulling a web in one direction, it distorts the shape of the web both near and far. Similarly, the words and behaviors of an individual certainly affect those next to us, but also reverberate to those connected to our immediate circle and so on (like a ripple in the water after a stone makes its initial splash).

Furthermore, webs can get messy when tugged suddenly and forcefully. Webs are fragile and need to be handled with care. Sudden movements can have irreparable consequences, so thoughtful approaches on how to shape your well-being culture are warranted.

One goal of building a well-being culture is to align workplace influences with healthy beliefs and behaviors. The individual and cultural approaches to building a well workplace and work team are complimentary. In my experience, a supportive culture provides the needed foundation for individual efforts to succeed. The more progress individuals make with their own well-being, the more they can contribute back to the well-being culture. Some of the advantages of creating and sustaining a healthy culture that are not inherent in traditional workplace well-being programs include:

- Healthy cultures touch everyone—not just those who are already interested in improving their well-being. You don't need to "sign up" or "show up" to reap the benefits of a healthy workplace culture. In

(Continued)

a workplace well-being culture, you are immersed in an environment supportive of your well-being journey.

- It is easier to make progress in employee health if people continue their healthy behaviors. Supportive cultures keep people on their healthy path, while unsupportive cultures thwart New Year's resolutions.
- Building new positive practices is easier in a supportive culture. A supportive culture increases the likelihood of developing new healthy habits, attitudes, and beliefs.
- A well-being culture improves employee morale. Most people want to feel cared for and benefit from caring for others. An organization with a well-being culture inherently has created a sense of community where everyone is rowing together, in the same direction, toward a healthier destination. This collective effort undoubtedly improves the sense of community and makes for a more resilient organization.

THE PATH TO A WELL-BEING CULTURE

For most of you, *well-being culture* is a new phrase, but *wellness* is not. However, my guess is that the meaning of "wellness" remains elusive given that it is used in so many ways. Understanding the history of wellness can make it easier to appreciate its contribution to individual well-being, as well as its shortcomings.

The history of "wellness" starts with "health." Just a few years after World War II ended, the World Health Organization offered this definition of "health": "Not merely the absence of disease or infirmity but a state of complete physical, mental and social wellbeing."[10] In 1959, Halbert L. Dunn, in his seminal article "High-Level Wellness for Man and Society," called for more research and greater effort for a "positive orientation toward life and society."[11]

Meanwhile, employers started taking an interest in the health of their employees. Blue Cross was founded in 1929 to help patients in Dallas, many of whom were public school teachers, pay for their healthcare.[12] Employee Assistance Programs (EAPs) can be traced back to the 1930s, when some companies began to offer interventions over concerns about alcoholism and the resource expanded in the 1950s to support mental health issues.[13,14]

The postwar cultural shift that promoted fitness spanned decades. Depending on when you were born, you might remember Jack LaLanne from the 1960s, Rocky Balboa from the 1970s, or Jane Fonda from the 1980s. EAPs expanded their offerings in the 1970s as companies took interest in workplace wellness as a cost containment strategy.[15]

Big corporate wellness programs, such as Johnson & Johnson's *Live for Life* program, began leading the way in 1978, and were mostly concerned with exercise and weight control. Around the same time, the National Wellness Institute (NWI) was formed. Dr. Hettler (one of the founders of NWI) released the "Six Dimensions of Wellness Model,"[16] one of the earliest of many other wellness models to follow suit. The 1980s brought rise to other wellness-oriented organizations, such as the Wellness Councils of America.

Evidence of the advantages of worksite wellness grew gradually, until in the 1990s the federal government launched the Healthy People 2000 initiative encouraging 75 percent of employers with 50 or more employees to offer health promotion services as a benefit.[17]

As the science of medicine started to accelerate and new drugs, surgical techniques, and diagnostic tests became available, healthcare continued to move away from the foundation of health—nutrition, exercise, sleep, and the rest of what we inherently know to be good for us. Healthcare was leaving a void. As more advances were deployed, healthcare costs started to rise. Good relationships, movement, sleeping well, and basking in nature are free (or at least a lot less expensive)! Conditions were ripe for a new industry to emerge that improves health at a much lower cost than remedial or diagnostic measures. Employers were sure to be interested since most were starting to cover the cost of health insurance as a benefit to attract and retain employees. As health insurance costs started to rise, a less costly option grew more attractive.

For decades, workplace-wellness companies popped up to offer simple solutions to complex problems. While these companies had the best intentions, they mostly failed to produce the results they promised because they didn't address the root causes of why individuals weren't reaching their optimal state of being. When "wellness" business started to suffer, the adoption of "well-being" was eagerly promoted. It was a chance to give their company a makeover. However, like previous attempts, and although programs and outcomes vary from one organization to another, collectively, their effectiveness is questionable.[18]

Current well-being strategies don't address the essential elements of building a healthy culture that are shared in this book. To make matters more complicated, now "culture of health" is becoming a buzz phrase. Again, many of the same people driving a for-profit industry looking to genuinely help, but not completely understanding the science, are just rebranding the same old stuff.[19]

The current wellness market includes supplements, anti-aging products, and a dizzying array of self-help apps. This wellness economy is a colossal global industry, estimated to be $4.5 trillion in "value"![20] In this book, I am offering you a path to achieve a well-being culture for your team and organization that doesn't require you to put a mud pack on your face each night (although I am not opposed to smooth skin). You can create a well-being culture that supports the continuum of well-being. That means happiness, health, and resilience are included!

IS IT WELLNESS OR WELL-BEING?

If you're looking for a conversation that might not have an end, ask a friend to explain the difference between wellness and well-being. The World Health Organization defines *wellness* as "a state of complete physical, mental, and social well-being, and not merely the absence of disease or infirmity." I think of well-being as a state of mind and body that fluctuates on a continuum, based on countless variables. To me, well-being is not a constant state, but rather an ongoing journey with a destination of wellness. For the purposes of this book, I will use *well-being* to describe a journey to wellness.

Frankly, I think you can embrace either term. Given that everyone is on their own well-being journey (we're all different), it makes sense that I'm encouraging you to embrace your own definition of well-being, which might be the same as your definition of wellness. If someone tries correcting you, pay no attention to this minutia. What's important is that you learn what you need to feel well and then come to understand how to attain the state of well-being that you desire.

Different segments of the healthcare industry use related phrases. In the occupational medicine field, *employee health and productivity management* is quite similar to *employee health and well-being*. Even the trending *population health* can be used to refer to employee health and well-being when working with employee populations. A well-being culture in the workplace though, is a separate concept from each of these terms. If I'm doing my job right, you'll come to embrace the full meaning of this phrase by the end of this book.

Johnson & Johnson: Early Adopters of the Well-Being Culture

Johnson & Johnson (J&J) is one of the largest companies at the forefront in addressing employee health and well-being. More than 75 years ago, J&J created a credo that squarely focused on health and well-being; not only for its customers, but also for its employees.

A central portion of the Johnson & Johnson Credo is:

> We are responsible to our employees who work with us throughout the world. We must provide an inclusive work environment where each person must be considered as an individual. We must respect their diversity and dignity and recognize their merit. They must have a sense of security, fulfillment, and purpose in their jobs. Compensation must be fair and adequate and working conditions clean, orderly, and safe. **We must support the health and well-being of our employees and help them fulfill their family and other personal responsibilities.** Employees must feel free to make suggestions and complaints. There must be equal opportunity for employment, development, and advancement for those qualified. We must provide highly capable leaders and their actions must be just and ethical.

While only one sentence of the excerpt is highlighted to make a point, every sentence of the paragraph reflects and impacts employee health and well-being. In the context of the full credo, health and well-being are raised well before the financial obligations to shareholders. The way J&J conducts business serves as an exemplary model.

THE EMBERS ARE HOT

Whether you get the news from an actual newspaper or the internet, you are likely aware that chronic diseases (such as heart disease, cancer, and type II diabetes) have not been cured. If anything, more people are getting diagnosed with these conditions each year. Unhealthy behaviors are primary factors in the seven leading causes of death—heart disease, cancer, stroke, respiratory diseases, accidents, Alzheimer's, and diabetes. Together they account for more than 70 percent of all deaths in the United States. The COVID-19 pandemic illustrates the benefit of healthy lifestyles. Those with healthy behaviors have stronger immune systems, which are more likely to protect us from the devastating possibilities of this infection.

Behaviors, such as walking outside, eating nutritious food, and getting good sleep not only help our physical health but also our mental health; which, by the way, for many people, is also in shambles. More than 1 in 10 adult Americans are depressed,[21] and more than half report an unhealthy amount of stress in their lives from a number of different sources—including work.[22] The economic and social costs are a tremendous additional burden to individuals, businesses, and communities.

COVID-19 also challenged our resilience as individuals, and collectively as teams and organizations. Why is it some people, some teams, and some companies were able to withstand the uncertainty and the new challenges of the swiftly changing public health and social dynamics? They were equipped with healthy behaviors and constructive attitudes, combined with supportive and competent leadership and peers as well as necessary tools and resources.

We must respect the many cultures within which our employees live. Our employees are part of their family culture, community, ethnic, and possibly religious cultures, as well as sports, hobbies, and a variety of other subcultures (to be explored in Chapter 2). All these cultures add up to the individual's collective experiences, which play a role in how one impacts, and is impacted by, the culture in the workplace. By understanding the complexity of the human experience, employers stand a better chance of being more supportive so that employees can have a healthy workday, which will carry over outside of the workplace. You can't do this alone, however. You need a team.

WHO IS ON THE WELL-BEING CULTURE TEAM?

To increase the likelihood of creating a well workplace culture, everyone needs to be rowing in the same direction. We each affect the happiness and health of the individuals on our team and every person with whom we work. Leaders and managers have been ill-equipped to guide their organizations and teams forward on this path. The following subsections identify the other key players who can be significant contributors to healthy workplace cultures.

Human Resources

The human resources (HR) department is at the core of the employee experience. HR is responsible for policies, hiring practices, benefits, and many of the other ingredients (culture connection points) that shape the culture. Yet, the conversation usually falls short of a comprehensive look at the influence of the workplace on health and well-being. This could change. It's not unreasonable to think a well workplace culture rises to the same level of importance (or higher) as the disability claims, retention strategies, and benefit analysis, all of which, by the way, would be improved with a meaningful well-being culture.

There are plenty of examples of how experts in the human resources community have made substantial contributions, albeit often unknowingly, to create a well-being culture, by owning many practices, such as creating a safe space to work and fostering respect, diversity, inclusion, and professional development. There is, however, room for growth in developing human resources professionals to expand their repertoire to include happiness, health, and resilience. In fact, such efforts will serve to further improve existing efforts to promote employee engagement, high performance, and ethical behavior.

Occupational Health

For more than 50 years, occupational medicine has made an important contribution to protecting the health and promoting the safety of the workforce. These healthcare professionals (I was one of them in my third job) are experts in identifying safety risks and treating injuries and diseases born out of workplace lapses in precautions. Thanks to this group of professionals, we have created cultures of safety in the workplace. The Occupational Safety and Health Administration was established to evaluate the science in this field, make policy recommendations, provide support to employers, and oversee the maintenance of safe working environments.

While these professionals make an important contribution to the health and well-being of the workforce, there is always room for growth. Occupational medicine practitioners could be leading the charge of building healthy workplace cultures (or at least supporting and reinforcing the efforts). There is a clear connection between health, well-being, and workplace safety. When employees come to work well rested, physically fit, and well nourished, they are less likely to have accidents. Employees who have substance-abuse addictions and mental health challenges are more likely to have accidents. The success of creating a culture of safety by the occupational medicine community should not overshadow the need to create a culture of health and well-being. This is a key gap in many occupational medicine programs, a gap that can be filled by these practitioners learning the key concepts and strategies shared in this book.

Health Promotion Specialists

Health promotion specialists have a broad portfolio, but at its core, their education and training make them highly qualified to help shape positive health behaviors, attitudes, and beliefs. Perhaps there is already a health promotion specialist within your organization. They specifically chose this path to help others adopt healthy behaviors. Unfortunately, all too often their goals aren't given adequate support. Many organizations incorrectly conclude that if they have a health promotion specialist in place, the health and well-being of the workforce is being addressed. It doesn't work this way. Cultures only shift when a critical mass of folks rows in the same direction.

Lifestyle Medicine

Let me add one last layer to the mix. Lifestyle medicine is the use of behaviors such as healthier eating, movement, not smoking or drinking alcohol, getting adequate rest, building positive relationships, and limiting stress levels to treat and prevent disease. Lifestyle medicine is a growing field of medicine, often embraced by clinicians tired of doing the same thing (writing prescriptions) and getting the same results (surgeries and hospitalizations). Lifestyle medicine makes a valuable contribution to the range of options patients may use to address their health concerns. However, too often it is an individual sport. It puts the onus on the patient. While this may work for some, it falls short of the support a well-being culture brings that can make it easier to build and maintain healthy lifestyle habits. I will use the term *lifestyle* throughout this book to refer to the examples of positive behaviors stated earlier in this paragraph.

A lifestyle medicine practitioner might be a valuable addition to your organization. However, to give your employees a fighting chance to benefit from the clinician's wisdom, you'll be well served to create a well-being culture so they can build and sustain the healthy lifestyle habits their doctors, coaches, or nurses are teaching and preparing them to embrace.

THE WELL-BEING CULTURE BUILDING BLOCKS

In the same article that my colleague Judd Allen and I defined a culture of health, we also laid out six building blocks described below and in Figure 1.1.[23] Collectively they provide a conceptual map for culture change and analysis. These building blocks overlap and sometimes the bricks are hard to differentiate from the mortar. Together they make a strong foundation.

1. Shared Values—Organizations have shared values, often articulated through mission and vision statements, business, and strategic objectives. For a workplace culture of health to flourish, well-being needs to be a priority.
2. Social Climate—The social cohesiveness and morale of a group are determinants of health. How people treat each other greatly influences our emotional and mental health, which in turn influences our behaviors that impact our physical health. Working in a nonjudgmental, supportive environment contributes to a positive approach, which in turn contributes to feeling good about the individuals with whom one works.
3. Norms—Norms are the collective behaviors of a group. People often conform to group behavior. This can be great when the group is making healthy choices and harmful when the team has unhealthy habits.

Figure 1.1   The Well-Being Culture Building Blocks

Source: R. Safeer and J. Allen, "Defining a Culture of Health in the Workplace," *JOEM*, 61, no. 11 (2019): 863–867. Reproduced with permission of Wolters Kluwer Health, Inc.

4. Culture Connection Points—Cultures have formal and informal ways of "connecting" with the individuals who make up the culture. Culture Connection Points are any form of interaction between the organization and the employee which has the potential to influence their well-being. For example, policies and programs.

5. Peer Support—Co-workers and friends play a major role in the choices we make and how we feel about ourselves. Whether or not we succeed in building and maintaining healthy habits is largely dependent on the support we get from those around us. Employers can provide strategies that encourage peers to support each other.

6. Leadership Engagement—Organizational leaders play an important role in fostering a workplace well-being culture. Executives, managers, health promotion professionals, and wellness committee members are all influential. Leaders can make it easier for members of the team to practice healthy lifestyles and feel good about themselves, their job, and their employer. Leaders can create conditions that support people in their quest for better health and well-being.

HOW I HELP HOPKINS GET HEALTHY

I was hired in 2012 to be the medical director for the employer health program (EHP—employee self-insured health plan). I really wasn't looking to stay in the insurance side of healthcare (I had just left BlueCross BlueShield). I accepted the job because I discovered during the recruitment process that EHP didn't have what I knew to be a viable plan to support the health and well-being of the workforce. Not only did that turn out to be the case, but also the human resources department was juggling a number of other priorities and wasn't focused on the well-being culture. Having become passionate about the role the employer can play in the happiness and health of the workforce (and their families and community), I took the calculated bet that I would grow my job into something bigger than figuring out which health screenings should be promoted.

The tie between employee health and well-being and offering world class patient care was obvious to me. However, with few visible signs of a healthy workplace culture, I wondered if I was alone in this conclusion. After studying many documents and presentations and interviewing many people who were at Hopkins long before I arrived, this is what I learned: I found that in 2007, leaders from across the Johns Hopkins Health System and the Johns Hopkins University banded together to take a coordinated step in supporting the health and well-being of the 60,000 people who make up the organization. Our marketing and communications department dreamed up the pithy name "Healthy at Hopkins" and gave us a contemporary logo. The big kick-off event drew many leaders and many more employees for a grand gesture display of a group walk.

With such a grandiose inauguration, what went wrong? Several things. Unfortunately, not as much planning effort was invested in the long-term strategy and success. The presentations that had been given leading up to the launch spelled out the problems (what health maladies afflicted the employees), but didn't provide the solutions. As a result, the enthusiasm quickly waned and all that was left was a few people sitting in a room together trying to figure out what to do next. The leaders who had the energy to launch the ambitious movement didn't have the energy to keep their attention on the initiative. The founders of Healthy at Hopkins never built an infrastructure to sustain the effort or determined a path to follow.

When I arrived in 2012, Healthy at Hopkins mostly lay dormant for the previous five years, except for the name and annual walk. Knowing there was a lot of work to do, I began conversations with a few stakeholders about how to create a comprehensive approach. One of the essential pieces I recommended was for this core group to start by adopting some best practices and to get a roadmap in place.[24] A second was to convey that our strategy needed to be more than a series of programs. We needed to build a well-being culture. Finally, we needed to realign priorities such that the focus of success was neither on the performance of the EHP, the profitability of an outside well-being vendor, nor the academic achievement of involved faculty (the stakeholders currently leading the discussions), but rather on supporting the happiness, health, and resilience of the workforce. It seems intuitive, but think about what competing priorities are interfering with your company's success in creating a well-being culture.

After making the connection between the soda truck parked outside the old emergency room and the impact of soda on the health of our employees, I redirected my walk to inside the building. Sure enough, there was soda everywhere: the cafeteria, vending machines, gift shops, and served at our meetings! Our culture embraced unhealthy beverages. The widespread presence of soda, along with the visual cues, product placement, and financial incentive (at the time, a soda cost less than the same size bottle of water) were all contributing to a culture of unhealthy nutrition. This approach was making it easier for our workforce to accept that drinking soda was the norm—that it's okay. While we might be caring for patients who are harmed by these drinks, it's okay for us. How was I going to change this culture? My first order of business would be to propose creating a healthy beverage norm where healthy beverages are more available and desirable. This symbolic step would turn heads and put a stake in the ground. We were going to create a healthy and well workplace culture.

Put Your Own Mask on First

While this is not a self-help book, it is essential you address your own happiness and health so that you are ready and able to support the well-being of your team. Just as a flight attendant instructs you to put your own oxygen mask on first before you can help those around you, you can't be your best self without self-care. Your well-being affords you the capacity and skills necessary to fill your role in building and supporting a well-being culture. You certainly don't need to be perfect, but you must continue to explore your own well-being needs (and take steps on your path to wellness) in order to better appreciate the possible well-being challenges of those on your team. Rest assured, when you build a well-being culture with your team, you will also benefit.

THAT'S A WRAP—LET'S GET STARTED

There's one small problem with the title of this book, *A Cure for the Common Company*. There's nothing common about any company. Every company is different. While this book provides the framework for creating a well-being culture, it's not as simple as getting the brownie mix out of the cupboard (maybe a bad analogy for a health-related book) and following the recipe. Human behavior is messy stuff. Put a bunch of humans together in one workplace and it is even messier!

Instead of using the word *create*, you'll often see me use the word *shape* or *support*. Following the tenets in this book will allow you to shape the culture. You can't control everything. Not when it comes to human behavior at least. That's what makes this work so challenging. However, the more closely you follow the prescription, the more quickly you and your colleagues will begin to benefit. Shaping a well-being culture is a very intentional strategy. Following the framework shared in this book will increase the likelihood of a successful transformation of your work team and organization. This book will provide you the essence of what constitutes a well-being culture. It's best if several stakeholders within your organization read the book so that you share a common language and understanding of the process of well-being culture building. By the end of the book, you will be prepared to make a plan, and implement, measure, and improve your strategy.

You must pay special attention to your own unique circumstances. You can't look over the shoulder of your friend at a different company and get the right answers. You can get some good ideas (and some bad ones too), but every company is unique. While you will succeed if you follow the culture building strategy, you will likely have some failures along the way. It's okay. It's to be expected. Hasn't your company failed at something else before? It's just important to set expectations and don't give up the first time something doesn't go as planned. Step back, assess, and re-address.

Any leader who is serious about supporting their team and any organization that is serious about supporting their workforce needs to shape and support a well-being culture. I think you'll be surprised by the number and type of ingredients necessary to create this healthy culture — things that traditional workplace wellness never comes close to touching. Your daily behaviors and the complex set of beliefs and attitudes that exist within your social constructs at work, at home, and in your community are what truly influences our happiness, health, and resiliency.

2

Getting Personal

How Our Subcultures Influence Our Well-Being

——

WHEN SARAH KAPLAN WORKED THE night shift for *The Washington Post*, she wound up averaging three to four hours of sleep a day. Her sleep-inducing strategies for off hours included soothing music, dull podcasts, yoga, meditation, and chamomile tea, all with poor results. The prescription sleep aids she tried left her unrested and groggy. When she finally did fall asleep, at work, with her cheek pressed against her notes, her boss sent her home, and she wasn't upset about it. In her 14 months on a 9 p.m. to 6 a.m., five-day-a-week shift, her short-term memory faded, her hair fell out, and she said she had the sleep habits "of a colicky infant."[1] The health risks for such shift workers are high, ranging from upset stomach, nausea, diarrhea, heartburn, insomnia, greater risk of injuries or accidents, to diabetes, cardiovascular disease, obesity, ulcers, and depression.[2] Not a pretty picture.

It's hard to believe that Sarah will feel better without addressing the underlying reason for her poor health, and it's also difficult to conceive of any person achieving their ideal well-being state if they're not living and working in supportive cultures. Fortunately, there is a process for shaping a well-being workplace culture. As you can imagine, the larger the team or organization, the more planning, time, and resources are needed to influence and shape the well-being culture. One of the main reasons for this additional challenge tied to the size of your organization is the number of subcultures.

A workplace well-being culture is the outcome of a complex set of social influences that are in essence shaped by the six building blocks introduced in Chapter 1. A subculture is the collection of behaviors and attitudes of a specific group of people within the larger culture, who share a commonality like working the night shift.

Most employees are part of many subcultures, some more influential than others, such as their immediate work team, family, and friends. While the well-being culture of the organization may be pointing in one direction, subcultures can align closely, somewhat, or possibly point in the opposite direction to the culture (like that faction of smokers behind the building). How well the culture and subculture match depend on the collective actions and thoughts of the people making up the subculture. If you are a manager, you'll want to think about how you influence the subculture of your work team. Recognizing Sarah's work group, the night shift, as a subculture, with its own specific health risks and needs, helps tailor a response that supports their well-being.

There are companies taking specific steps to support their nightshift subcultures. Veolia, a refuse and recycling company, is receiving help from The Impact on Urban Health group to protect the health of the 300 night shift workers at their Southwark center in the United Kingdom. They sought to address sleep and health issues caused by disrupted circadian rhythms. These issues intensified after the onslaught of COVID-19 and they devised a Night Club aimed at supporting the mental health of employees and promoting good quality sleep while providing advice on relationships and anxiety. Employees could also get a free consult with "Dr Sleep," a sleep science expert.[3] Seventy-three percent of this subculture committed to changing their behavior as a result of the support received.

Well-being subcultures at work are created by people with commonalities in the workplace. The work team is likely the most influential subculture. Other subculture examples include occupation and work location. Subcultures do not have to be solely formed around work-related elements. They can be formed around common interests of a group, such as jogging or sharing the same religious beliefs. Subcultures vary on how they impact different aspects of health behavior and beliefs. For example, a subculture defined by an employee's work team may be more influential on the employee's stress level than the subculture of the employee's work location. There are likely many teams on the same campus. The stress level of these teams will vary depending on many things, including the attitudes of those within the team, how those in the subculture treat each other, and how the supervisor manages.

While building a healthy workplace culture is critical for organizations to reach their full potential, that pinnacle cannot be reached without respecting and supporting healthy subcultures. Cultures set the tone and pace while subcultures personalize the experience. It is like walking into an ice cream shop. You love ice cream, so you are happy to be there. Your experience is made even better when you see your favorite flavor is available. The ice cream store is the culture and the different flavors each represent a subculture. Granted, I probably could have used a healthier example for this book, but keep in mind there are ice creams that are soy and nut based!

Subcultures often have a more powerful influence on their members than the broader culture because the behaviors, attitudes, and beliefs of the members of a subculture are more deeply intertwined with each other. When working within a robust well-being subculture, you are likely to find acceptance, support, optimism, and psychological safety. Healthy subcultures help you maintain your healthy practices and build new ones. A rich well-being subculture lends itself to engaging in workplace health promoting activities, supporting each other's emotional health, and taking advantage of wellness-related benefits. Ultimately, workers who are part of healthy subcultures are happier and tend to be more engaged and satisfied with their jobs.

It is perhaps easier to recognize unhealthy subcultures. A team that always eats lunch at their desks while working has room for improvement. However, there are many subcultures that are unhealthy because of their attitudes. For example, there are groups of employees who are more apt to identify what's wrong than celebrate what's right. Their negativity is toxic and casts gloom across the room. Groups formed around unhealthy subcultures can be skeptical of the employer and thus be reluctant to participate in productive solutions to challenges and any program that is voluntary.

One of the greatest dangers to an organization is a manager who creates or contributes to an unwell subculture. There are many management practices that lead to an unhealthy subculture such as micromanaging, criticism, withholding information, favoritism, negativity, and lack of acknowledging contributions, to name a few. Be careful how you manage. The number-one reason people leave your company is because of their bosses![4] It's not always the job or the pay or the hours. This is why it is so important to include your managers in your effort to build a well-being culture in the workplace.

───────

INFLUENCE OF SUBCULTURES ON LIFESTYLE HABITS

Every health behavior and the entire spectrum of emotions are potentially influenced by subcultures at work. Subcultures have the potential of a Swiss Army knife. Some part of this tool can help you address your health and well-being needs. For example, our subcultures influence what we eat, how often we eat, and how much we eat. For those who physically work at a location outside their home, it is highly likely you eat either on the way to work, during the workday, or on the way home (or all three times). The subculture defined by your team influences your food choices. Ever notice what kind of food is left in the break room on Monday morning with a note that says "Help yourself"? It is not likely a bowl of fruit. It is more often leftover cake or cookies. Someone decided they really needed to watch their weight and one way to quickly change course is to give this unhealthy food to someone else. What a quick way to be "generous" with your work colleagues and get yourself away from the day-old birthday cake.

The influence of our team subculture changed for many because of the COVID-19 pandemic. It brought a huge surge in remote workers, and the work location for millions suddenly moved to just around the corner from the refrigerator and pantry. How do you think that's affecting body weight in the subculture of remote workers? Remote workers are a subculture defined by work location. Their work location influences their eating patterns and choices differently than those going into the workplace.

Let's go back to the team that doesn't take a lunch break. The culture may have a policy, break rooms, cafeteria, and other culture connection points that promote breaking for lunch, but the subculture may have an attitude that runs counter to this behavior. If the team perceives taking a lunch break as something only lazy people do or people without enough work, then those on the team may eat at their desk while working through their lunch break. In this case, the norm of the subculture is more powerful than the greater organization's cultural influences.

Subcultures at work can even influence your lifestyle patterns at home. Imagine you are part of a work team that has too much to do and not enough hours in the day. Sounds familiar, right? The team could try to keep up with the workload and put in extra hours, not take breaks, and check emails in the evening. Another subculture might decide they will think more clearly and do a better job if they take work breaks, address the priorities, and leave their work at work. Which subculture do you think sleeps better at night?

Many organizations benefit from well-being subcultures that have formed around shared sport and recreational interests. While the company softball team may not be that common now, it was once the oldest and most treasured well-being program. It's much more common to see groups of employees walking (a subculture of walkers). There might even be employees who run together at lunch or who form a bowling team. It's in the employer's interest to foster subcultures that promote well-being, whether it is through the installation of a shower and changing room or sponsoring the team T-shirt (complete with well-being program name and logo).

Healthy subcultures provide support for more than physical health. They can provide an emotional network and social connectedness. As we work, our life goes on around us and family members fall ill, children struggle on the playground, and perhaps financial pressures start to mount. If we're lucky (well, maybe it doesn't have to be luck, as we'll find out in Chapter 4), we are part of a supportive and caring subculture (or more than one) that helps us navigate life's turbulence.

THE REMOTE WORKER SUBCULTURE

In March of 2020, many companies sent part or all of their workforce home, either to work remotely or to wait idly as the COVID-19 pandemic unfolded. Overnight, millions of employees lost a big part of their social network, and with it, a portion of their emotional support. The benefit of our work team, of belonging to a group, to our well-being was never so apparent.

Once an exception, the COVID-19 pandemic has forced American businesses and organizations to evaluate the feasibility of a remote workforce. Many have found that working remotely has increased productivity and improved employee satisfaction. Many of the myths about remote workers not being as productive or not being able to participate have been dispelled. Remote workers have their own subcultures. Once largely overlooked in health and well-being strategies, they can no longer be ignored!

Special considerations are needed to support the health and well-being of the remote worker subculture. Primarily, let's focus on the intersection of work and home, where the boundaries are getting more difficult to set, given the 24/7 internet and the ever-growing remote worker population.

Are there boundaries? As a manager and leader, have you made it clear that there is work time and private time? The most difficult part of separating the two might be our computers. For people who work remotely, it's too easy now to work.

There are several longstanding misconceptions that we need to overcome. One is that more time working means you're a better employee. The quality of our work isn't always at the forefront. It's hard to deliver high-quality results without adequate rest of both mind and body. Nonetheless, remote workers often feel the need to prove that they are carrying their load and, therefore, some compensate by working longer hours—eating into family time, exercise, food preparation, and other activities that support employee well-being.

Do set boundaries! As the leader, you can give permission for your team to turn off and recuperate. Ideally, your team will decide on email etiquette together. In other words, before and after what hours is it unacceptable to send emails because of the pressure it places on others to do the same? This is a great example of how a team can work together to create a healthy norm and support each others' health.

Then there is break time. At work, there is the break room. For the remote worker there is the rest of the home. Think about how this affects the health of your colleagues. Is the desk in the bedroom, really blurring the lines between work and rest? Is the workspace situated in the basement, making daylight an all too infrequent occurrence? It's worth spending some time creating a strategy and the infrastructure to support your remote workforce.

HOW TO SUPPORT HEALTHY SUBCULTURES

Supporting Subcultures Gathered Around Healthy Themes

As a leader, manager, human resource representative, or other decision maker, you have some discretion on how to allocate resources. You don't have to spend a lot of money to foster healthy subcultures. Instead of a holiday gift that ends up in the drawer, how about one that ends up on the desk? For the cost of a plant, your team can have a little bit of nature on their desk every day. Nature is a well-being ingredient. Just be sure to get one that is low maintenance. The last thing you want is team morale to plummet if these newfound friends don't stay around very long.

Supporting healthy subcultures can cost even less than a plant! Maybe all you need to do is allow groups to borrow a room or other part of the facility. Can you let the employees use the grounds to play softball? Of course, you'll want to make sure the batters are aiming away from the building. Don't be stingy with resources that already exist and just need to be repurposed. Maybe groups aren't even thinking this is a possibility, so you might need to have a message or a campaign to advocate for groups interested in gathering around healthy activities to "apply" for resource support.

If your organization can afford to, giving small grants to different subculture applicants that have demonstrated how the money would be effectively used to promote well-being can be a good investment.[5] The money is used in a very targeted and specific way to bolster the well-being of a subculture that may not have what they need to achieve their goals through the resources that are available to the population at large. For example, perhaps the nightshift workers have a common challenge of feeling sleep deprived. While there are programs that address insomnia for the general workforce, perhaps a grant is needed to work with interested nightshift workers to specifically learn coping skills for working against the circadian rhythm. Maybe this group needs assistance in creating a home environment conducive to sleeping during daytime hours.

Customize the Organizational Experience at the Team Level

Company programs and campaigns can be great to show the support for healthy choices and to engage the workforce in behaviors that support well-being. These efforts might even be better if the infrastructure is in place to allow subcultures to emerge in alignment with the overall effort.

It can be easy to get lost in a sea of hundreds (or thousands). Providing a process whereby smaller groups can participate in the overall effort together can enhance the experience. For example, if your company offers mindfulness programs, is there a way to allow a work team to participate in this well-being practice together? This approach normalizes the experience (let's face it, some people still think meditation is weird), shows the boss is on board, encourages peer support, and creates a shared experience that the team can return to and encourage each other to deploy when needed. The team that "ohms" together, stays together.

Talk About Health and Well-Being

You may be comfortable talking about a variety of health and well-being topics, or perhaps you will be by the end of this book. At the very least, try to share parts of your own well-being journey. It will help others feel more comfortable to do the same. Of course, we want to make sure no one feels coaxed into disclosing information they'd rather keep private. Listening to and affirmation of employee concerns is always a welcome contribution.

Don't be surprised if you cringe at the thought of leading a discussion on many well-being topics. Perhaps your work team needs help discussing health in the workplace. Maybe this topic has been taboo in the past and even breaching this invisible line is too much to overcome. As a leader, you can secure the tools and strategies to allow your team to embark on this path such that it is easier to have a meaningful conversation about what the team members need to have a healthy workday.

Although relationship qualities such as trust, appreciation, respect, and other social expectations are becoming more commonplace for organizational focus, at the manager level, approaching these topics can be daunting. When in doubt, give a shout (for help). The last thing you want to do is inadvertently offend or make someone uncomfortable. In your attempt to take the team one step forward, you might end up taking two steps back.

Of course, be prepared to support the outcome of the discussion. This doesn't mean that if the group asks for support to relax during the day, that you need to open an onsite spa or salon. However, if your team lands on lack of movement during the workday as a common concern, be creative in how you allow time during the day for walks or group activity. Can a conference room be turned into a dance studio at lunch time? Is it possible to connect a video game system to a monitor already available in one location so employees can play games that require movement? Is there anyone on staff who is a certified instructor and wants to volunteer to lead an exercise class? Give permission to be creative to support subcultures.

Give Your Leaders Driving Lessons

When your child is legally old enough to drive, it's unlikely you will hand them the keys and close your eyes to nap as they start the car (. . . if they even know how to start the car). Train and support executives, managers, supervisors, and union representatives to better support the well-being effort in your organization. Leaders from the C-suite to front line managers need to be trained on their roles in creating a well-being culture in order to optimize the overall effect.

Training managers and leaders on how to identify signs of stress and mental health issues will better enable them to spot and respond to their team's needs. Employees who may be apprehensive about contacting the employee assistance program (EAP) may act differently if you have been trained and are vocal about what you've learned. Employees may then see the EAP as a trusted source and may be more likely to be open and communicate when they are struggling. Trained managers and leaders are better able to have a supportive conversation and guide employees to the help and resources they need.[6]

You can create and share a well-being vision that meets the needs of your group. You can align your team's practices with well-being, and you can track and celebrate well-being efforts. Perhaps most importantly, you can help make well-being acceptable and fun. Training need not be difficult. It can be as simple as developing a method to routinely inform these leaders of the current resources, programs, and efforts related to health and well-being. However, to make the most out of the influence these leaders have on the organization, it is worth going several steps further.

Managers have a lot on their plate, so perhaps in your organization it is more practical to train champions on how to lead conversations on well-being. Or perhaps an easy-to-follow toolkit might be provided to team leaders. If you are in a position that influences the well-being strategy at your organization, consider giving teams a roadmap to follow so health and well-being topics can be introduced and team members who are comfortable can share their thoughts and ideas. Perhaps someone from the core well-being team can be trained as a facilitator and can moderate these discussions.

Some training that is currently viewed as traditional human resource skills has a profound effect on the well-being of staff. This training includes:

- Communication
- Diversity and inclusion
- Conflict resolution

Even core management training has an impact on the well-being of the workforce:

- Prioritizing deliverables
- Autonomy versus micromanagement
- Providing feedback

Training more directly linked to employee health and well-being could include:

- Managing to limit workplace stress
- Identifying signs and symptoms of depression
- Recognizing sleep deprivation

HOW I HELP HOPKINS GET HEALTHY

Stress is a huge problem for most people. The American Psychological Association had previously found that work is the greatest stressor in the lives of Americans. Not surprisingly, the COVID-19 pandemic has ramped up the level of stress above previously existing societal stressors. In its "Stress in America™ 2020" report, the APA found that 78 percent (8 out of 10 adults) said that the pandemic was a significant source of stress in their lives.[7]

Healthy at Hopkins has the usual solutions to help our employees reduce their stress. We have presentations, workshops, and portal resources. They all focus on what the individual can do to manage or cope with stressors. While these resources can be helpful, it puts the onus squarely on the employee. How about shifting some of the responsibility to a major source of stress? Their managers!

It occurred to me that I've had many supervisors over the years, and while many were a source of positivity, some caused me grief. I can immediately identify the one who was responsible for a lot of lost sleep. The leader of the work team not only influences the quality and quantity of the work produced but also influences the mood of the team. I knew focusing on managers and supervisors could make a difference.

At Hopkins, when you become a new manager or supervisor, you get to participate in the Hopkins Leadership Essentials (HLE) program. This training program helps you learn the necessary skills and resources needed to be a team leader, covering topics such as benefits, organizational equity, and patient safety. It had covered everything a human resource team would want you to know as a new leader except how your actions and words influence the stress level of your team. That is, up until a few years ago.

As our broader team came to appreciate the many facets of building a well-being culture, it became apparent that our new managers needed driving lessons. It was critical to Johns Hopkins that we equip these new leaders with the skills needed to manage with care. We delivered The Role of a Leader: Managing Employee Stress in person, and then shifted to an online format to adjust to COVID-19. The training raises awareness of the preponderance of stress in the workplace, how it impacts our ability to deliver high-quality patient care, how it affects the health of our employees, and what managers can do to help limit workplace stress. The program introduces new skills that can help leaders as well as their teams.

By training managers, the time spent multiplies the impact on the organization. While hundreds of managers have been trained, thousands of employees have been touched. The same can be true with any other training you provide leaders. Training is not your typical wellness program, but it sure does influence well-being and contributes to a healthy workplace culture.

Pushing Back on Unhealthy Subcultures

While your organization may have a strategy to support an overall culture of health and even strategies for specific health behaviors, it is likely there are pockets of employees, who together have created a subculture that runs counter to your organization's goal. Pushback is one culture connection point for countering unhealthy attitudes and behaviors.

One of the most common unhealthy subcultures is a group of employees who smoke (and now we can include vaping). If tobacco use is no longer a problem at your company, count yourself lucky and mentally substitute another unhealthy behavior running amok in your organization.

Even when you have aligned culture connection points to dissuade your employees from smoking (i.e., no smoking signs, a policy) and provided culture connection points that support quitting (i.e., counseling, nicotine replacement therapy), at the end of the day tobacco use is an addiction. For many, it is hard to quit. Like bees to honey, smokers will find each other and form relationships, and before you know it, they have created their own subculture. The time they spend smoking is time they spend sharing stories, getting to know each other, and forming relationships. Their subculture persists by stopping by each other's desks and asking if they want to share a smoke break so they can pick up their conversation where they left off from the last break.

While an employer can't think of every possible way to dissuade their employees from smoking, you can certainly remove ways that make it easier to smoke and add ways to make it less attractive. While benches may have been placed for employees to relax and take a break from the stressors of work for a few minutes, some of them might have been placed in unobtrusive places, perfect for a smoke break. Figure out where the smokers congregate, and if there's a bench, move it to a more visible location. Smokers are less likely to flout your no smoking campus policy if they know they are being watched. Even if they choose to stay in the same location and stand, at least they are getting more core strength work by standing up during that time.

Don't make it easier for smokers to take a puff during inclement weather. Make sure your organization didn't previously erect shelters for a time when smoking was more acceptable and that your company never got around to taking them down. If you have shelters for transportation on your campus that have been hijacked by employees who smoke, it could be easy enough to place a video camera inside the shelter to record the rule breakers. It's not fair to the nonsmokers who want to stay dry while waiting for the company shuttle or bus.

Create a Smoke-Free Workday by adopting a policy whereby employees are not allowed to smoke during their shift, not even during their breaks. While the employee may choose to smoke at home, they can't smoke while engaged in their workday. Leaving campus to smoke and then returning to work is not allowed. The odor that permeates from a smoker can be offensive to those who are nearby, or, worse, spark breathing difficulties for those who are susceptible. Your company may just decide that's not acceptable.

Offer a health plan premium difference. Smokers generate more healthcare costs than nonsmokers.[8] It's reasonable, then, for an employee who smokes to pitch in more for health insurance. At the annual enrollment period, the higher premium for smokers listed next to the lower premium for nonsmokers sends messages to two different subcultures. To the smokers, it says, you need to share the higher cost of your unhealthy habit. To the nonsmokers, it recognizes and rewards their healthy behavior and reinforces their good choice. Sometimes the purse speaks louder than your voice. In fact, taxes on cigarettes are the single most effective way to reduce tobacco use.[9]

Finally, if you really want to squash smoking subcultures altogether, send that message before they are even hired. Include a statement in the job announcement that your company has a smoke-free policy. That may dissuade those who are addicted and don't think they can quit before a start date. Some companies have a policy of not hiring smokers.

This requires either an affidavit or a tobacco test as part of the hiring process, with rescinding the job offer if the results aren't favorable. You'll, of course, need to check with your legal counsel as the state laws vary on employee rights.

If there is an unhealthy subculture in your workplace, you don't have to accept it as permanent. Although this book focuses on creating healthy cultures, you can use the same building blocks to dismantle unhealthy subcultures. Be mindful along the way. Some of your employees have serious well-being challenges, so take a measured approach when pushing back to minimize their distress.

One Company. Two Different Worlds

Dr. Oyebode Taiwo, 3M's Global Medical Director (95,000 employees), knows health isn't just the absence of disease, but is also about feeling well. Also, one size doesn't fit all when it comes to global companies. National and geographic subcultures raise specific health issues for companies. While visiting facilities around the world, he once observed that training was needed in one African location for the use of mosquito repellent, nets, and antimalarial drugs to combat malaria.[10] Locals were unaware that walking long distances to and from their jobs exposed them to malaria, and they needed to be educated, as well as provided with the means to protect themselves. Education, encouragement, and providing resources seems like a more egalitarian approach than that taken by the Chinese company, New South. Its CEO Zhu Layi was seeking to test a controversial MDA (mass drug administration) approach on 10,000 people in Kenya's Indian Ocean coast near the port city of Mombasa, where native workers have similar long walks to work and malaria is endemic. It was a starkly different way of dealing with the health issues of a subculture.[11]

3M faced a different challenge at home in Saint Paul, Minnesota, where the culture of tolerance and respect needed to be addressed. Following the death of George Floyd at the hands of Minneapolis police officers on May 25, 2020, racial tension and community stress were at an all-time high. Saying, "Progress requires us all to stand up as advocates for racial inclusion and social justice," 3M's Chairman and CEO, Mike Roman, announced the company would invest $50 million to

(Continued)

address racial opportunity gaps. Intending to "listen, understand, and act," the company planned to listen to its employees, understand the needs of its community, and take positive and meaningful actions. The company put its words into actions by donating millions for local scholarships and social justice partners while accelerating the company's representation globally in all dimensions of diversity. That included a focus in 3M's US workforce on people who are Black/African American or Hispanic/Latino. 3M also took aim at adjusting its practices for fairness and equality, training and developing all company leaders in racial inclusion advocacy, and using that advocacy at home and in its global workplaces.[12]

CULTURAL HEALTH AWARENESS

The World Health Organization released a policy brief in 2017, helping policy writers and other leaders be aware of the important relationship between culture and health.[13] Starting with self-awareness, one of the first steps to understanding complex cultural contexts is to assess what you take for granted and to reassess your assumptions.

Prudential Financial's employee wellness program was enjoying a high participation rate in 2002. Executives were feeling good about the numbers until they looked at who was signed up. They found that African Americans were greatly underrepresented.[14]

The company initiated a communications strategy to get more African Americans on board, only to find another problem. Dr. K. Andrew Crighton, chief medical officer at Prudential Financial, looked more closely at the company's healthcare data and found that African American employees had much higher rates of diabetes and hypertension than those from other racial and ethnic groups.

To address those disparities, the company collected and analyzed employee health information by race, ethnicity, gender, age, and job levels. They were able to track chronic conditions like diabetes, cardiac disease, and asthma. Based on that information, Prudential launched the Healthy Diabetic program in 2011 to address the disproportionate incidences of the disease among various employee groups.

Aware that physical well-being is often tied to financial well-being, Prudential Financial observed that during the years between 2007 and 2016 the number of Hispanic households at risk of not being able to maintain their standard of living in retirement rose to 61 percent according to the Center of Retirement Research (CRR) at Boston College.[15] The median income for black families was also significantly lower than white households. Prudential Financial realized that closing the retirement security gap would not be easy, but they could increase partnering between private corporations and nonprofit institutions, improve access to workplace retirement plans, engage financial services firms in grassroots marketing partnership with trusted community leaders, and increase access to financial wellness programs.[16]

Another subculture getting attention from Prudential Financial is that of unpaid caregivers. During the COVID-19 pandemic, the shift to working at home as well as children attending school at home caused regular distractions leading to reduced productivity at work and strains on employees' financial, emotional, and physical health. Also, the caregiving duties most often fell on women and people of color. Employers can offer a wide range of solutions, such as helping secure child- and elder-care services, to help employees balance caregiving and work responsibilities. In addition to doing the right thing, the payoff for employers comes in improvements in employee engagement and productivity, talent recruitment and retention, cost containment, and workforce management and diversity.[17]

Prudential Financial backed its observations by partnering with Wellthy, a service for caregivers, which enables the company to offer no-cost access to Wellthy's digital caregiving tools, including educational content; digital care plan creation; the storage of caregiving documents, like prescriptions, medical records, and wills; a shared calendar to track appointments; and the ability to establish a group caregiving discussion.[18]

Shaping Your Team Subculture

Being a manager is not always easy. In addition to the responsibility of steering the team to getting the work done, you have a lot of different personalities on the team as well as the collective persona of the group, or the subculture. Your team has specific beliefs, behaviors, and attitudes that may be similar or different from the culture of the larger organization. While your company may provide many different resources, benefits, and strategies that support a well-being culture, the needs of your team may be different based on the members of

(Continued)

your subculture. To optimize your approach to supporting well-being on your team, ask yourself these questions:

- How do the jobs or the function of our team influence our well-being needs? The needs of employees who work at desks all day are different than those who are on their feet all day.
- How does the time of day or length of our shift influence our well-being needs that are different from the larger organization?
- What family relationships influence the subculture on our team? Are there parents on the team? Is everyone single or are some people married?
- Is the team cohesive or have they broken into two or more groups on a social level? This may interfere with creating a sense of community. How will you address this schism?

Take subcultures into consideration when planning ways to support well-being on your team. Your favorite flavor of ice cream deserves special attention.[19]

HOW I HELP HOPKINS GET HEALTHY

When the pandemic struck Maryland in March of 2020, a sizeable portion of our workforce needed to leave campus. Suddenly, we had thousands of remote workers. While most of our healthcare providers and those that keep our hospitals open and running stayed on campus, we realized those with desk jobs would likely be working from home for some time; a remote workers subculture, so we went to work.

Among our challenges was how to prevent the aches and pains from working long hours at a desk, such as carpel tunnel syndrome, headaches, backaches, and more. None of these feel good and all of them ultimately will interfere with your employee's ability to work, so do not overlook how your employees are working.

Our colleagues no longer had our company-furnished, ergonomically friendly office equipment. We pulled together our "How to Create a Body Friendly Workplace at Home," a one-page summary that includes a diagram as well as written instructions on how to set up a workstation that wouldn't cause aches and pains over time. Not only did we make this available through different marketing and communication avenues, but we also dedicated one of our "Ask the Expert" sessions to bring in someone from our physical therapy department to share his expertise and take questions from our employees.

More of our "Ask the Expert" sessions were focused on the impact of the public health crisis and the new workplace paradigm on mental health. Topics included loneliness, new parenting challenges, anxiety, and insomnia. We created a list of "socially safe" fun activities and participated in remote baby showers, happy hours, and birthday celebrations. When addressing well-being needs, be creative.

Put Your Own Mask on First

You probably hadn't realized how much you're influenced by the many subcultures in which you belong. There's no time like the present to take stock of how to support your well-being by understanding your subcultures.

- List at least three subcultures you belong to at work (for example, a shift, a team, a professional or trade group, a friend group).
- Identify a healthy practice in one of these subcultures. If you desire to make this healthy behavior or attitude a habit, figure out how to spend more time with this subculture.
- Identify an unhealthy influence from one of these subcultures. If you are trying to avoid this unhealthy behavior or unhelpful attitude, either express your concerns to the group and see if they can support your needs or simply be conscious of this subculture's bad influence and work on ways to minimize its potential impact.

THAT'S A WRAP

Subcultures in the workplace are created when groups of employees share the same interests or circumstances. The work teams in your organization are prime examples, including the group of people who report to you directly, if you are a manager. Throughout this book, I'll provide you managerial tips so that you can apply the well-being culture principals to your subculture, from the perspective of a leader. It works looking *up* the organization as well. You are part of the subculture of the team in which you report. So, here's a not-so-subtle suggestion for a not-so-subtle gift for your boss: give them a copy of this book.

Team subcultures can be supportive and, unfortunately at times, just the opposite. It is important for the team leader to advocate for health and well-being in all its shapes and sizes. There are those within our midst who are too shy, timid, or have other reasons for not asking for help or for not achieving their well-being goals. The benefit of a healthy subculture is to raise the well-being of the entire group. You can start by making well-being a priority, a shared value.

3

Best Companies Value Well-Being

Shared Values

ROBERT B. WEGMANS'S PORTRAIT IS posted near the front of every Wegmans store, along with his credo, "Never think about yourself; always help others." What a great world we'd live in if we all lived by that mantra, and what a great value to work by. *Fortune* magazine agrees, putting Wegmans on its 100 Best Companies to Work For every one of the 25 years the ranking has been made available.

If it were only so easy to articulate a great commitment that supported both employees and customers and then have it come to fruition. Companies like Zappos work hard and are very intentional in shaping their core values. "Create Fun and a Little Weirdness" and "Build a Positive Team and Family Spirit" are just 2 of their 10 core values that clearly support well-being. Zappos builds cultural fit into their interview process and, once on board, there is a training team to impart wisdom about each core value. The result? Zappos is a Fortune 100 Best Companies to Work For seven years in a row.[1]

Are you getting the picture? Shared values matter. But it's unusual for a company to put employee health and well-being on the high-priority list, alongside goals like profitability, outstanding customer service, and new product innovation. However, we have clear evidence that a culture that puts employee well-being at the top, starting with its values, will lead to success. In fact, guess what shared values show up in *Fortune*'s Best Companies to Work For?

It's a common misunderstanding that employee health and well-being only benefits the individual or only the employer. Everyone benefits. These mutual benefits stem from shared values, the priorities that both employees and the employer embrace. When employees appreciate that their job and their employer value their well-being, then companies flourish. According to research by McKinsey & Company (and found true by others), companies with the healthiest cultures perform the best, and those with the worst flounder or dissolve altogether.[2]

THE VALUE OF SHARED VALUES

If you already work at a company where employee health and well-being are valued, like Johnson & Johnson, Wegmans, and Marriott International, count yourself lucky! However, don't despair if not, because it's quite likely that your organization does have at least one shared value that sits hand-in-hand with health and well-being, such as respect, trust, equality, inclusion, and diversity.

Pause for a moment. How are your company's shared values working for your team? For your organization? Do you even know what they are? This isn't just something to check off the human resource "must do" list. An organization's values can substantially impact its success. In Richard Barrett's book *The Values-Driven Organization*, he explains that those companies that adopt "care or love-driven cultures" through values such as teamwork, balance (work and life), and fun support well-being.[3] These companies focus on the needs of their employees. When employees feel cared for, the employees will care for the company.

There are other companies that may be living values that promote a "fear-driven culture," even if these aren't the values written on the company website. Values in this group include hard work (aka long hours) and results (aka productivity). The values in this type of culture are focused on the needs of the leaders, owners, and shareholders. This culture promotes stress, distrust, and self-interest.

The contrast between love-driven and fear-driven cultures is vast. Your company's current values are likely a mix of both love- and fear-driven types. Even when the company's values are written in a way that clearly supports well-being, if leaders (from the CEO to the manager) don't live these values, then they aren't meaningful.

Don't always trust what you read, even when it's chiseled in marble in the main lobby of a corporate headquarters.[4] This was the case for a once highly valued company. Enron was one of the world's biggest utility companies. They proudly espoused their values of integrity, communication, respect, and excellence.[5] They hardly had integrity, manipulating their financial records to appear more profitable than was reality. What part of hiding the truth fulfills the values of communication and respect? It's not even worth commenting on excellence when referring to a bankrupt company.

CHOOSING THE SHARED VALUES

Organizations have their own personalities, often greatly influenced by characteristics of the president or CEO, the sector of the economy, or the community in which the company is located (or all the above). Those personalities may come out in their commercials or can be seen by visiting their stores or websites. They may also be reflected in their core values. There's a retailer whose commercials include bright colors (predominantly red), energy, multiple smiling actors and actresses, and a dog with a black ring around one eye, eerily similar to the company's red bull's-eye logo. You guessed it, and Target Corporation's advertisements reflect their values. Their values of inclusivity and connection are represented by the ethnically diverse group of people having fun together.

A company's values serve as the beacon for how the company makes decisions, behaves, and prioritizes its resources and effort. Values = priorities. It's worth the time and energy to focus on the company values because they serve as a rudder to keep the company on course.

Hopefully, when assessing your core values, you're starting from a place where values include health and well-being themes. The themes don't have to be blatant, like exercise. An organization that values work–life balance is doing wonders for well-being by allowing families to flourish, employees to recharge before coming back to the office, and keeping stress levels down as employees deal with life's speed bumps.

Target's core value of connection is not a blatant affirmation of health, but as you'll read in the next chapter, feeling like part of a team and feeling cared for are big parts of well-being. This value of connection helps Target recruit new talent because Target knows that Millennials aren't seeking a boss (which infers separation), but rather a coach (which infers connection).[6] The human experience plays a huge role in job satisfaction and well-being and has regularly placed Target on the list of Fortune 100 Best Places to Work For.

When asked what your values are, most people can't limit the answer to one or two things. In fact, we can probably rattle off a list of things we hold in high regard and are important parts of our life. The broad question of values can provoke a broad set of answers, from honesty to fun and even religion. When trying to hone our values down to health and well-being, the list can still be long and include many of the things on the original list, such as honesty, fun, and religion, all of which have health implications. Now imagine asking 1,000 employees for their well-being values and trying to figure out which to focus on to unify the workforce on a common path. Not an easy task.

However, there are certainly many ways to include broad representation when choosing or revising the organization's shared values. Zappos went low tech in 2005 when an email to the workforce invited employees to reply with their shared values—what was meaningful to them as individuals. That's not a difficult exercise when there are only 300 employees.[7]

It doesn't take too many more employees before you start to realize that maybe an online survey tool would be more efficient (and practical). Focus groups could work as well or maybe randomized samples of employees from every part of the organization. Shaping the shared values is best achieved when the people that make up the organization are represented.

Johnson & Johnson has revisited its credo several times since it was first unveiled. In 1987, language was added to articulate the company's support for work–life balance. More recently, in 2017 they invited more than 2,000 global employees to participate in small focus groups led by executives.[8] True to their unwavering support of employee health and well-being, the group added inclusion, fulfillment, and purpose, all great ingredients for employee morale and elements of optimal well-being. Including thousands of employees in the process is a sure way to know the values are shared.

Let's Hear It for Yay Days

REI is another company to be a regular on *Fortune*'s 100 Best Companies to Work For, and has been on the list for 21 consecutive years. Begun in 1938 as a co-op by 23 avid outdoors adventurers to get better prices on gear, the company remains a purpose-led organization that prioritizes stewardship of the outdoors. Raquel Karls, senior vice president of human resources, said of REI's 12,000 employees, "It's an incredible honor, in our 80th year as a co-op, that our employees feel so strongly about the work we do."[9]

REI's core values are:

- Authenticity—We are true to the outdoors.
- Quality—We provide trustworthy products and services.
- Service—We serve others with expertise and enthusiasm.
- Respect—We listen and learn from each other.
- Integrity—We live by a code of rock-solid ethics, honesty, and decency.
- Balance—We encourage each other to enjoy all aspects of life.

But, as Amy Lyman puts it in her book, *The Trustworthy Leader*, "The words contained in the values are not much different from those found in the value statements of any organization. So what makes it different at REI? The people at REI actively seek to live out their values."[10]

The co-op invests 70 percent of its profits annually in the outdoor community and is committed to the long-term health of the outdoors. According to the company's annual employee survey, 96 percent of employees fully support the co-op's values. Among the retailer's unique benefits are days off to play outside. Each employee receives two paid "Yay Days" a year that allow them to enjoy their favorite outdoor activity, learn a new skill, or to help maintain outdoor spaces through the stewardship project. The reward of a Yay Day hits a bulls-eye with two values: being true to the outdoors, and encouraging each other to enjoy all aspects of life.

REI's vision statement says its "core purpose is to inspire, educate, and outfit for a lifetime of outdoor adventure and stewardship. As a cooperative, everyone in the company and customers, producers, and suppliers are invited in to the mission of REI and asked to play a part

(Continued)

in creating the unique REI experience." In REI's employee alignment survey, the majority said they were motivated by the company's mission, vision, and values.[11]

REI gives out their annual Anderson Award (a culture connection point) to nonmanagement employees, who in the eyes of their fellow employees, live REI's core values and embody the co-op spirit. Employees drive the award's selection process (a peer support strategy) each year with a task force led by a previous winner of the award. Among the honors that go with the award, the one hundred-plus winning employees are flown to the Seattle headquarters for a three-day event that includes tours and outdoor activities.[12]

MAKE WELL-BEING A SHARED VISION

I'm sure your exploration of shared values will land on some very meaningful themes if you're not already starting with a strong well-being value foundation. One step toward making your shared values meaningful is to translate them to a vision for your well-being culture. Your well-being vision helps employees understand what well-being ideally looks like as it pertains to the organization. It allows everyone to move in the same direction and inspires the workforce to seek their own well-being path as well as contribute to the well-being of their colleagues.

Among the shared core values of HUB International Limited, a 10,000-employee insurance brokerage firm based in Chicago, were: "Integrity - We do the right thing every time" and "Teamwork - We work together to maximize results." HUB's approach to refreshing and expanding its well-being culture was motivated out of caring for its employees rather than cost-containment. Healthy and happy employees are more engaged, resilient, and productive—a win-win philosophy of "employees win when the organization wins, and the organization wins when the employees win." That attitude promotes shared values, purpose, goals, vision, and results.[14]

HUB began putting its "value of caring" into action by:

- Visiting its locations across the United States to find what was most needed to create an environment of health and long-term well-being.

- Establishing a network of wellness coordinators to work with employee needs and support their cultures.
- Working with management teams to break down barriers to caring and support an open door to creating a healthy culture.

The result was "H3 – HUB Healthy Habits." Although this incidentally led to financial advantages for the company, the most important part of the initiative was that it demonstrated to HUB employees that caring for them was at the heart of creating a positive work environment.[15]

Hopkins Highlight
The Johns Hopkins Medicine Strategic Plan

Including employee health and well-being in strategic objectives is a green light for building a well-being culture. In 2014, the leaders of Johns Hopkins Medicine (JHM) released its five-year strategic plan. These six pillars created focus for our collective effort. The first goal of the five year strategic plan was to "invest in the health, development, mentoring and advancement of JHM's people at all levels." To be more specific about how to reach this goal, the first strategy was "Actively support a healthy workforce through the expansion of Healthy@ Hopkins and population-management initiatives." If not for this highly visible proclamation from our executive team, the energy, resources, and attention needed to move forward on a healthy-culture path were not likely to have been as fruitful. Building off the initial five years of success, our current five year strategic plan calls on us to "actively support a healthy workforce."

CHARACTERISTICS OF A SHARED VISION

Ideally, the vision of the organization would include a reference to health and well-being. Sometimes the vision naturally dovetails with well-being. For example, Martin Luther King's vision is inextricably tied to social well-being. A vision can have benefits beyond pointing the organization in the right direction. When a vision is inspirational, such as putting a man on the moon, it can unify a team toward a common goal. If your organization doesn't have a shared vision that includes a well workforce or some other message of well-being as part of the journey or destination, then creating one specific for the purposes of inspiring a healthy workplace culture is warranted. Ideally, the well-being vision will motivate not only the persons responsible for driving the employee health and well-being agenda, but to also engage the broader workforce.

For instance, with over 345,000 employees, IBM's corporate Responsibility Report states: "Employee well-being is integrated into every aspect of IBM's global business. It underpins our total health management system and demonstrates a commitment to employee health and safety that values the whole person—at work, at home, or as a member of a larger community."

The company's vision is guided by its well-being mission statements:

- Address local and global health priorities
- Improve the overall health and vitality of our employees
- Provide safe and healthy work environments
- Design health benefits and health-promotion programs to improve access, increase quality, reduce costs, and drive innovation
- Support business continuity and growth[16]

It is helpful to think of the shared vision not only for the specific aspect of well-being that your organization will pursue, but also in the context of either your organization's history, current events, or business objectives. In other words, can you tie the shared value of your well-being strategy to something that is already meaningful to your workforce? In this manner, it's more likely your shared vision will resonate.

IBM has a long history of caring for its employees—90 years long. At the New York Safety Conference in 1932, IBM's first president declared that safety was not only the responsibility of each worker, but also each foreman, executive, and president. IBM shared its well-being vision, and you should too.

SHARING THE WELL-BEING VALUES AND VISION

Once the health and well-being values and vision are identified and recognized, the message needs to be broadcast frequently and through a myriad of avenues to reinforce and amplify the importance of this value to the community. This is not the kind of thing you want to keep a secret.

It's most helpful when the message comes from the top of the organization and from you, the team leader. However, well-written and meaningful values and a good vision are easily remembered and resonate with everyone. They therefore can be easily repeated, making it easy for everyone to share the vision, not just the president.

Optimize your well-being shared values and vision message. Communicate the myriad of benefits that come with the shared value and vision, so that your team is likely to find relevance in at least one of them, according to their individual circumstance. By sharing the multiple benefits of a healthy workplace culture, the message is likely to resonate with the most recipients and avoid alienating portions of the workforce. Announcing only a single benefit of the value of a healthy workplace risks disenfranchising some subcultures if they disagree with that reason for the organization pursuing the strategy. Employees are particularly wary of seeing health strategies as a cost-saving measure for the company without benefit for the individual.

MAYBE NOT EVERYONE AGREES

Gallup analytics show that only one in four employees "strongly agree" they believe in their company's values, and again, only one in four employees "strongly agree" they can apply their organization's values to their work every day.[17] That's a shame, because we know that companies with much higher degrees of shared values attract more qualified applicants and retain their workforce, which is a critical challenge right now.

Even if health and well-being make it to the final slate of shared values, it is likely that not everyone will agree they should be a top priority for the organization. In fact, there might be some who don't even think health and well-being is a priority at all. It's best to anticipate these laggards and plan accordingly. Don't try to sweep discontent under the rug. As a manager or leader, if you interact with an employee who doesn't care for the shared values of the organization, try to help them find their personal connection.

Change is a given in all organizations and industries. It's unlikely that an employee at Marriott International can't find meaning in their core value, "embracing change," because of all the changes we're all experiencing with the pandemic response, political upheaval, and social unrest. However, please imagine that an employee doesn't understand how the shared value of embracing change applies to them. This is an opportunity to discuss how change can cause stress and facing it together as a team can make it easier. Discussions around core values strengthen allegiance to the organization. It's okay if not everyone is cheering for the company core values, but it's not okay to let someone on the team be an impediment to everyone else's acceptance. Marriott has been a "best company to work for" for more than two decades and has a place for "Core Values & Heritage" on its website landing page. It's that important.

MAKING THE SHARED VALUES COME TO LIFE

Zappos sees itself as both a team and a family (a company-shared value). Zappos invests a lot of time and energy creating and sustaining its culture. Its leaders embrace leading by example, including letting every employee be heard. Zappos has explicitly stated, "we believe that in general, the best ideas and decisions can come from the bottom up, meaning by those on the front lines that are closest to the issues and/or the customers."[18] Fueled by ideas from team members, the company is able to innovate and stay ahead of the competition. That two-way street of communication and sharing also means employees are participants in shaping as well as living the shared values. Open, honest, communication is critical to relationship-building, and that's how a family like Zappos works.

The conception and production of the Post-it note is possibly one of the best examples of ideas coming from team members. Although a 3M scientist was assigned to discover stronger and tougher adhesives, Dr. Spencer Silver's interest was piqued by the happenstance of finding an adhesive that wasn't strong enough to bond, but nonetheless had a sticky property. Voilà . . . the Post-it Note.[19] 3M provided an innovative breeding ground that allowed Dr. Silver to move his idea to an actual product (even though it took time and persistence).

You can make your well-being culture sticky by making it a top priority—a head above the many competing goals that an organization might define.[20] Some companies lean toward too many priorities, which can muddy the water and makes it difficult to see where to start and where to give the most attention. Employee well-being needs to be held in high regard, like customer service and productivity. Fortunately, employee well-being is synergistic with good customer service and high productivity and enhances other business objectives as well.

Sometimes practicing a shared value means walking away from a profitable market. Target and Wegmans were among the earliest retailers to stop selling tobacco products.[21,22]

The last thing your organization wants to do is spend time and energy creating shared values and letting them sit on the shelf. If you indeed get your employees involved with creating the shared values (hence "shared"), it will be particularly disheartening and demoralizing if the workforce doesn't see the shared values lived. The shared values need to be reinforced not only through marketing and communications, but also through the same means other business objectives are supported, such as assigning goals to employee health and well-being.

Nothing gets more priority than the goals the company sets out for the year. Many teams and organizations set annual goals, like the number of widgets sold, or how fast the phones are answered, or number of members in their club. Getting health and well-being as part of these metrics is a true testament to the importance of this value within the organization. Without it, health and well-being may not get the attention they deserve.

Nestlé, Not Just About Chocolate

Nestlé, a company that may bring an image of chocolate to mind, says: "Driven by our purpose we want to share a better world and inspire people to live healthier lives."[23]

Nestlé's values are respect for ourselves, respect for others, respect for diversity, and respect for the future. Among the ways it lives up to those values is that they "work resourcefully and tirelessly to understand the needs of individuals and families across the world and serve those needs with passion."[24]

For example, to take on malnutrition, the company sent a team of researchers to India, where they found that 70 percent of children under the age of 3 and 57 percent of women were anemic. The team visited 1,500 households to observe diets and cooking customs. The spicy food was low in micronutrients like iron, iodine, and vitamin A. So the company produced a micronutrient-reinforced spice called Masala-ae-Magic that sold for only three rupees, affordable even to low-income families. The company relied on existing and new nonprofit distribution channels to reach the more remote and affected areas of India.[25]

INCLUDE EMPLOYEE HEALTH AND WELL-BEING IN THE ANNUAL PERFORMANCE EVALUATION

Despite their flaws, performance evaluations are still a ritual in most organizations. Although ideally we are giving feedback literally every day, we also need specific times set aside to reflect and discuss how we're contributing to the organization as well as how the organization is meeting the needs of the individual (aka shared values). Organizations measure what's important. If you're intent on supporting a well-being culture, why not assess everyone's contribution?

We're much more likely to focus on those areas that are measured and for which we are responsible. We are asked to excel in customer service, financial responsibility, and quality improvement, so why not in our role in the team and in an organizational well-being culture? Given we know that our well-being and those of our colleagues is critical to the organization's success, it makes sense to include this area in our performance evaluation.

Now many of you might be squirming in your seats right now. "We can't evaluate and measure our employees on their health or their well-being!" That's correct. However, you can assess how well they are honoring and demonstrating the company-shared values. If one of your company-shared values is either employee health or well-being (or both) or something related, there are many ways to ask your employee whether they are contributing to the desired well-being culture:

- Are they supporting and encouraging those teammates who are openly striving to adopt healthier habits or shed unhealthy ones (peer support)?
- Does the employee find ways to be optimistic and upbeat, even during tough times (positivity)?
- Is the employee kind and respectful, and do they make others feel accepted (sense of community)?
- Does the person on your team collaborate and work toward the team's collective goals (shared vision)?

Shaping Your Team Subculture

It's one thing for the company to arrive at shared values and it's another for the team to embrace them and live by them. You don't have to wait for the organization at large or the human resource department to

(Continued)

bring the shared values to life on your team. Here are a few ways to keep the shared values front and center:

- Make it a point to choose one shared value each month and have a discussion with the team on how you're practicing that value.
- Recognize someone on the team for exemplifying one of the shared values.
- Post the shared values in a common space so that there is a regular reminder of how you're working together.
- Include a reflection on the shared values when welcoming a new team member.
- When someone's behavior runs contrary to a company shared value, take them aside, discuss the problem, and remind them of expectations.

Southwest Airlines' stated purpose is to connect people to what's important in their lives through friendly, reliable, and low-cost air travel. The company's vision is to be the world's most loved, most efficient, and most profitable airline.

The airline has a three-part value set:

1. Me: How I show up. These values serve as guideposts for how I conduct myself each day—pride, integrity, and humility.
2. We: How we treat each other. These values describe how we interact with people and win as a team—teamwork, honesty, and service with LUV.
3. Southwest: How Southwest succeeds. These values convey how we all work together—efficiency, discipline, and excellence.

The trademark humor of flight attendants and even pilots underscores the friendliness and wit that puts passengers at ease. During the normally boring emergency exit speech, a flight attendant might well say, "There may be 50 ways to leave your lover, but there are only five ways to leave a Boeing 737." Or the female pilot could surprise you with, "Yes, I'm a female pilot, and as a benefit, if we get lost on the way, I won't be afraid to stop and ask for directions."

Southwest's careers.southwestair.com features the following: our purpose, our vision, our company promise, our employee promise, the three-part values, and a Southwest citizenship statement, including,

"At Southwest Airlines. It's always been about heart." A photo of inflight instructor Roshaun Casey shares her own statement: "I am naturally a fun-loving, free-spirited person who loves to be around people—helping, serving, and building bonds. Southwest has given me the opportunity to be me. I get to turn it all the way up and enjoy myself at work."[26]

Put Your Own Mask on First

Within all of the humorous Southwest announcements, the message to put your own mask on first still gets conveyed. It's that important.

- How are you living your values during the workday?
- Identify the company's shared value that resonates most with you.
- Identify the company's shared value that you find most difficult to practice, and make a plan to grow in this area.
- Stick to your job priorities. Learning to say no (politely of course) to requests for work and meetings unrelated to your job will lift a huge weight off of your shoulders.
- What well-being challenges are keeping you from reaching your business goals? Take time to recognize what health behaviors and thought patterns make it easier to get your job done (i.e., sleep, optimism) and which ones make it difficult (i.e., sugary foods, pessimism).

THAT'S A WRAP

The values that drive your healthy-culture effort can be captured by crafting a definition of employee well-being tailored to your unique organization, in a way that is vital and relevant to your employees. In a manufacturing company, it might focus on physical well-being that supports health and safety. In a retail business, it might focus on psychological well-being, with an emphasis on kindness and patience. The challenge, of course, is getting to a refined set of values and definition of well-being with the buy-in of dozens, hundreds, or thousands of employees, all of whom have their own values and cultures they bring to work with them every day.

The values should be easily remembered and therefore easily repeated. They should resonate with everyone on some level, making it easy to turn to them for direction and inspiration, and they should be tailored to the organization's language and mission. Finally, to be meaningful to the organization, the shared values need to be integrated into the business goals. If we don't regularly bring the shared values to life, they may be nothing more than words chiseled into marble (and you know how that turned out for Enron).

I was once a job applicant for an organization that appeared to have great values. However, once I became an employee, it quickly became apparent that the values were only seen periodically, like the sun peeking through on an overcast day. The weather pattern inside this organization was influenced by far more than the shared values, which left many of us running for cover when storm clouds began to form.

4

Oh, the Weather Outside
Is Frightful
Social Climate

"WHAT'S THE DIFFERENCE BETWEEN WEATHER and climate?" the quiz show host asked.

"Time," the beaming contestant answered. "Weather is what's going on today, but climate is what we have year round."

The social climate at some companies is sunny and warm, while at others it is cloudy and can even be downright frosty sometimes, like the Arctic. I once worked at a company with a warm and collegial work environment that went sour quickly when a new CEO was hired. The new CEO started his rampage within a month by letting go of all but two executives. Sometimes the layoffs occurred in waves after shutting down whole programs. Other times it was one or two individuals. Often, new hires to replace those who were fired didn't make it a year. Guessing who would be fired next was a nonstop water cooler topic. Even I wondered when I would be let go. It was a revolving door. The turnover was so high I stopped recognizing most faces!

If you were lucky (although many thought it to be unlucky) to be part of a meeting with the CEO, you didn't want to sit in the "hot seat."

That was the seat to the immediate right of the source of our discontent. I sat there on many occasions. My job and ethical obligation were to advise the CEO on the science of prevention and behavior change. Unfortunately, I had a lot of advising to do, and most often it wasn't solicited. One day my boss called me into his office. My position had been eliminated. No surprise. Indeed, part of me was relieved. Working in a toxic environment had been wreaking havoc on my sleep schedule for years.

Obviously, it doesn't have to be this way. From frontline supervisors to the C-suite, leaders can promote a positive social climate by building a sense of community, fostering positive attitudes, and creating a shared vision. Leaders set the tone by making people feel included and united in their efforts. Feeling good about where you work and the people you work with is a big, big part of well-being.

The social climate is akin to the weather over a long period of time. When it's mostly sunny out, we're more likely to feel happy, upbeat, and energetic. A little rain one day isn't so bothersome, but if it's cloudy every day, we can start to feel depressed! Unlike the weather though, you can influence your social climate and the long-term forecast.

A good social climate is also good for the organization. Research that goes back 50 years show that a good social climate positively impacts the organization in the following ways:[1]

- Improves recruitment and retention—When your organization has a good reputation (and it will if there is a positive social climate), it is easier to attract the right talent because word of mouth will be your best friend. Turnover will decrease because employees will want to stay with the organization longer. Employees won't mind getting out of bed in the morning! Easier recruitment and better retention have multiple financial benefits for the organization (and for your own sanity).

- Enhances trust—Positive social climates allow more flexibility for candid conversation. If employees aren't allowed to voice their opinion and take risks, then businesses can't adapt to meet new challenges. This culture of trust also makes it easier to give and receive feedback, making it easier to modify workflow, products, and other essential aspects that contribute to organizational success.

- Increases resilience—Teams that trust each other are not only more likely to collaborate, they are also more resilient! Trusting and collaborative teams stick together in difficult times and can work through crises, both business and personal. The positive social environment makes it easy for teammates to help each other. An inherent nature of encouragement flourishes and individuals thrive.[2]

- Lowers the cost of doing business—A good social climate breeds positive problem solving and optimistic thinking, increases knowledge sharing, and improves customer satisfaction as well as productivity.[3,4]

A good social climate contributes to happier, healthier, and more resilient teams (and a more financially sound organization). Teams that work together for longer periods of time, that collaborate and trust each other can support each other's well-being in ways that are not possible with colleagues who don't share the same cohesiveness. This support extends from developing healthier habits to managing crises with less turbulence and simply just enjoying work! It's really the essence of creating a "work family." Most of us yearn to be part of a caring, uplifting, positive community; when that's not available to us, we may look elsewhere.

GETTING TO KNOW YOUR COMMUNITY OF METEOROLOGISTS

If you can remember the first day of any grade in elementary school, you were probably a little nervous. Why? Probably for many reasons, including whether you would "fit in." Over the course of the year, the kids in your class interacted more through team assignments, lunch period, and recess. Eventually some of them came over after school to play and joined your birthday party roster. Your class became your community. Your friends were indispensable.

Fitting in, being part of the group, and feeling included are crucial parts of being well. When people feel like they are on the outside and the last to know, and overhear "inside jokes," they are less likely to be engaged. Why would they be? Who liked being the kid who was picked last for dodge ball?

Being part of a group fills a human need. Socializing is not a "nice to have." Socializing keeps us from catching colds and developing chronic diseases.[5] Those with social support are not only less likely to get sick, but also likely to recover more quickly from an illness.[6] The absence of feeling socially connected increases our health risks as much as smoking 15 cigarettes a day![7] Indisputably, those with social support will live healthier, happier, and longer.[8]

Unfortunately, the exponential integration of technology that is connecting us on one hand, is also contributing to astonishing levels of loneliness. Amazingly, even with all the people around us in the workplace, many employees feel lonely at work, even CEOs.[9] Loneliness comes with its own baggage, like depression and greater risk for burnout. It's imperative that we create a sense of community within the workplace if we expect healthy and happy employees (and a thriving organization).

Here are some ways to enhance your sense of community.

Onboarding

You've found your perfect candidate and they accepted the job. They are ready to start. In addition to providing them with passwords, schedules, and the company ID badge, this is the time to set the expectations for how they will contribute to the greater workplace community. Don't leave the important messages of collegiality, trust, and collaboration to a self-paced mandatory prerecorded training. This approach will not do justice in terms of highlighting the organization's emphasis on building a strong community.

When the probation period is over or whenever it is that your company deems your recruit to be done with their onboarding experience, give this employee the opportunity to share their early impressions. We can always learn from each other, and getting fresh input can be very valuable. Feeling like you are part of something special doesn't require putting your employee on a plane to a tropical island (although, granted, I wouldn't mind). Creating a sense of belonging does not require that the employee be showered with material goods (but it doesn't hurt to have apparel with the company name and logo).

Meet and Greet

Creating spaces where employees can congregate and socialize is one way to creating a sense of community. If you were to visit Amazon's office building in Seattle, you would find numerous common areas where the company's 45,000 employees can mingle, relax, and have fun. Under displays of rotating art you could play foosball, shuffleboard, or ping-pong. There are also six eateries, a coffee stand, a video game lab, an art studio, and a market.

Like Amazon, Google has gone to great lengths to encourage employees to get away from their computers. Google employees, called "Googlers," enjoy several amenities, including a number of themed cafés serving free food for all three meals of the day.[10] There are also two swimming pools, two beach volleyball courts, a bowling alley, GBikes to ride from building to building, and group cooking and fitness classes.

These campuses do provide plenty of opportunities for employees to get to know each other and have fun together. Assuming your workplace is not close to matching Googleplex, take some solace knowing that providing every amenity possible and making it easy to live at work is not a great way to encourage your employees to step away and enjoy their lives outside of work.[11]

Vulnerability and Trust

The Society for Human Resources Management makes it clear that trust is more important than perks when it comes to great places to work. Trust works best when it's a two way street; managers must trust employees and vice versa. Furthermore, employees must trust each other.[12]

Stephen Covey, businessman and best-selling author, said it best, "Without trust we don't truly collaborate; we merely coordinate or, at best, cooperate. It is trust that transforms a group of people into a team." When we trust our colleagues, we feel safe, which lowers our stress level, by allowing us to not be on guard. It is only then that we can be our authentic selves and allow our full collaboration with those on the team.

One very important way to improve trust within the organization is to foster a willingness to make oneself vulnerable. It probably comes more naturally to share intimate details of your life with a family member or close friend than it does with co-workers. When we choose to show that we are human, that we put our pants on the same way as everyone else in the organization, we begin to help our teams understand that we are fallible. This not only opens the idea that we can accept those around us for their imperfections, but they too might accept us as imperfect leaders. This is a step toward empathy and building trust. University of Houston professor and best-selling author Brené Brown emphasizes the importance of vulnerability in leadership by dedicating more than half of her book *Dare to Lead* to the topic.

Mark Bertolini, Aetna's former CEO, had a skiing accident in 2004 in which he slammed into a tree, breaking his neck in five places, and then tumbled into an icy river that froze his spinal cord and kept it from fatally rupturing. Taking several prescribed narcotics did little to ease the pain until, while wearing a neck and arm brace, he sat in his car contemplating suicide by driving into a bridge abutment. A police officer asked if he was drunk, and he admitted to being high on drugs.

After the close call with nearly ending his life, he turned to alternative healing with yoga and mindfulness. After finding relief, he made these healing methods available to Aetna employees as well, as a way for him to "open his heart to the organization." His aim became to leave a legacy of compassion. By sharing his inner feelings, by making himself vulnerable to the company and, frankly, to the world, Mark made it easier for others at Aetna to share their struggles, to let their colleagues into their lives. This creates trust and allows us to forge closer bonds to the people we work with.

When leaders display their human side, as Mark did with his story of emotional turmoil, it makes it easier for employees to show their human side as well. After an employee came to him to ask if she could donate some of her own paid time off to a co-worker who needed to tend to a sick child, Mark created Aetna's Paid Time Off (PTO) bank for just that sort of thing. Along with handwritten thank you notes and publicly recognizing employees, the PTO bank was one more way of encouraging Aetna employees to support each other through difficult times.[13]

Feeling Respected and Having Our Opinions Count

A key step in feeling comfortable with offering an opinion at work is our trust in the organization. If we think there will be retribution if we disagree with our boss, our peers, or the greater workforce, not only will it stifle our contribution but it will also add to our stress level. Organizations that build a high level of trust take their employees' opinions into account. This contributes to greater levels of creativity, collaboration, and productive solutions, as well as increasing collegiality.

Knowing that our ideas will be respected keeps communication lines open. Giving and receiving feedback shows respect for our colleagues, builds trust, and supports teamwork.[14] Employees who feel their opinions count are more engaged and productive. Collectively, these work traits of sharing and respect help us nurture a resilient team that will rise to the occasion when a crisis sets in.

Communication

Keeping everyone informed can be difficult, especially in large organizations. However, if you want everyone to feel like they're on the same team, you'll have to master communications.

Southwest Airlines (SWA) embodies the notion of building a strong social climate through communication.[15] If you've ever flown SWA, you're familiar with the humor used during the announcements.

You may not know, though, that leadership meetings are recorded and made available to employees. Can you think of a better way to let the workforce know what's going on at the top? SWA's social climate translates to a low 4 percent employee turnover and a number-one ranking in customer satisfaction by the US Department of Transportation.[16]

Having Fun Together

"Fun" is the last word we likely think of when we hear "work," "assignment," and "project." Having fun has a lot of team benefits. Teams that have fun together stress less and accomplish more.[17] Organizations that integrate fun into work have lower levels of absenteeism, greater job satisfaction, increased morale, and a greater sense of team bonding. The weather is sunny!

Having fun is great for individual well-being. Fun is especially valuable when it leads to laughter. Laughing relaxes our muscles, gives us a break from negativity, and boosts our immune system. Laughter can serve as a great "time out" from a heated discussion. What ever happened to the company softball team?

Volunteering

At Colgate-Palmolive, caring is as important as a healthy smile. Their Colgate Cares Day offers free dental screenings and oral health education to underserved children without access to dental care. Their "Clean Hands, Good Health" effort encourages children to wash their hands while providing free soap and guidance.[18] The company gives its employees the opportunity to be dental or community volunteers. Employees have the chance to make positive impacts on communities. That includes staffing the mobile dental vans, which functions as a dental office on wheels.[19] This program generates smiles—both for the children and the employees.

Volunteering brings all kinds of benefits to not only the recipient, but the volunteers as well. Volunteering lends itself to being grateful, which contributes to happiness. Volunteering helps bring purpose to the day, creates teamwork, and generates positive feelings about the contribution one is making. For each of these reasons, having your team volunteer together in the community adds to your team's positive social climate.

My favorite volunteering opportunity with our team was a spring cleanup of the grounds outside an adult custodial home. We got outside for half the day to pull weeds, plant flowers, and remove garbage to beautify the yard. Not only did we get fresh air and exercise, but we also gained a sense of pride for helping the residents. Wearing our Johns Hopkins volunteer shirts really added to our sense of team.

Volunteering doesn't mean you have to get dirty (although being outside in nature does help our well-being). Volunteering might be just a few clicks away. Instacart, a leader in grocery delivery, partners with Feeding America to remove barriers and provide hunger relief to underserved communities, while raising awareness of a growing inequality. The company supports areas impacted by natural disasters, and every year gives its employees opportunities to donate groceries and funds to support their local communities. Employees are encouraged to place an Instacart order to be delivered directly to local food banks.[20]

Egalitarian Companies

Egalitarian companies are on the other end of the spectrum from traditional hierarchal company structures. In egalitarian organizations, individuals are given a high degree of autonomy and are trusted to make decisions. Title is less important. What matters is who has the talent and experience for a particular job. In contrast to a more conventional model, subordinates are encouraged to provide feedback on managerial effectiveness.

W.L. Gore & Associates, a material science company, is one such workplace, and 88 percent of its employees say it is a great place to work.[21] The company views all employees as capable decision-makers. An employee can be a team leader on some jobs and follow colleagues on another.[22] Leaders emerge naturally by demonstrating some special knowledge.

"Too many organizations view human beings as mere 'resources.' Until this changes, our organizations will be less energetic, less creative, and less resilient than the people within them," said Terri Kelly, former president and CEO of W.L. Gore, talking about the company's long-running experiment in natural leadership and managing without managers.[23] What better way to feel like you have a seat at the table?

SINGIN' IN THE RAIN

The 1952 musical *Singin' in the Rain* forever changed the notion that the weather dictates our mood. Our attitudes come from within and can't be blamed on Mother Nature. Imagine if everyone in your company was singing in the rain. More positive people and fewer negative attitudes equals a better forecast. In fact, we know that when hope and optimism abound, employee performance improves, as does job satisfaction, happiness with work, and organizational commitment—all of which translates into greater employee health, happiness, resilience, and retention.[24,25]

Having an upbeat attitude comes hand-in-hand with collaborating and working toward creative solutions to challenging problems. Yes, an upbeat attitude helps us weather the storm and is an attribute of a resilient worker. Employees who take a "doom and gloom" approach to project setbacks and new competitors in the market will have a difficult time adjusting and getting the results needed.

There is no shortage of potentially stress-inducing events during the workday. However, how we are prepared to meet these stressors impacts our health. Organizations that present challenges in optimistic ways and lead with a can-do attitude are not only enhancing the likelihood of a successful outcome; they're also helping protect their workforce from the elevated blood pressure and weakened immune system that may result from stress.[26] Expressing positive emotions such as happiness and hope translates to a longer life.[27]

The benefits of an organization that takes an upbeat, positive, and optimistic approach extend to supporting employees in their efforts to create healthy habits. Encouragement helps overcome obstacles. Positive attitudes allow more problem solving and make it easier to weather setbacks.

Every employer can create a positive atmosphere. A friend from Austin once had a rock smash through his car windshield. Imagine his surprise when he pulled into Longhorn Glass, across Highway I-35 from the University of Texas campus, and found everyone smiling, quick to help him, and in a jovial mood. Inside, the waiting room was spotless, and the walls were covered with motivational posters. Everyone seemed to be having a jolly good time at work. In under 20 minutes he was pulling out of the business's lot with a grin on his own face. Imagine that! Of all things, a windshield repair shop was the source of uplifting his spirits. Of course, he recommended them to everyone.

All this being said, everyone has a bad day and we all experience losses. Be understanding and don't force positivity on your team and co-workers inappropriately.

Recruitment and Orientation

Do yourself and your organization a favor and include attitude in your job applicant considerations. Look for candidates who emit positive energy and carry optimism and warmth. While we can all learn new skills, why not start out with people on the right end of the positive attitude spectrum?

Orientation is an opportunity to set a positive tone for your new team member. Be sure that all presenters and materials used in orientation follow the best practices of seeing the cup half full and respecting the different parts of the organization. This is not the time for sarcastic or deprecating humor. Get your new employee off on the right foot by showing them that the company is about teamwork, and everyone brings something valuable to the table. How the new employee perceives the attitudes of those providing orientation will shape their outlook. It's an overused expression, but it works: Make a good first impression.

Self-Care

Some people make us feel good inside and others not so much. We are impacting them the same way. If we don't practice self-care, it's going to be difficult for us to be at our best for those around us. Sleeping, eating nutritious food, getting outdoors, and exercise all make it easier for us to feel good inside and emit those positive emotions to those around us. This is important because our emotions are contagious. Your happiness can influence not only the people you work with, but also the people they work with and even one more degree of connection further away.[28] Imagine what would happen if the entire leadership team made their annual professional development goal to learn the skills needed to be more optimistic, grateful, and upbeat—happiness would spread throughout your organization!

Feedback

It should come as no surprise that we prefer to hear what we're doing right rather than what we're doing wrong. Research from Barbara Frederickson, distinguished professor of psychology and leader on the subject of positive emotions, indicates high-functioning teams enjoy sharing three times more positive experiences than negative ones. Since then, a study at Harvard concluded that employees ideally need six pieces of positive feedback for every one critical improvement received.[29] Regardless, we need a lot of sunshine to be a happier and a more productive team. It's probably worth your while to reassess the way your organization not only does performance evaluations, but also integrates identifying what's going right during the day versus what's going wrong. This is easier said when we practice gratitude and appreciation.

Gratitude, Appreciation, and Recognition

It turns out we can learn a new trick. We can enhance our happiness through the practice of feeling thankful. By recognizing our good fortune regularly, we reinforce the positive things in our life. Gratitude's cousin, appreciation, is also an easy strategy for your organization to deploy.

American CEOs agree that gratitude is important—90 percent! Too bad only one out of every three employees are satisfied with the amount of gratitude they receive.[30] It's no surprise that companies extend a heaping portion of gratitude on their customers. Why not on their employees? Your company may already have an appreciation and recognition program. But are you using it?

Be careful that your appreciation is consistent with a well-being message. Does an employee appreciation day that serves hot dogs, cookies, and soda show you really care? I have been "appreciated" this way more than once during my career.

Celebrating

People respond to praise and encouragement. Try not to let success go unacknowledged. Sometimes we wait too long to recognize forward movement. Your organization would fare much better if small achievements were recognized along the way to milestones. This applies not only to good customer service and increased sales, but also to cheering on those employees who are succeeding in reaching their well-being goals. Ask for permission to publicly acknowledge your employee's effort. Acknowledging success not only feels good, but it reinforces desirable practices to the recipient as well as those in the vicinity.

Holidays

Holidays are a perfect opportunity for injecting positivity into the workplace. While not every company can afford to bring in Snoop Dogg for a private performance, like CarGurus did, it's likely you can still create fun on a more modest budget. For your remote workers, how about a "Fuzzy Socks White Elephant End of the Year Party" like they had at Blockstack (now Hiro PBC, a technology company focused on secure data sharing). Get your feet in front of the camera![31]

Smiling

When in doubt, smile! It turns out that a simple smile can be a surprisingly effective way to promote health and happiness! Smiling has many positive health effects, including lowering blood pressure, reducing stress, and improving our attitude. Plus, while you might think that happiness produces smiling, the reverse is also true. Smiling can produce happiness. The physical act of smiling triggers the release of serotonin and dopamine in the brain. These chemicals help us feel happier and calmer. In essence, it's possible to change your outlook and make yourself feel better by just faking a smile. As a bonus, when others see you smiling, they'll smile too![32]

Bupa, a company that offers health insurance, health services, and elder care, aptly named their global well-being program "Smile." Bupa knows that smiling helps our energy levels—the focus of their well-being culture effort.[33]

PACKING FOR THE SAME VACATION

Heading out of town on vacation can be one of the best experiences to forge bonds with your family—or one of the worst. Plenty of preparation is needed. Agreeing on the location, the accommodations, and what to pack are among the decisions the group needs to make. When the family is aligned, has the same ideas of how the vacation will be, and anticipates the same experience together, it's much more enjoyable. When your son shows up for a beach vacation without a bathing suit, maybe he didn't have the same vision of the destination.

"A shared vision happens when both leadership and employees not only want the same things for the company but also work together to accomplish these things. It's an effort from the top to the bottom, and back up—and repeat. It begins with everyone, not solely a leadership team, thus creating common interests and an organic sense of shared purpose across everything that happens in the organization. It should be palpable to your audience. That's the goal."[34]

The primary reason that an organization's shared vision plays a role in employee health and well-being is related to its role in creating unity toward a common destination. The ability of a shared vision to bring everyone together and rowing in the same direction is a great gift to improve collegiality and create a sense of purpose, which you may find instrumental in your own well-being. A strong, shared vision serves to not only unite groups of people with inherent differences, but also helps individuals understand their contribution in getting to the destination. Everyone wants to play a valuable role on the team. Who wants to be the player on the bench? We all want to be in the starting line-up.

Sticking with the sports analogy for a minute . . . inspiration is another benefit from a shared vision. When we are inspired, we can accomplish things we hadn't thought imaginable. How many stories have we heard about individuals and teams rising to the occasion to overcome the odds because they were inspired by their goal or their situation? I think of the 1980 Olympics, US men's hockey team taking on the Russian team in what became known as the Miracle on Ice. At the time, the United States was playing with an amateur team (mostly college students) while the Russians enrolled veteran players. The Cold War was still present, and Russia had recently invaded Afghanistan. Tension was high. The Russian team hadn't lost an Olympic hockey game in more than a decade. Unified by their underdog status as well as the strength they derived from the perception of the United States as a moral leader, the US team defied the odds and beat the four-time defending gold medal champions.

Their coach, Herb Brooks, drove the team with grinding purpose to aim for gold. When he asked each of them who they were, he got answers like, "I play for Boston University," or "I play for the University of Wisconsin." He kept at them until they would shout back, "I play for team USA!"[35] With a shared vision, they were at last ready to fix their sights on gold. No one thought they could do it, but they did.

According to John Kotter, Harvard Business School professor, when organizations need to change, having a shared vision makes it easier because the vision states the direction of the change and motivates employees to act together in the same direction (which limits conflict, wasted time, and resources).[36] Unfortunately, only one in five employees can see the connection between their work and their team's and organization's goals.[37]

Most people like feeling part of a team, especially a winning team. Everyone wants to feel like they are contributing to something bigger than themselves and that they are part of a group that is bound together with a common purpose (which incidentally fosters resilience). This sense of belonging is a valuable contributor to a sense of well-being that is very different from the value brought by healthy eating and good sleep. It is one more facet that contributes to the whole personal well-being journey.

THERE'S NO PLACE LIKE HOME

Our home is of prime importance for creating the social conditions needed to show up at work, ready to be a team player and contribute to the goals, mission, and vision of our organization. If things aren't great at home, they won't be great at work. It's hard to find a family that isn't struggling to address a challenge. There are so many to choose from! Marital challenges, learning difficulties, peer pressure, financial challenges, and lack of recreation time together all pull at the foundation of family unity and are likely to affect one's ability to work effectively.

If you want your employee to show up and be fully engaged at work, then your company needs to be sure it's doing what it can to support the challenges its employees face at home. It's for this reason that employee assistance programs have expanded greatly over the years. When your organization has the resources, be sure to care for your employee's family and address concerns beyond the workplace. It will allow your employee to focus more on their job and company.

For most organizations, the company family picnic is long gone. However, are there other ways to bring the family into the mix? If there is a holiday party, can your employees bring a "plus one"? Is there a benefit to help strengthen marriages, like a subscription to Our.Love app (a gamified skill-building app that improves relationships)? How about a bulletin board in the break room where members of your team can post a picture or two of a family member or pet? It's a great way to start a conversation about the special people in each other's lives. These types of strategies can help break down barriers of talking about one's home life and potentially open the door to understanding the challenges we all face, which could then lead to providing the support we yearn.

Zoom Video Communications' Denver office has a happiness crew whose aim is to ensure the company's culture is maintained through events, celebrations, and community involvement. As Denver sales leader Ben Volkman said, "One of my favorite events that the happiness crew put on was Bring Your Parent to Work Day. During my interviews, I ask, 'What motivates you?' After a lot of probing, it usually comes down to family and how the employee was raised. To meet the parents and family members who motivate our employees brings it all full circle. After spending time with their parents, I can see where they get their drive and tenacity to be successful."[38] Such events serve to further bond employees together.

For many, pets are part of the family. Companies like Amazon in Seattle, PetSmart in Phoenix, Ceros in New York, and Splendid Spoon in

Brooklyn all have pet-friendly workplaces. Amazon even has a dog park for its 6,000 registered dogs, and that comes with free treats and poop bags.[39] Just petting a dog lowers stress levels quickly.

Salesforce has been listed on several Best Place to Work lists, in part because the company believes a good work–life balance is vital for a great culture. While the employees work hard, they also enjoy how the company respects peoples' lives outside of work. During the earliest part of the COVID-19 pandemic, the company closed all its major global offices. They offered employees financial support to ensure their home office was suitable, and they supported their employees' physical and mental well-being. They were one of the largest employers to announce the end of the 9-to-5 workday as they moved to a semiremote model, a progressive move for a company with over 50,000 employees.[40]

If you really want to extend the social climate of your company, extend it into your community. Texas-based grocery chain H-E-B, with more than 340 stores and over 100,000 employees, is committed to serving its communities. In addition to sponsoring many well-being events, like an annual Fiesta FitFest,[41] the company is quick to offer its own disaster relief to communities in times of crisis, with employees as well as customers among the volunteers delivering emergency supplies and drinking water.[42] Along with supporting many proud H-E-B volunteers, the company supplies over 3 million meals a year to Texas food banks.[43,44]

When the company's annual in-person Thanksgiving effort to offer 250,000 meals to 33 communities seemed stymied by the COVID-19 pandemic, the company scrambled to deploy a mobile operation "where we can enjoy the holiday with our neighbors," said Winnell Herron, Group Vice President of Public Affairs, Diversity and Environmental Affairs.[45] Volunteers from H-E-B employees, customers, and community organizations worked together to make the feast happen once more. This consistent effort to engage their community has led to very proud employees and very loyal customers. Employees voting in Glassdoor's "Employees' Choice Awards" cite culture, earning H-E-B a spot on their list of Best Places to Work.[46]

LET'S NOT SELL HAPPINESS SHORT!

HubSpot, an American developer and marketer of software products for inbound marketing, sales, and customer service, ranks high on the *Business Insider* top 25 companies where employees feel happy and fulfilled. Voted number 1 for employee happiness by Comparably (a human resource information consolidator and disseminator), the company is dedicated to creating a culture in which employees are happy, engaged, and included.[47] Beyond a robust perks and benefits package, which includes flexibility, along with praise and recognition, happiness is dead center in why the company thinks emotional well-being matters at work.

The big difference at HubSpot is that they believe the model of job success leading to happiness is a model that is backward. The company believes that happiness isn't a destination, but rather it is a starting point. Four important ways the company keeps its employees happy are:

1. Giving employees a variety of assignments
2. Allowing employees to work independently from management
3. Sharing work-related intelligence with them (transparency)
4. Fostering collaboration between managers and employees

HubSpot also encourages employees to achieve and maintain happiness at work by finding meaning in their work, doing work that helps others, remembering what they love about their work, searching within for any sign of unhappiness, eating with and interacting with others, learning something new, and planning a vacation. HubSpot's progressive model, sharply focused on happiness, serves as an exemplary model offering specific ways in which other organizations may wish to emulate.

DYING FOR A PAYCHECK

In stark contrast to HubSpot's happy environment, toxic workplaces are at the opposite end of a good social climate. In Jeffrey Pfeffer's book *Dying for a Paycheck*, he describes 10 characteristics of a toxic workplace. [48] All 10 of Jeffrey's "workplace exposures" demonstrate a lack of caring by the employer—a general breakdown of a social climate. The physical and psychological toll of toxic workplaces is as harmful as exposure to secondhand smoke and results in more deaths annually than from diabetes.[49]

Working in an atmosphere of regular layoffs certainly doesn't create a sense of community. And it's not just bad for the employees. Companies that engage in toxic practices, such as annual layoffs, are less profitable and successful by other measures than those organizations that are more intentional with their human resources.[50]

You're probably not working for a toxic organization. However, there's probably room for improvement. The workforce is no longer waiting to be dismissed. Employees are voting with their feet and leaving on their own. Give your workforce a reason to stay and new employees to join, by building a great social climate. Without a good social climate, trying to develop healthy norms or navigate turbulent times will be difficult if not impossible.

Shaping Your Team Subculture

While the company might think that being a good manager is about getting payroll done on time and accomplishing the team's goals, your job extends well into the human experience. How you, as the manager, make your employees feel is vitally important. Without a cohesive and enthusiastic team, you won't meet those goals or even possibly have a payroll to complete if everyone leaves!

Shaping a good social climate may not be an inherent manager responsibility. The good news is that there are ways to improve team cohesiveness, create more optimism, and inspire a shared vision, which will ultimately lead to greater joy in working together. Here's a checklist from the "weatherman":

- Communicate! No one likes to be kept in the dark.
- Be fair. People want to feel as if they are being treated justly. If we perceive favoritism, it's a sure way to alienate members of the team.
- Don't rush to judgment. Keep your foot out of your mouth by avoiding swift conclusions.
- Give employees choices. People don't like to be told what to do, but rather prefer to be involved with decision-making. Give them a high degree of autonomy.
- Create opportunities for collaboration.
- Enlist a facilitator to lead a trust building exercise.
- Be caring. Who hasn't had a bad day or gone through a challenging period? People want to feel supported during these times.

(Continued)

- Establish a no tolerance policy for sharing protected information and sensitive information about team members as well as other co-workers in the organization. Gossip is a trust-buster.
- Give your team permission to have fun. They may think it's against the rules!
- You can just be kind! Practicing consistent acts of kindness helps everyone feel welcome.

These strategies amount to being a good manager. If they don't come naturally to you, check with your human resource department. It's possible they have resources to help build some new skills and extinguish some unfavorable habits. The additional time spent learning how to be a good manager will be worth the effort spent trying to get your team to perform their best work. You don't need to be a well-being expert, therapist, or counselor to assist.

HOW I HELP HOPKINS GET HEALTHY

When the pandemic hit, we had to adjust quickly on many levels. In addition to the obvious challenges of identifying and treating those infected with COVID-19 as well as protecting our workforce from contracting the virus, we knew there would be the added assault of fear, stress, and social separation. Our team had to adjust and meet our employees where they were—but safely.

Most of our programs and services had been delivered in person. The idea of providing programming through a teleconference service hadn't been entertained. Who would attend such a program and how could it be meaningful? Challenging circumstances call for creative solutions. Like so many other organizations, we pivoted to address both stress and the social disconnectedness our employees were experiencing. Our "Worksite Wellness Menu" allows *teams* to choose from a list of stress-reducing activities to experience together. Examples include progressive muscle relaxation, breathing exercises, and chair yoga. Not only do the participants benefit from the activity, but they also benefit from the shared experience. Additionally, the stress-reducing activities were designed with the intent of creating a space to discuss new stressors and gave permission to the team to acknowledge that stress is real and something that needs to be addressed.

Put Your Own Mask on First

You'll benefit when you feel like you belong, embrace positivity, and align your work with the organization. Consider the following:

- When was the last time you were goofy, silly, or otherwise had fun at work?
- Lighten up and enjoy your day a little more.
- Make yourself vulnerable. Share something about your personal life with your team or even just one work colleague. Doing so will draw you closer to the people around you and help you feel more connected.
- Practice self-compassion. Turn off your inner critic.
- Check in with yourself—when we're feeling down, angry, or negative in another way, it's hard to hide. Emotions can be contagious. Be sure to learn how to understand and assess your own well-being. How do you show up for a meeting? If you're not well, seek help!
- Focus on the present and don't dwell on the past—rehashing a failed project isn't a path to happiness.
- Stop complaining and start appreciating. The change will replace the cloud over your head with sun and clear skies.
- Learn how to be happier, read *Positivity* by Barbara Fredrickson or *Authentic Happiness* by Martin Seligman.

THAT'S A WRAP

Having a good social climate makes it easier to establish and maintain relationships. These relationships can extend well beyond your immediate team when the atmosphere fosters accessibility and approachability. When a positive social climate exists, people look forward to coming to work. It's not just a paycheck, but rather a source of fulfillment. We've all heard about the companies where the CEO knows everyone by their first name. What do you think their social climate is like?

Consider how your organization can implement strategies that support a good social climate across the entire organization.

- What process does your organization have in place to help new employees feel like they are part of the team right away?
- What opportunities do you create for employees to socialize? What do you do for those working remotely?

- What volunteering opportunities has the organization provided for your employees? Favor those that require people to work together.
- How are you assessing attitude in your talent acquisition strategy?
- What resources do you have in place to train managers as effective leaders, including having a positive attitude?
- What strategies are in place to optimize the alignment between the employee's role and the organization's vision?

Cheers was a popular television series that aired from 1982 to 1993. Set in a fictional bar in Boston, this dramedy depicted what many of us hope for ourselves. For some of us, going to work is like going to the bar from *Cheers*. There is a sense of community, where people enjoy each other's company, can laugh together, celebrate each other's success, and lean on each other in times of distress. Even the show's theme music conveys the desire to be part of a community and ends with the lyrics, "you wanna go where everybody knows your name."

One of the main characters, Norm Peterson, is warmly greeted every time he enters the tavern. When Norm opens the door and enters, the patrons shout out his name, "Norm." This ritual, this expectation of the staff and customers, actually has a name. The regularity of the patrons singing out "Norm" is aptly called a "norm"—a pattern of group behavior and the next well-being culture building block.

5

All the Cool Kids Are Doing It (or Thinking It)

Norms

PRIOR TO ARRIVING AT JOHNS HOPKINS Medicine, I was never much of a coffee person. I might have had four or five cups across the seven years it took me to finish medical school and residency training. For the most part, I was not a "normal" physician. We face early mornings and long days, and many of us use caffeine to keep us on our feet, especially in medical school and during residency. In my first role at Hopkins, I was hardly ever on my feet. I moved from sitting at my desk to sitting in meetings and then back again—and all the sitting was making me tired, not rested.

When I found I could no longer keep my eyes open through the afternoon, I decided to give coffee a try again (partially thanks to my wife, who suggested ways to make the taste more agreeable). Soon, I was making it through the afternoon alert and productive.

But why did I change my behavior, really?

The break rooms on the Johns Hopkins Glen Burnie, Maryland, campus had coffee machines with single-serve disposable pods. The free and decent coffee was a perk, and I had noticed my co-workers gathering around the machine, enjoying each other's company, as I passed on my way to the refrigerator for my lunch. At Johns Hopkins, coffee drinking is a strong *norm*—a shared behavior—and I was exposed to this norm every day. My inactivity and afternoon slump primed the appeal, but the cultural norm made the idea of coffee drinking more attractive. I could have chosen tea, right? Despite my more than 40 years of avoiding coffee, I changed my behavior and my habit. You might say I succumbed to the norm. Now, it would be difficult for me to change back.

This is the power of norms to influence individual behavior when the circumstances are right—and the leverage they give us when we're trying to create a well workforce. Starting to drink coffee is easy compared to someone trying to stop eating pizza or start exercising daily. Think about your own struggles to adopt a healthy behavior. It's hard when our goals go against norms in our immediate social circles. Likewise, it's much easier to adopt a behavior when all the cool kids are doing it and when norms align with our own goals.

Norms are one of the key building blocks of culture. Back in 1871, the pioneering anthropologist Edward Tylor defined culture as "that complex whole which includes knowledge, belief, art, law, morals, custom, and any other capabilities and habits acquired by man as a member of society."[1] Norms are "the way we do things around here," the usual way of acting in a given circumstance, behaviors that are done without much thought. Norms also include the attitudes and beliefs prevalent in the culture that support those common behaviors and habits.

Consider handwashing for healthcare workers. We don't give it much thought. It's just part of the routine. But it wasn't always. Somebody had to create that norm for the betterment of patients and staff (thank you, Ignaz Semmelweis). Even once the healthcare community understood it was important, it took decades of hard work, education, and adjustments to the physical environment to turn it into a norm—and that work is still ongoing.

This example, or your own experiences, might have you thinking that you're facing a long, tough climb with certain behaviors in your workplace. The difference is that we know so much more about how to create norms and thus how to influence behavior than we once did. Norms can be shaped much more quickly now.

HOW NORMS WORK ON US AND OUR ORGANIZATIONS

If you went to college or have ever watched any movie about the college experience, you're likely familiar with the culture of drinking—and I'm not talking about coffee anymore. Even if you weren't inclined to drink alcohol, it's possible you held a cup in your hand and occasionally lifted it to your lips to give the allusion that you were part of the group. You were cool. You were accepted. Not drinking would potentially mean you were on your own, or at least in a quandary as you tried to find the few like-minded individuals whose values deviated from those of the general culture. These nonconformists avoided an unhealthy norm that landed some college students in the ER, some on probation, some kicked out of school, or worse. But it wasn't easy. Socially, it made things difficult, even stressful.

Norms are established much earlier in life than college, though. Even in early childhood, we prioritize being accepted by our peers, and we recognize that norms help. In one study, preschoolers were observed acting out punishment on puppets, their make-believe peers, who weren't "playing" according to prescribed norms.[2] Even when kindergarten students had just observed their peers give the wrong answer to a picture book with cartoon animals, they were more likely to give the same incorrect answer than when students were asked questions separately from onlookers.[3] Privacy blunted the power of conformity. When they know they're not being observed, children are also less likely to conform to a norm.[4] It appears that behaving in a collective manner, via norms, is innate![5] But what's the biological imperative?

In any culture or society, we all experience a personal benefit to conforming to group norms. Consider David Rock's brain-based SCARF (status, certainty, autonomy, relatedness, fairness) model for leading and engaging employees, based on the decades of research into social neuroscience by psychologists, anthropologists, and neuroscientists. A core theme is that "social needs are treated in much the same way in the brain as the need for food and water."[6] Our brains are constantly looking to maximize reward and minimize threat in social situations, to get what we think we need and avoid the things we don't want, and conformity helps us do that.

The first element of the SCARF model is status. Status gives us a place at the table. Being part of the team often means conforming with the group. Innately, we understand that conforming improves our reputation as someone who can be trusted and therefore included. Bucking team norms is a path to being excluded. Three more elements of the SCARF model—certainty, relatedness, and fairness—tie directly to the power of group norms. If everybody follows them, we can feel more certain about the future (we can roughly predict how people will behave), we feel a sense of relatedness or connection through our behaviors, and we experience fairness because everybody is held accountable to the same expectations, rules, or policies. When we comply with the norm, it helps others see us in a positive light and at minimum, keeps us from being shunned.[7]

The last element, autonomy, may at first intuitively run counter to norms. When a team leader mandates norms, such that group behaviors are no longer the collective action but rather the decree, that's a problem. Autonomy decreases stress because it provides some control over our situation and surrounding. As you navigate supporting healthy norms, be aware that a reduction in autonomy may drive some team members away. Tread carefully and don't impose your behavior preferences on your team.[8]

Take a moment to think about it. You probably work with or have worked with somebody who regularly defies the norms in your team or organization. What kinds of words have been used for that person? "Difficult"? Even "troublemaker"? And what happens if that person defies too many norms for too long? They get pushed out, right? Norms are an important construct when we think about the workplace and the behaviors individuals adopt to keep their jobs or get promoted. Who is going to buck the group behaviors and attitudes and risk being cast in a *negative* light? Remember, norms can be healthy or unhealthy, and if people are afraid to defy them, unhealthy norms can have a profound impact on people's well-being.

The power of norms explains in part why anonymous feedback is so valuable. It allows individuals to break from the norms and share their own beliefs and attitudes.[9] Even our kindergarten students got the answer correct more often when given the opportunity to answer in private. Don't underestimate the importance of giving employees ample opportunity to offer candid feedback without repercussion if you are trying to understand the truth of your culture. It may even be worth the cost of hiring an outside company to run the survey or interviews.

Because they are so powerful, norms can have a profound impact on the organization's well-being. Cultural forces "interpret" an organization's policies and official procedures and heavily influence whether they work as intended. So, for example, the written policy may be to have a half-hour lunch break, but the cultural norm could be an hour. The written value statement might include "respect," but the norm might be for leaders to be demanding, condescending, or rude. The official HR policy might be that new parents can take three months of leave, but the norm might be six weeks—and anybody who takes more might feel judged or feel as though their job is at stake.

The reverse is also true: everyday healthy norms are helping organizations achieve goals, support and engage employees, and align policy and reality. Look at Johnson & Johnson, a pioneer in investing in the health and well-being of their employees around the world. They have focused on consistently building norms that support their culture and values and align with their policies. For instance, they were one of the first companies to become tobacco free. When they weren't getting the participation they had hoped for in the health-risk assessments, they offered a $500 reduction in healthcare deductibles for anybody who participated. In 2020, they made healthy eating a priority and set a policy to ensure that 80 percent of the food offered at their facilities around the world is healthy. The result is that J&J has one of the healthiest workforces in the world. "In 2016, 30% of people nationwide had hypertension, compared to just 9.2% of the Johnson & Johnson population," and their healthcare costs are 2 to 3 percent lower than other large corporations, which translates into hundreds of millions in savings.[10]

The real takeaway here is that a culture is in trouble when you have to be a hero, an outcast, or a social psychologist to do what is healthy and right. Luckily, it doesn't have to be that way.

SPOTTING THE HEALTH NORMS IN YOUR CULTURE

Too often the different cultures to which we belong, such as our family or community, have strong norms for unhealthy behaviors. When we try to build healthy lifestyle habits in opposition to those norms, it's like swimming upstream. Yes, it's possible to say "no thank you" to the cake your mom makes every Sunday, but it gets a lot harder if there are donuts on the table every morning at the team huddle. Swimming upstream for long periods of time can really tire our arms out and eventually our willpower sinks.

In organizations around the world, norms that run counter to what is healthy for most people are rampant. For example, in most workplaces, the idea of a 9-to-5 business day is long gone. Now it's 8-to-6 . . . and then a little more after dinner . . . and a bit more on the weekend. It's common to get emails from our managers and co-workers at all hours of the day and every day of the week. And as we head into a time when a hybrid home-and-office workplace becomes a norm, ending our workday will only become harder. Our American cultural norm for working nonstop is killing us (literally, as well documented in *Dying for a*

Paycheck by Jeffery Pfeffer). Conforming is a powerful force. When we're in the midst of conforming, we may not even perceive the behavior as problematic.

This is why it's so crucial for all of us, and especially leaders, to be able to identify the norms influencing our behaviors, our teams, and our organizations. You are in a position to turn the tide; put the brakes on unhealthy norms and push the pedal on the healthy ones.

So, let me take a few moments to help you start spotting health norms in your culture. Consider the following questions:

- Have you been trying to eradicate an unhealthy behavior across your team, such as sending emails after work hours or on weekends, working through the lunch hour and eating in front of the computer, or loading up the break room with leftover cookies, candy, and cake on Monday morning? If you've been struggling to change it, what influences might be working against your efforts?
- Have you observed a stronger focus on health or a stronger team atmosphere in another department in your organization? What are some of the specific behaviors or attitudes feeding their team culture?
- Have you successfully built a healthy norm in your team culture, even if you weren't thinking of it in those terms? What is it? How is it helping your team?

Now that you have a sense of the norms at play in your team or organization, let's look at how you can change them or develop new ones.

NORMS CAN BE INTENTIONALLY CHANGED OR CREATED

Our need to belong, to be thought of in high regard, and for structure and predictability all contribute to the consistency of norms. Yet as conditions change, so can norms. When our environment calls for adopting new beliefs or behaviors, we adjust.[11] As I shared at the beginning of the chapter, I needed an afternoon pick-me-up, so after decades of one behavior, I adopted a new one. On a large, community-wide scale, I can think of no better illustration of how quickly health norms can shift than the response to the COVID-19 pandemic. In many subcultures in America, social distancing, wearing a mask, and washing hands gelled very quickly. At the same time, these behaviors didn't become norms in other subcultures, because they didn't align with the shared values or beliefs. The leaders of different subcultures (i.e., clergy, politicians, company presidents) heavily influenced the development of these norms or discouraged their adoption.

How does this play out within organizations or companies, where individuals with different beliefs and desires and views come together?

Remember my firetruck revelation in Chapter 1? Well, after making the connection between the soda truck parked outside the old emergency room and the impact of soda on the health of our employees, I took a stroll inside our buildings. Sure enough, there was soda everywhere: the cafeteria, vending machines, gift shops. It was served at our meetings! Our culture embraced unhealthy beverages. The widespread presence of soda, along with the visual cues, product placement, and financial incentive (at the time, a soda cost less than the same size bottle of water) were all contributing to a culture of unhealthy nutrition and making it easier for our workforce to accept that drinking soda was the norm, that it was okay—while we actively cared for patients (some of whom were our own co-workers) who were harmed by these drinks.

In the meantime, tackling "big soda" was gaining traction at other hospitals and communities. We were seeing a broader norm shift at play. And in terms of my work to build a culture of health at Johns Hopkins Medicine (JHM), I felt addressing unhealthy beverages in our workplace would be a tangible and relatively straightforward starting point. It would help send a message that we wanted to actively support the health of our workforce. So, I set out to change that part of our culture, to change the norm.

To succeed, we needed to build the infrastructure. We created alliances with communications, human resources, and procurement departments. We pressed for integration of the effort with our business goals. Some norm changes are better managed over a longer time; a cataclysmic shift that happens too fast can provoke resistance. Maybe that's just an excuse to make me feel better that despite our focus, it took several years to see our collective attitude and behaviors change across the organization. Over those years, we took a series of incremental steps:

- We stopped offering soda and sugary beverages in containers larger than 12 ounces.
- We set a policy for cafeterias and other food services that soda and other sugary beverages can make up no more than 20 percent of the beverage options. The rest of the options need to be low-calorie

or no-calorie drinks. We didn't eliminate choice. We just provided more healthy choices.

- We set a policy that water must always cost less than the sugary beverages.
- We created a point-of-purchase marketing plan, putting red dots on unhealthy beverages and green dots on healthy beverages.
- We made the healthy beverages more visible by placing them at eye level.
- We created a policy to only offer healthy beverages at our company meetings and events (with an exception or two for holidays and celebrations).

Some leaders were concerned these changes would create an uproar, but we actually received thank-you notes! Many employees asked why we hadn't made the changes sooner. Members of the workforce even helped by spotting areas where the strategy wasn't fully implemented or had a setback after product stocking. The transformation of our beverage norms along with the marketing and communication strategy that accompanied the process sent a clear message to our workforce that they can drink whatever they like *and* we're going to make it easier for our employees to choose healthy drinks *because we care*. And we saw real behavior change. For instance, the percentage of "green dot" beverages purchased from our vending machines doubled!

Norms can be intentionally shaped, and that work is the crux of change management of almost any kind. Shaping norms to support healthy behaviors can be more complex because we don't have the right to dictate how people behave when it comes to their well-being. The key to remember is that in a culture of health, personal choice is respected. Norms encourage healthy practices *and* support individual discretion. You can choose to drink sugary beverages at JHM, but we will only be selling them in 12-ounce containers, there will be fewer choices, and they will cost more than our healthy choices.

Despite the subtle balancing act required, healthy norms are being developed in organizations around the world every day.

CHOOSING NORMS TO CHANGE

What are you trying to change? What behavior or attitude is not serving your organization well? What values does your organization want to support? With so many unhealthy behaviors in almost any culture, it may not seem difficult to choose a few norms to shift or shape. But your team and your boss may have opinions. People may have their own health issues they want to address, biasing their perspective. Trending health behaviors might influence the discussion. Before you know it, the decision becomes a little less straightforward. There are a lot of opinions to balance and if you only rely on opinions, you might miss the best path! To increase the chance of arriving at a decision that is most likely to benefit your organization, you have to be strategic and focused. Consider three fundamentals.

The right norm aligns with the organization's values. In Chapter 3, we explored shared values and the critical role they play in shaping a culture of health and well-being. Every culture needs a foundation and guidelines, and values can offer that. When choosing norms to build or eradicate, look to the shared values for guidance. The more aligned a norm is with the values, the easier it will be to adopt and maintain. An organization that values work–life balance might develop a norm that eliminates company communication after 6 p.m. An organization that values kindness and giving might develop a norm for supporting employees in need. When choosing norms, consider your organizational values first.

The right norm has to be meaningful to employees. As Michele Gelfand and Joshua Jackson write in their analysis of the science behind norms, "Humans are meaning-makers" and norms "serve as perfect solutions to our need for cognitive closure."[12] But norms have to be functionally meaningful, too. If a "socially learned behavior repeatedly has a low payoff"—if an employee simply can't see any real benefit from repeating it, either physically, emotionally, or even just to gain social approval—it won't stick. And a poorly chosen norm could even result in defiant behaviors.

The right norm needs to be meaningful to the organization. While the health and well-being of employees impacts every aspect of the success of an organization, some norms might more directly impact certain organizational needs or goals. Think about the most pressing needs of your organization. For instance, if you're in the manufacturing industry, norms that help you support employee health while achieving safety goals and targets could be important. If you're in the retail industry, where turnover tends to be high, norms that could have a long-term impact on employee engagement and retention might be an important North Star. When norms are meaningful to employees and to the organization, the alignment makes change much easier.

―――――――

THERE'S NO PLACE LIKE HOME

When possible, consider extending the norm into other cultures influencing your employees.

Some workplace norms are shaped more quickly when they are also addressed in other cultures simultaneously. Often our habits are influenced more by someone we live with than someone we work with. For example, a major influence on our food choices is the person who is shopping for or preparing the food in our home. If you want to create a norm related to good nutrition, only applying strategies that resonate and influence behaviors during the workday will make it difficult for your employees to maintain the healthy habit outside of work. The results for them and for the organization may not be stellar. You might need strategies that help them share the habits with friends and family. For instance, you might invite spouses or partners to join healthy skill-building programs or allow them to eat at employee cafeterias. You might offer programs outside of the workplace, such as at a local grocery store or food co-op, and invite the broader community.

Sometimes, though, we have to go even further. Let's keep going with the healthy eating example. If your company owns a factory in a neighborhood that is essentially a "food desert"—an area with highly limited access to healthful or varied foods—all the education in the world won't help them make better choices outside of work hours because the choices don't exist. To really shape the norm, you may have to partner with local community organizations to help address the lack of healthy foods. JHM, like some other employers I've seen, began working with local farmers to create farmers' markets on campus, across our locations, making it easier for employees to access healthy produce and bring it home to their families.

―――――――

AVOID GOING TO EXTREMES

The influence of norms in cultures falls into a range, and the two extremes of that range are authoritarian and anomie. Neither is good for the population within that culture. In authoritarian societies, norms have the power usually assigned to laws—individuals adhere to whatever commandment the leader professes, whether or not it infringes on individual rights or autonomy. This is obviously not ideal. Authoritarianism restricts freedoms, which are inherently essential to well-being. In fact, mandates run counter to the "A" in David Rock's SCARF model. Despite the fact that we want to feel that we belong to a group and that we're included in and respected by the group, we also want enough autonomy to feel like we're making our own choices and can shape our lives as we see fit.

Rarely are norms written into laws. However, in the workplace, some norms are written into policies. A nonsmoking policy is a common example. This policy may define where smoking is acceptable and the number of smoke breaks an employee is allowed to take in a day. As long as the policy respects the law, it can define acceptable behaviors in the workplace. But if policies are too restrictive or are punitive, our norm-building efforts can backfire. While not law, punitive action might feel like law when it is applied to your behavior. Using laws and penalties that apply strict definitions of norms and don't allow individual choice are ripe for problems. The result can range from individuals feeling bad about themselves for a behavior they can't achieve, thereby possibly creating a situation that detracts from their well-being, to outright dissent that runs counter to building a positive social climate. Either way, the individuals and the organization are worse off for this approach.

On the other end of the spectrum is anomie—a culture without norms. This circumstance can occur when there is rapid change, such as leadership, economic, or social upheaval, and commonly accepted norms and values disappear. This period of transition can contribute to unethical behavior. One example might be when a company acquires another company.[13] If the acquisition isn't handled well, employees from the acquired company might feel disconnected from the new organization. This feeling of not belonging may then result in talent leaving the organization. Anomie can also lead to deviant behavior.[14] Perhaps an employee will feel less inhibited to take home office supplies.

The Motley Fool, the investment media and education company founded to "speak truth to Wall Street," dealt with a challenge after 24 years of functioning with a very specific norm. The Motley Fool produces content, or intellectual property, and if employees aren't feeling good, aren't mentally engaged, aren't creative, everything suffers. They need employees to work hard but also feel trusted and respected, critical elements of psychological safety. Early on, they worked to build a culture of low hierarchy, high autonomy, and minimal management. Their goal is to never have an adversarial relationship develop between leadership and employees. They establish norms like everybody choosing their own title and their unlimited "take what you need when you need it" vacation policy. And it works. They've been called a recruiting power-house and were named to the *Inc*. Best Places to Work list in 2020.

But any well-intentioned leadership team can go too far. Because the company culture is laid back, low hierarchy, and low "policy" oriented, project teams have always been created informally. For 24 years, people would simply invite other team members onto their projects to help, and the invitees would accept or not—no rules, no policies, no parameters. It was a norm of no norms. Once the company got to a certain size and age, people started to feel the approach was unfair and unequal, especially because, as Lee Burbage, chief people officer, explained, "Most people look at reward and recognition and think cash, but our currency is get-ting on the right project. That's how you know you're getting ahead."[15] By trying to avoid one type of hierarchy or inequality, they inadvertently created another. People felt they didn't necessarily have the opportunity to work on the projects they wanted or that would boost their careers. Remember, we all desire fairness (the F in SCARF). When the leader-ship team discovered the problem, through employee surveys, they shifted. Now the norm is that the company posts all projects and jobs internally and people apply. It feels fair, which helps reduce stress and disengagement.

Shaping Your Team Subculture

I've shared a few examples of successful norm changes, and by now you may be excited enough about the possibilities to be thinking, "Okay, so how do I do this?" First, remember that the building blocks of a healthy culture are interdependent. Deciding to build or support healthy norms is part of shaping a culture of health, but to be successful you have to leverage every tool. Basically, to successfully shape norms, you really need to read the rest of the book!

- What norms are creating problems for your team?
- What does the conversation around the watercooler say about the norms the team wants to either get rid of or build?
- Which health norms do you think would be readily embraced by your team? Which would prompt resistance?

With a good social climate, prompting a conversation will be easy. Be sure to listen, acknowledge, and invite everyone to be heard.

(Continued)

Well-being is personal and not everyone will want to share. Respect their privacy. Although it might be tempting to change multiple ways of doing business, land on just one or two to make it easier to succeed. You'll want to steer the team toward a norm goal that is likely to be easily attained in order to build confidence in the team so that when you succeed, they'll want to address another behavior. Starting with a norm goal that is too challenging or doesn't have broad support might set the team up for failure, making a future attempt unlikely.

A CASE STUDY IN A LOW-STRESS START TO THE DAY

I don't know about you, but I have almost unlimited admiration for teachers, especially elementary school teachers. I can't imagine managing a group of 20 or so young ones for seven hours a day while trying to make sure they actually learn something, and nobody gets something stuck in a nostril. It may be why I'm so fascinated by the work of the Vermont Public School System to help reduce stress for both teachers and kids, especially in one large elementary school.

When they looked at the highest points of stress throughout the day, what they uncovered was a sense of chaos when the kids arrived each morning, especially during the winter months. If you're a parent, I'm sure you're familiar. It could take a half hour just to get the youngest kids out of their snow gear. Then kids were expected to shift from the high-energy arrival directly into sitting still to learn, with almost no transition.

The leaders believed that a chaotic start was translating into higher stress throughout the day, so they set a path to changing the norm and creating an effective and calmer "ramping up the day" ritual. Everybody in the school had a role to play. They established a staff gathering before the kids arrived to check in and run through a mindfulness exercise. The food service team baked bread or other foods that would create a warm, homey, calming smell to greet the kids. They created areas and learning games to help the kids stomp snow off their feet and then take off and store their outerwear. Counselors stood near the entryways to identify kids who were struggling and take them to the gym to burn off energy or for a quick rest in the nurse's office. Sometimes, all it took was a hug. Once in the classroom, teachers would allow time for morning hellos and a glass of water before the whole school would spend time on mindfulness activities. Kids could choose to draw, stretch, or do breathing exercises.

It was an eye-opening process for everybody. Even talking through the existing norms helped staff understand why mornings seemed so hard. And working through some resistance to required mindfulness exercises helped leaders see where they needed to offer more staff education and training. The real eye-opener, though, was the result. They measured stress levels before the norm change and again six months after and found that people reported experiencing significantly less stress throughout the whole day! It's amazing what even one norm change can do to help shape a culture of health and well-being.

Put Your Own Mask on First

New Year's resolutions are tough to keep, and sometimes our family, friends, and work team seem to be conspiring against our best intention. Have you noticed that despite your best effort to make healthy food choices, when you're out with your friends, you tend to succumb to agreeing to pizza for lunch? Recognizing how group behaviors are influencing your health is a good step on your well-being journey.

- Pick a healthy habit you are trying to achieve.
- Create a table with three columns and two rows.
- Label the top columns, family, friends, and work, three subcultures you'll address.
- In the first row, list the positive influences the subculture has on your health goal.
- In the second row, name the unhealthy norm that is getting in the way of your well-being. Make a plan to address these distractions.

THAT'S A WRAP

Every culture is full of norms, whether we're acknowledging them or not. In too many organizations, more of the norms fall on the wrong side of the health and well-being scale. But this is not an insurmountable problem. Norms can be identified, and they can be changed, and when we make the effort, we can have a profound positive impact on people, teams, and organizations.

However, most norms don't change quickly or easily. Remember, you are attempting to get a group of people to adopt a new behavior, a new attitude, or a new belief—or all three! And you're trying to make this shift while creating a sense of security so that employees don't feel they're deviating from a norm or are in danger of being shunned for adopting a new behavior. This is hard, gradual work!

Leveraging multiple sources of cultural influence to nudge the workforce in the direction you're seeking takes time to plan, execute, and maintain. Not every part of the process is in your control. You'll have to rely on the work of other people, teams, and departments, and you'll have to adjust as you learn. It might take six months to embed a norm, and depending on the size of your team or organization (the larger the longer) and the complexity of the norm change, it could take years. Persistence is a real attribute in this work! Even early and smaller behavior shifts matter, and the effects accumulate over time.

Before you even attempt to build or shape a healthy norm, address your team social climate. You'll be much more likely to succeed with your norm strategy if the team is cohesive, has a can-do attitude, and has a shared well-being vision. Tie your effort to the shared values of the organization so that its importance is clearly communicated. And make sure it's receiving strong leadership support and engagement. This is what we did at JHM to reduce soda consumption. You'll need a good dose of culture connection points—opportunities for the employer to shape the norms. This is where we are headed next.

6

More Than My Love Handles
Culture Connection Points

WHEN I WAS SOMEWHERE IN my mid-forties, my doctor said he'd like me to start a medication to lower my blood pressure. I was sitting on one of those super comfortable exam tables in my super comfortable paper gown. It was one of those times when the voice in my head was saying, "This just got real." I had a few elevated readings previously. Nothing dramatic and there were certainly enough normal readings in between for me not to be concerned. Then again, most of us don't want to believe that we might not be as healthy as we think.

As with most concerning messages I receive about my health, I paused to appreciate that I could influence my path and not accept the fate of a prescription. I politely declined and asked for a grace period. I had already transitioned to a vegan diet (with a side of chocolate) and shed a pinch off my waist.

Almost half of adult Americans have hypertension, so why should I have been surprised?[1] For starters, I don't smoke, I don't drink, I exercise regularly, and I eat healthier than most. However, I hadn't yet addressed my stress and poor sleep, significant contributors to my elevated blood pressure and frankly overall well-being. A few more tweaks, I told myself, and my blood pressure would be fine.

Employers should be concerned as well. Not only is hypertension likely the most common chronic disease among your workforce, but it is also among the costliest. The risks for hypertension, (i.e., excess body weight, lack of exercise, stress, smoking) are the same risks for all the other common serious illnesses such as diabetes, heart disease, and cancer. A well-being culture in the workplace could make a significant dent in addressing health problems.

Your organization is making innumerable decisions every day that not only impact your organization's success, but also the well-being of your team and workforce at large. Many of these decisions either make having a healthy day easier or harder. The prompts can be subtle and happen throughout the day or they can be overt and have a long-term presence. Our well-being is shaped by cues and levers developed and deployed by our organization. Collectively, these culture connection points shape our behaviors, attitudes, and beliefs.

A culture connection point is defined by the intersection between the design of our workplace experience and our well-being. Culture connection points can influence healthy behaviors and attitudes, or they can be complicit in unhealthy behaviors and attitudes. This chapter is about positioning workplace levers that influence human behavior so that they are all pointing toward supporting healthy beliefs and choices aimed at achieving a healthy workplace culture.

Achieving daily health and well-being practices requires examining the culture connection points and then making strategic adjustments. Faced with innumerable choices that impact our well-being every day at work, employers can design the employee experience so that it's easier to support a well-being culture and keep our New Year's resolutions.

RECRUITMENT AND SELECTION

When a college is listed in magazines as a "party school," guess what is on the mind of the high school applicants? Just as winning sports teams find it easier to recruit the most promising athletes, you will find it easier to draw health-oriented people if you already have a winning well-being culture.

Dell Technologies is a leading developer of personal computers, including the one I'm currently using to type this sentence. When you sample their job postings, you'll be met by "What's most important to us is that you are respected, feel like you can be yourself and have the opportunity to do the best work of your life—while still having your life." Sounds like your well-being will be supported if you work there, right? Shaping a well-being culture starts before a new employee even walks in the door. Your well-being culture can be embedded into your job announcement.

Interview questions can be designed to ask how applicants will contribute to the well-being of their future team. What would the applicants do to support their peer's well-being? Not questions about their own health (which might land you in front of your legal counsel). It won't take long to figure out which applicants will add to the well-being culture.

In addition to conducting formal interviews for the job vacancy, make sure one or more people on the hiring team has an opportunity for a conversation as a prospective peer. While the manager has the final decision on whom to offer the job, a team member may have a better perspective on how the candidate will influence the social climate. Part of that meeting should include having your team member share how the organization supports their health and well-being. Like-minded candidates particularly interested in their health and well-being will take note that your company makes well-being a priority.

When you "land" on the Southwest Airlines (SWA) careers website page, you'll notice well-being has a prominent place.[2] The company's culture is highlighted, specifically articulating their three "vital elements": appreciation, recognition, and celebration—all ingredients of a good social climate. It's no wonder that *Forbes* has named Southwest one of America's Best Employers.[3] Fun is also part of the company culture, which not only improves customer satisfaction but also attracts job candidates.[4]

FIRST IMPRESSIONS

Talmundo, a European HR tech company, believes that there is a well-being crisis, and that stress makes it particularly hard for employees to perform their best. In response they champion the idea that, "Employee well-being starts with smarter onboarding." They believe in setting a culture of well-being from the moment new hires start. Onboarding itself can be a big source of stress: What will I wear? Where do I park?

Among the steps Talmundo feels are important to seize the well-being bull by the horns, they encourage:

- Introducing new hires to colleagues and assigning a mentor before they start.
- Providing prestart information and training.
- Giving new hires a voice by inviting feedback from them.[5]

All these culture connection points set the tone for future interactions with the new hire.

Onboarding refers to the mechanisms through which new employees acquire the necessary knowledge, skills, and behaviors to become effective organizational colleagues and insiders. Employees' early experiences make a strong impression. It is an all-too-common mistake to neglect well-being in the haste to get a new employee working. You can ensure that employees' early impressions are positive ones by explaining the wellness vision, team well-being norms, and the importance of self-care throughout the workday. And it certainly wouldn't hurt for a team member to invite them along for a coffee break.

The commitment you are articulating will quickly be washed away if your actions are inconsistent with your words. If you serve an unhealthy lunch after introducing the organization's well-being resources, strategies, and policies, you will squash the expectations you were trying to build. In addition to talking about well-being, it would be a great idea to do an exercise to practice well-being. A simple breathing exercise, stretch break, or walk can set the right tone. Actions speak louder than words.

After the formal orientation is over and your recruit joins the team for their first team meeting, take some time to get to know each other in a more informal way. In addition to the standard, mundane background information of where you live and what hobbies you have, prompt the veterans on your team to share what they do to stay active and what other healthy practices they maintain during the workday. These stories give implicit permission to the new team member to continue or to build their health and well-being practices while working. Get your new teammate engaged with the collective effort to build a team well-being culture that fosters healthy workdays.

New hires at Twitter go through 75 steps and handoffs as they pass through recruiting, HR, IT, and an introduction to the facilities. Before they sit down at their desk, they have an email address and a bottle of wine waiting. A Twitter T-shirt is an inexpensive way to make the new hire feel as though they're part of the team.[6] Remember, feeling included is part of social climate, one of our well-being building blocks.

Be careful not to take your eye off your new team member a few days into their welcome. Feeling part of the company will take more than a welcome party. LinkedIn provides employees with a 90-day "New Hire Onboarding Plan," designed as a weekly guide to help the newbie feel grounded within the organization (aka, sense of community) and contributing to the team (aka, shared vision).

The remote workforce can find it particularly challenging to feel the well-being benefits of social connectedness. The home office of Equalture is located in The Netherlands, but new hires work from locations as remote as Latvia. To ensure the mental well-being of onboarding employees who have never had the opportunity to shake hands with co-workers or meet them in person, the company initiated three principles for new hires that help them better feel part of the team:

1. Stay connected.
2. Keep listening to your team!
3. Don't forget about the social aspect.

They had to find new ways to establish social connection among team members, so they devised virtual coffee moments during which employees can chat with each other and 15-minute check-ins that are more about sharing jokes and humor than charts and graphs. TGIF is celebrated with a game played through Google Meets. Bi-weekly one-on-one talks to collect feedback and address concerns round out the way Equalture promotes connectedness among employees who are countries apart.[7]

INFORMATION AND COMMUNICATION

Health education has limited impact on our behavior.[8] If it was uniformly effective, then everybody would be eating an apple a day. However, some methods of communicating and sharing information are more effective than others and can make a difference. Massachusetts General Hospital is one of the most respected hospitals in the United States (I can name another). As the science poured in (wait for it . . .) about the dire consequences of regular soda and other sugary beverage consumption (good one, right?), Massachusetts General laid out a plan to encourage healthy beverages.[9] Communicating through a traffic-light campaign (red equals unhealthy, yellow equals less healthy, and green equals healthy) at the point of purchase, researchers found increased sales of healthy beverages and decreased sales of unhealthy beverages.[10] We just need to be creative in how we communicate!

We all know that many doctors speak gibberish when it comes to explaining health information (that's why I have an editor).[11] Let's not make the same mistake in the workplace. All too often, to be complete, health content is written above what many can comprehend.[12] Quizzify, an employee learning platform, provides health information to employees through interactive online health quizzes, made easily understandable using health literacy practices.

While you'll want to avoid the gibberish, if your organization is fortunate to include a physician, it can be helpful to have this person's endorsement. Doctors serve as credible sources of health information, which makes messages from this uniquely qualified group more believable. If not a physician, how about an employee who is known to be healthy, positive, and generally a great well-being role model?

Humor is a great way to communicate. There are plenty of opportunities to have fun while promoting health and well-being. Using shame, guilt, and fear is counterproductive. Remember, creating a positive outlook is part of our social climate building block. Be careful, however. Sometimes humor might be funny for one person, but not for another.

Word of mouth is another source of information. Co-workers are often trusted sources. If you can have some degree of confidence that certain workers have a genuine understanding of health and can stick with content reviewed by a health and well-being professional, these people would be a great choice for sharing the well-being message. Some companies have "champions" or "ambassador" programs for this very reason.

Since family can be both major sources of support when making healthy choices, as well as significant obstacles to good health, if you are able to include spouses, housemates, and other persons that your employees live with in your messages, it can multiply the impact. For example, many companies provide information at open enrollment to help with choosing benefits. You can presume some of your employees will make their benefit decisions with others, making this a good time to share information about company-sponsored resources that support health and well-being for the entire family.

Communication is likely to be the most common culture connection point used in our well-being culture toolkit. While I agree that its omnipresence is vital, unfortunately, communication alone won't be enough to change behavior. It's important to use several culture connection points simultaneously to foster adoption and maintenance of healthy choices.

Hopkins Highlight

We use many different communication avenues because we have a wide variety of job types, which creates different opportunities for sending and receiving messages. For example, we write a wellness weekly newsletter. This newsletter is inserted into the Tuesday edition of our daily institutional email, "Inside Hopkins," posted on our Office of Well-being website and distributed through email to department heads who've requested direct receipt for redistribution to their own teams. These are all electronic avenues. But you have to know your audience. Most of our workforce isn't sitting in front of a computer all day. One food service supervisor made the newsletter into a poster and secured it to the wall behind the cafeteria where the workers congregate. Some HR departments leave a few copies on their reception desk for visiting employees. We also place our wellness weekly newsletter on our wellness carts (literally pushing a cart while handing out healthy snacks and water while simultaneously pushing camaraderie and a dose of self-care messaging) for easy pick-up when we're making visits around campuses.

BENEFITS AND PROGRAMS

Undoubtedly, you think you've checked the boxes on benefits with a retirement plan, days off, and health insurance. The opportunities to support the well-being of your workforce through benefits are countless. Programs at many companies are also abundant. With so much attention on this culture connection point, it's worth the time to consider how benefits and programs can support the larger well-being culture goals.

I personally benefit from a free home blood pressure monitoring kit. I can take my blood pressure at home or at work, because sometimes I put it in my bag and bring it with me for the day. I don't have to make a special trip to the pharmacy or doctor's office to get a reading and the immediate feedback may be followed by a breathing exercise if I don't like the numbers.

Beyond the employee knowing the benefit exists (via communication culture connection points), consider how easy it is to access the benefit. Maybe install a self-serve blood pressure station in a convenient location at work. Want to draw even more attention to high blood pressure? While at first blush, an onsite blood pressure screening event might seem costly, consider the bigger picture. Hypertension is already costing you a huge amount of money. It's the "silent killer." Why not make some noise around blood pressure so your workforce pays attention, takes care, and addresses the problem? Did you know that almost one in five of your employees has undiagnosed hypertension?[13] Remember, high blood pressure is silent . . . until it's not. Until it makes itself known by a heart attack or stroke. It's certainly easier to get your blood pressure checked at work than making a special trip to the doctor or pharmacy. This is not, however, a blanket endorsement of biometric screening, most of which is inappropriate and potentially harmful unless tailored to the individual.

Benefits have become much more extensive in the past couple of decades. Onsite childcare, assistance with eldercare, legal assistance, and other support services are commonly offered to help manage the stressors that come with being a grown up. Companies like Google and Genentech have even gone to the extent of providing haircuts on campus to make life easier for their employees. Some companies offer laundry, bike repair, and sabbatical to those who've been in their role a minimum number of years. It seems anything is possible now.

Benefits can simultaneously support occupational health. Think about how many of your employees are sitting in front of a computer, all day, every day. Sitting for long periods of time isn't great for our health. Why not make lemonade out of lemons? Companies like obVus Solutions and Upright offer wearable devices that provide immediate feedback on posture, likely helping to avoid aches and pains. These tools also provide cues to breathe regularly and take breaks, integrating well-being practices into a desk job.

Often (and sometimes in a panic) in an attempt to solve a problem, a leader will give the order to create a program. "Stress is a problem! Create a gratitude challenge." "The number of employees with diabetes is rising; make sure we offer a cooking class." Programs, programs, programs. Sometimes it may seem that programs are all your employer is doing to support health and well-being, and that indeed may be the case. Programs tend to consume a large amount of the budget as well as time for planning. For some employees, the workplace may be the only source of getting help with their well-being challenges. If you are successful in building a strong well-being culture on your team, your programs will be impactful because the participants will have the workplace support needed on all levels.

Not long ago, mindfulness was thought to be only for the tie-dye-wearing Woodstock crowd. Now it's much more accepted and available. Some companies might even consider mindfulness practice a norm within their walls. Companies like Merck, Aetna, and General Mills provide mindfulness programs. Even Johns Hopkins Medicine, a stalwart of excellence in delivering Western medicine, now offers a variety of mindfulness programs and access to the Calm app (an app that teaches the user how to reduce stress and anxiety through meditation and other mindfulness practices).

Don't have the wherewithal to stand up a mindfulness program yourself? Do not despair! Bring in Mindful Life, Mindful Work, Inc., a leadership development company, which can create custom-designed mindfulness programs for your leadership team or the whole company. Mindfulness experiences can be literally delivered to your door. MindSpa booths, a space to close the door behind you, and immerse yourself in acoustic bliss, provides a window of tranquility in an otherwise sea of workplace frenzy. The options are plentiful.

While there may be a lot of programs, there might not be a lot of participation. One thing you can do as a manager is negotiate a consensus among your team for which program you will attend together. Peer support amplifies our effort to be well. Another option is to go rogue and create your own program. It's possible that your human resource department or health and wellness team can support your effort. Taking this path allows you to customize the experience to your team's needs and could prove to be a team-bonding experience, which in itself is good for your well-being.

If you are in a decision-making position for benefits, consider a needs assessment to better understand what would be most meaningful to your workforce. In the United States, benefits account for 31 percent of employee compensation.[14] With that much money at stake, it might be worth getting professional help from an organization like the International Federation of Employee Benefit Plans.

STORIES AND NARRATIVES

When I was a kid, one of my favorite books was *The Monster at the End of This Book*, where Grover, a self-described "cute, furry little monster," spends the entire book fretting about the readers finishing the book, because he was afraid of the monster the title warned about. As the end crept closer, Grover's anxiety grew, and despite his pleas to keep the reader (my mother) from turning the page, we finally did reach the end of the book only to see Grover looking into a mirror, seeing himself as the monster.

Stories draw listeners in and hold our attention. Stories are easier to share with others because they resonate much better than school lessons, facts, and numbers. Good stories, ones that are picked specifically for an audience, have elements that allow the listener to imagine that they too could have been the person in the story. We can remember stories decades later—in my case, five to be exact. As Chip and Dan Heath make clear in their book *Made to Stick*, stories resonate with listeners and readers and ensure you get your message across and it stays with them.[15]

The story subject will influence the appeal and reach of the story. It's quite likely when the story is about one of the organization's leaders that many people will take interest. A leader's story about his/her journey to a healthier place can resonate and stick. Recall the story that Aetna's CEO Mark Bertolini, who had a skiing accident in 2004, shared of his fight against pain killers and suicidal thoughts with employees, giving them a well-being message they would remember.

There are health and well-being stories all around us. Whether or not these stories originate, propagate, or are otherwise bolstered by the workplace is likely irrelevant to whether the story will be meaningful to those who listen. It's not difficult to find health and well-being stories if you look for them. It does take an extra step though to realize there is a story in front of you that needs to be shared with a broader audience. A story that illustrates how a company cares for its employees is going to be far more effective (and welcomed) than one that hints that the company's concern is about saving money on healthcare costs.

Stories that the listener or reader can imagine happening to themselves are more impactful. These stories can be about successful strategies that one employee used to lower blood pressure or how a group of employees made taking a break during the workday a norm. Stories of employees volunteering or lending a hand to help someone complete an assignment can be great messaging for others to follow suit.

The same story written or conveyed by two different people can have different impacts not only because of who is telling the story and how the story is told (the narrative), but because of their storytelling skills. Word choice, voice inflection, body language, and tone are just a few of the ingredients that will vary among storytellers. Be thoughtful about which stories you highlight, not only for the content, but also for the messenger. Where needed, recruit help from your marketing and communications colleagues to create a more impactful message.

The team narrative can focus on how a decision was made to collectively address well-being. While it might include the leader's own well-being journey or the role of the wellness champion on the team, to foster a sense of community, the focus should be on how the whole team is striving together for some healthier habit or practice. This will serve as a reminder to those on the team about their role in the well-being journey as well as a well-being orientation for new team members.

Unilever takes mental health seriously by addressing it up front before employees get to the point of needing acute care. Among other communication strategies, Unilever created storytelling films, including chief learning officer Tim Munden's, about post-traumatic stress disorder.[16]

Hopkins Highlight

We feature many stories on a regular basis, and they fall into three categories:

1. Success stories—these are individual employee stories of a person who was able to either achieve a goal or how they maintain their health. Excerpts from these success stories are posted in our Wellness Weekly newsletter and the full stories are available on our Healthy at Hopkins portal.
2. Feature stories—When groups of employees are engaged in healthy behaviors together, we recognize this health-culture-enhancing approach by featuring these stories periodically in "Inside Hopkins," the daily e-bulletin.
3. Leadership stories—Giving leaders a platform for sharing how they practice their health and well-being is an important message that needs to be conveyed. We provide leaders with a set of questions to choose from; whose answers provide the material needed to create their own well-being story. Leaders are chosen from across the organization to increase the likelihood that all employees will find a leader with whom they share a connection.

REWARDS AND RECOGNITION

I wouldn't be surprised that your first thought when seeing the word "reward" was big dollar signs. True, of the 68 percent of employers that offer a financial incentive tied to well-being, the incentive averages $600![17] Regardless of whether a formal financial incentive program is in place, it's likely that your employees' daily health and well-being decisions are influenced by rewards and recognition.

Creating an effective strategy is very challenging and wrought with nuances. Consider different income levels within your organization. The same amount of money in an incentive program will be much more meaningful for those earning the minimum wage compared to the executives.[18] The reward may be unobtainable for some if it is either all computer driven or based on a wearable device they don't own. Break down barriers. Maybe even give the lower-income employees a wearable device to get started.

You might consider fostering well-being as a collective effort. At Next Jump, a loyalty programs provider, teams compete in a weekly fitness challenge in which the group can earn virtual cash rewards as well as bragging rights. Working out and winning as a team helps create social cohesion and camaraderie as well as finding work fun and rewarding.[19]

Getting employee feedback on the well-being culture can be very helpful in assessing progress. However, for your employees, the prospect of filling out another survey might be as appealing as getting a cavity filled. There are times when a financial incentive can not only be helpful but also necessary to get people's attention. However, money alone isn't going to be enough to optimize the number of responses you're looking for. To maximize your investment, be sure to explain why you want their participation (create the imperative to contribute to the greater good—the community), acknowledge that the task might be boring (show empathy), and make it easy to complete (short, understandable, and easily accessible).[20]

For some, an incentive can be measured in cents, not dollars. Like cigarette taxes, changing the price of unhealthy food and drink demonstrates that price matters.[21] Transportation makes up a sizeable portion of our economy. Bus drivers, like many other employees in this field, are sedentary because of the nature of their job. When they do get a break away from the wheel, it's often at the station, where traditionally vending machines are stocked with unhealthy choices. It's no surprise this group of workers is at greater risk for obesity. Lowering the price of healthy beverages and foods in vending machines by only 10 percent and increasing the number of healthy choices increased sales of these items. Employees of the metropolitan transportation system of Minneapolis, Minnesota, who were vending machine customers purchased healthy foods twice as much after their machines got a makeover![22]

We don't need incentives for things we enjoy. No one is paying me a hundred dollars to play tennis with my friends (although I wouldn't mind). We seek activities that bring us joy and allow us to be creative and to learn. We want to direct our own work and contribute to larger causes. Wikipedia, an online encyclopedia, was conceived and flourished on the notion that volunteers would write the content, because they would derive pleasure by contributing, not because they would be paid.[23] Rewards most often come from within. They are intrinsic.

Sometimes it just takes common sense, not dollars and cents, to make an impact. Companies with the most robust well-being culture are likely to support intrinsic motivation for pursuing a healthy and well life — likely a more enduring approach than a chunk of change. An employee who is intrinsically motivated takes an action because it is fun, creative, or brings joy, rather than for financial rewards.

Johnson & Johnson created a culture of health in which it's easy for employees to act on their intrinsic motivation. The company not only makes engaging in healthy behaviors both convenient and accessible, but they also make being physically active the norm. A combination of manager accountability for supporting a culture of health and the company making it abundantly clear that it's okay to be physically active and visit the gym during company time fosters employee participation because it's something they want to do.[24,25]

Don't underestimate the power of a steady flow of recognition on shaping a well-being culture. Our employee success stories are not only inspirational for the readers, but they also recognize and reinforce the achievement for the featured employee. I personally write a thank-you note to each employee we select to be featured. I go out of my way to recognize their contribution to our well-being culture.

Recognition can backfire. What message are you sending through commonly recognized achievements? Is congratulations on "hard work" a frequent refrain? That might be great for now but may be a collective regret when people head for the door as they find another employer that gives them some breathing space. Earning lunch with the president for being this year's winner of "The Cup Half Full" award (for the employee with the best positive outlook) sends a very different message than company-wide recognition for the top sales performer (who, by the way, already received their commission as their reward).

One last word of caution. Incentives can become an expectation and trying to curtail or extinguish your strategy can become a thorny prospect. Before you start, or as you assess your current incentive plan, at minimum it's worth a little reading. One book you might consider, *Drive*, by Daniel Pink, articulates the science behind motivation. Another option, *Predictably Irrational,* by Daniel Ariely, explores the reasons why we make decisions. No, I don't have a bias toward Daniels (I don't think). It would probably be a good idea to get an expert involved, even if it's one through a book.

LEARNING AND TRAINING

We need a license to drive a vehicle because we can be a danger to ourselves and others if we don't know what we're doing. It's important we learn how to drive safely. Yet for every one person who dies each year from a car accident, more than three die because of illness and bad habits influenced by job and workplace conditions.[26,27]

We learn throughout grade school and, for many, college. However, we often learn most of our job on the job. Organizations often designate specific periods to learn new skills, like during orientation. It's an investment in the success of the company. Do we take for granted that our workforce knows how to have a healthy day? How to help others have a healthy day?

People tend to do what they know. Your employees come to their jobs with years of experience sleeping, eating, and practicing mostly ingrained workplace etiquette. This simple premise that we stick with the status quo works for and against well-being.[28] If your employees have healthy habits and treat their colleagues with respect and congeniality, your team and organization should be in great shape. However, less than 3 percent of American adults are sufficiently active, eat a healthy diet, maintain a healthy weight, and abstain from smoking.[29]

Well-being is much more than healthy habits. It's how we think and move through our day. Hilton, the hotel and hospitality giant, invests in training team members on resiliency, focus, and optimism—key ingredients to help their teams thrive and, not coincidentally, worked into the Hilton well-being program name, "Thrive@Hilton," and Arianna Huffington's company Thrive Global. Arianna herself leads a self-guided e-learning course focused on mind, body, and spiritual well-being, complimented with in-person training.[30] Provide opportunities for every employee to build happiness and resilience skills.

Managers have a lot of responsibilities. While it may be difficult to conceive adding one more, training managers to lead with a well-being lens will not only be good for the team's well-being, but for the manager's as well. Introducing Ten-Minute Well-Being Tips for Managers. Every week for just 10 minutes, my colleague and I share an important topic that influences team well-being. By participating, our managers learn to lead with an eye on well-being. In addition to exploring topics like how meetings can support or harm our well-being and breathing exercises to lower our stress, we have an open forum after our 10 minutes to exchange ideas and learn from each other.

SYMBOLS AND TRADITIONS

Southwest Airline pilots, as their ritual, touch the heart on the side of the plane before going through the boarding door. There is something wonderful about a symbolic act in that it represents our beliefs. For example, a fitness center can be symbolic of an organization's commitment to health and well-being. Releasing time for well-being activities not only helps eliminate a barrier to participation, but also symbolizes the priority being given to well-being. These are grand gestures. Simpler symbols can be created in the form of water bottles, T-shirts, pedometers and other wellness paraphernalia. An employee's work anniversary can be acknowledged without a pen! Try a jump rope or a yoga mat.

The UC Davis campus is aware of the impact of well-being symbols. A number of senior leaders showed their wellness support by moving their designated parking spots farther away from the front entrance, allowing themselves the opportunity to get more steps.[31]

One of the simplest symbols and yet possibly most powerful is to have and make visible a company well-being logo. By creating and utilizing a symbol, you can capture and message either the culture you have or the one you want to create. Logos are also easy to disseminate. They can be placed on flyers, book covers, and hand sanitizer and water bottles. In an organization with lots of communications, it is a quick way to allow your health and well-being program to stand out. The consistent use of a logo is a constant reminder to employees that health and well-being is important to this organization.

Like symbols, rituals have an influence that go beyond first appearances. For instance, an overhead announcement in a Wegmans store can prompt workers to take a stretch break. This simple act of stretching has become a wellness bond between employees. Other rituals can be seasonal. The annual 5K fun run/walk and the company picnic are rituals. Similarly, you could make it an annual ritual to complete a culture survey. You could transition the office birthday celebration to an occasion for fun (and not just a sugar icing binge). Perhaps the person whose birthday is next must "perform" a short demonstration of a skill, like juggling, singing (or lip synching). Blending well-being into customs makes it easier for health to be the norm.

It's also important to address unhealthy rituals. Is it possible your company sponsors a happy hour regularly that consists of unhealthy foods and drinks? How about transitioning that ritual into a regularly scheduled healthy program, like a weekly after-work softball game or Frisbee toss? You can still promote team bonding and support the health and well-being of your workforce if you take some thoughtful moments to create an inclusive activity that does not damage health. Call on your informal leaders to help you create the ideas and garner buy-in from some of the more ardent participants of the current unhealthy ritual.

DEATH BY SITTING: CUES FROM OUR WORK ENVIRONMENT

A decade ago, there was a flurry of headlines along the lines of "Sitting Kills."[32] I write this fully conscious that I am in a sitting position, dying as I type. The physical workplace attributes can be powerful culture connection points. Energy provider Chesapeake Energy has made a serious investment in providing lots of options to not sit. Their 72,000-square-foot fitness center is complete with swimming pool, rock climbing wall, and personal trainers.[33]

Don't dismay if your workplace hasn't committed such a generous budget. The cost of standing desks has come down and a little ingenuity goes a long way. For two years I used an old wooden bookshelf as my portable standing desk before they were commonly commercially available. Let's not overlook the power and simplicity of stairs. Even bus drivers, who obviously are sitting while they work, can cut their risk of a heart attack by taking a minimal number of stairs during the workday.[34]

Just having stairs though won't make a difference if you don't design them to be used. My favorite example is at the Kaohsiung Municipal Ta-Tung Hospital in Taiwan. The staircase is designed as a piano, both with the paint to show the typical features of a piano key as well as the technology for the body weight of the piano "player" to trigger a piano sound with each step. Yes, it did increase stair use.[35]

Your investment though doesn't have to be as elaborate. Paint, paintings, and even just keeping your stairwells clean can be a good start. Add signs near the elevator bank pointing toward the stairwell and you may just start to see some movement in that direction. This strategy of encouraging stair use isn't new, but what is your organization doing to make it come to life? Stairs not only provide some physical activity during the day, but their use can also wake us up, give us some needed distraction, and reset our minds before returning to our tasks. Stairs are just one of many ways you could use your physical workplace to benefit the health and well-being of your organization.

Working on a single level doesn't exclude you from encouraging movement. Maybe an on-site health club is not financially viable (or necessary), but marking a walking path through or around the building and labeling the direction along with the distance traveled may be an option. Could bikes and bike paths be provided and maintained? A shower installed?

Stress is common in the workplace and no profession has been challenged more on this front recently than nurses. Getting some time during the workday to give our minds a break is an essential part of keeping our wits intact. While ideally the break would happen away from the action, sometimes we might need to bring the break right to the employee. Set up your work area to make a brain break feel like it fits into the workflow. Consider mounting a coloring sheet on a wall in an easily accessible location so that it's easy for a team member to stop for a few minutes, pick up their favorite crayon color and fill in a few spaces. Mindful coloring provides a few minutes of focusing on a soothing activity, and quickly lowers stress.[36]

USAA has "Energize Zones" that serve multiple needs: a place to do some light exercise or gather thoughts. USAA also posts messages about healthy behaviors on boards scattered throughout their building.[37] Brainstorm and find other changes you can make in your immediate and broader work areas that can make a difference in your well-being.

A lot of women work in healthcare. In fact, probably 70 percent of the JHM workforce is comprised of women, many of whom are of child-bearing age. The joy of a newborn is challenged by the stark reality of returning to work, making the transition back to the office stressful. For those breastfeeding, one of those stressors is figuring out how to continue during the workday. As such, over the past seven years, the number of lactation support rooms in our facilities has multiplied. Rooms were converted to allow breastfeeding women a quiet, private place for them to breast pump. Dedicated space for this practice is undoubtedly a big resource commitment. Even where space was tight, we placed a Mamava lactation pod nearby our food services and environmental service team areas, to be sure they had access. It's also an important symbol that motherhood and families are important to JHM.

POLICIES

While policies may not feel like the most creative strategy to influence the health and well-being of your workforce, they can be one of the most effective. Now, you can't mandate (nor do you want to) that people meditate, eat fruit, or do most other behaviors that you associate with health. However, there are plenty of ways to establish health and well-being as a formal part of business.

Safety protocols are a prime example of how policies can support health and well-being. Abstaining from tobacco use at work is another common health-related policy. Often policies have health implications that are not their primary intent. For example, a policy of allowing working remotely for certain jobs might be a strategy to improve recruitment opportunities, but it could also be a great retention strategy for those who find working from home better for their well-being. Remote workers often cite the flexibility this arrangement provides to accommodate other aspects of their lives, such as getting kids off to school or avoiding a stressful commute—both examples of well-being benefits that aren't the primary intent of the policy.

Consider memorializing a well-being strategy in a policy when a lot of time and effort have been taken to assemble a process and parameters to make it easier to engage in healthier choices. For example, when your food and beverage strategy includes nutrient content as well as product placement, price differentials, and marketing specifications, it's a lot to remember—not to mention that people leave organizations, and continuity is in jeopardy if not acknowledged in writing.

Policies shouldn't be perceived as tools to punish employees. They are very much available to protect employees, as noted by the number of policies that embed workplace safety practices. Policies can also protect employees from manager behavior. When managers overlook the lunch break policy, they may be getting short-term gain only to later bear long-term loss. There are likely employees who resent working through lunch and are only doing so because of perceived expectations given the practice was allowed to evolve. Those team members may not be around long. The employee may understand there is a policy that protects their lunch break, but the subculture is influencing otherwise and fear of retribution for complaining is real in some organizations.

Policies are easier to conceive than they are to consummate. Because of the business, financial, and legal implications of policies, many people within an organization will be involved with policy development. It can be a very long and challenging process that you may not want to undertake, but it might be a prudent path when many leaders want to move in a certain direction and other leaders resist. Don't take the idea of proposing a policy lightly.

Shape Your Team's Subculture

Once your team determines which healthy norms you want to adopt or which unhealthy norms you want to shed, you'll want to enlist the help of several culture connection points to make that transition stick. Follow these steps:

- Hold a brainstorming session.
- Break your team into smaller groups and assign each group a number of culture connection points.
- Each small group can think of one or two ways to use their assigned culture connection points to shape the desired norm.
- The team reconvenes and votes on which four or five culture connection points to pursue.
- Think about what culture connection points are harming your team and then create a path to change them.
- After a month of putting the selected culture connection points in place (and removing the unwanted ones), seek feedback from the team to see whether they feel the desired norm is starting to take shape. Adjust as needed.

HOW I HELP HOPKINS GET HEALTHY

After struggling to get momentum behind implementing a healthy food strategy, I was on the receiving end of a frank message from one of our food service leaders that this program wasn't going to get done because she had different goals. We were both getting directions from the same leaders that she felt ran counter to the co-existence of our plans. How can we maintain our revenue from food services while simultaneously offering healthier choices? While I knew research demonstrated that healthy foods and beverages could co-exist with increased revenue, I also knew that sometimes fear trumps science. Science also wasn't shaping up to be practical. Yes, science was having a bad hair day. We would need to hash this out in a forum and then cement it in a policy.

I couldn't believe the complexity of the food and beverage portion of our business. Procurement, contracts, food preparation, and distribution were some of the elements that made putting an effective and realistic plan in place difficult. Over the course of three years (yes, three) we discussed, tweaked, vetted, and otherwise explored the possibilities to arrive at a policy for signature. Talk about collaboration!

While not perfect, this policy is not only a document that keeps the institution pointed in a nutritious direction but it also serves as a testament to the value our organization places on health in general.

Put Your Own Mask on First

It's quite likely you aren't aware of all the different culture connection points that are influencing your own behaviors and thought patterns. Now is a great opportunity to see if your mindfulness practice, the art and science of being aware of the present moment, can allow you to identify the influencers shared in this chapter.

- Share your own well-being success story with your team. Not only might it inspire someone you work with, it will also reinforce your improved path and boost your confidence that you can continue.
- What motivates you? If needed, have a frank discussion with your manager to communicate how they can support your well-being and your job success.
- If you have annual job goals or professional development, make one related to your workplace well-being. Seek and engage in continued learning and training related to your well-being.
- What rituals do you have during the workday that run counter to your well-being? How can you change that practice? If you regularly grab a candy bar from the vending machine during your afternoon

(Continued)

> break, can you ask a peer to take a walk with you (away from the machine) instead?
>
> • Email is often a distraction from well-being. Set specific times during your workday to check emails and shun sporadic replies. The back and forth from your email box throughout the day adds to your stress level. Limit the periods you reply to emails, and you'll also save time.

THAT'S A WRAP

I personally appreciate the green leaf symbol tagged to the healthy foods in our cafeterias. This makes it easy for me to find the most nutritious foods, which include lower salt. In addition, these green leaf choices are priced lower (incentive) and placed at eye level when sold in refrigerator cases and vending machines (choice architecture). Our healthy food policy guarantees I'll find low-salt food options in the cafeteria and vending machines. With my tenuous blood pressure readings, I need all the help I can get with making healthy food choices.

Wegmans also addresses blood pressure. Optional onsite screenings make it easy to know your numbers. The availability of counseling by nutritionists and fitness classes (culture connection points) contributed to a reduction in the percent of employees with high blood pressure dropping 10 percent over a five-year period.[38] Merck & Company and Johnson & Johnson also boast of lower employee blood pressure.[39] Bus drivers and utility company employees have also lowered their blood pressure through workplace strategies.[40,41] Just about any employee can lower their blood pressure if enough culture connection points are in place (as well as the other culture building blocks).

Culture connection points give a plethora of opportunities to shape the culture of an organization and workplace. By using multiple ways to shift the culture in a healthier direction, you are bound to make progress. Sharing these culture connection points with a group of leaders can make it easier to brainstorm solutions for barriers to health and well-being during the workday. Healthy workplace cultures don't develop out of luck. A well-being culture in the workplace is the result of an intentional strategy, including the use of culture connection points.

Implementing some of the culture connection points will require resources. Be sure to propose your plans with colleagues from the highest level of the organization. When everyone shares the commitment, your organization will be much more likely to succeed. Well-being culture building is a team sport. Ask yourself:

- What are you doing to attract candidates that embrace well-being?
- How are you integrating well-being into orientation?
- Is the message understandable and "made to stick"?[42,43]
- What policies support or harm well-being?
- Is support available for norm change? No-smoking policies, for example, are better received when employees are given advanced notice, group support for quitting, and the option of tobacco cessation products.
- How do your company traditions line up with well-being? Do you promote well-being through a logo or catchphrase?

Even when an employer has taken great pains to craft the cultural connection points such that a healthy message, policies, and physical features align with a healthy workday, sometimes it only takes the sight of a tiny, colorful tinfoil-wrapped piece of chocolate to bring your New Year's resolution to a crashing halt.

In a previous job, one woman stands out as a super hard worker and a great teammate. Her stamina for working on her projects and lending a hand to others was remarkable. Mary (I'll call her) kept a bowl of chocolate on her desk for anyone who paid a visit. Unfortunately, my willpower was no match for the 20 yards between our desks. Employers would be wise to look at peer support as a core building block of a well-being culture. You'll see how things played out with Mary in the next chapter.

7

The Friends and Family Plan
Peer Support

WHEN I WAS GROWING UP, my friend Brad and I shot baskets, rode our bikes, and played tennis together. We were also part of a neighborhood group that played kickball, kick the can, and running bases. So many active outdoor games! When my family bought our Atari set, Brad was right there next to my brother and me as we learned how to play Space Invaders. Little did I know that kids 40 years later would, by and large, forsake the outdoor playground for connectedness through remote gaming and social media. Friends no longer encourage and support running, but rather sitting.

You can observe the similarities of the people around you. Not only are you likely similar in exercise (or lack thereof) patterns, but also in your weight. Our risk of being obese is more than 50 percent if we have an obese friend! If we have a friend who is a heavy alcohol drinker, then our risk of also drinking heavily is 50 percent more as well.[1]

Our friends and family also affect our happiness. Did you ever notice that even just a smile from someone nearby can cause us to smile? Try it! It's a quick experiment. Smile at your co-worker and see how quickly they smile back. It's a very simple way to boost someone else's mood as well as your own. Why not add smiling to your well-being culture strategy?

Unfortunately, other, less desirable emotions of our co-workers, such as feelings of sadness and stress, can also influence our mood. The good news is that we don't have to accept our own mood being dictated by our friends, co-workers, and family members. We can shape our behaviors and thought patterns if we're aware of the influences around us, including our peers.

Perhaps the greatest predictor of success for adopting and sustaining a healthy lifestyle habit is whether a friend, family member, or close co-worker practices that same healthy habit.[2] Peer support can make the difference between success and failure. Friends, family, and co-workers are in a unique position to provide the ongoing support needed to achieve lasting lifestyle change.

You've likely heard about WW (formerly Weight Watchers) and Alcoholics Anonymous. Their success is in part based on this concept of peer support and creating an encouraging environment. Not only do groups lose more weight when they set out to accomplish this goal together, they are also likely to sustain the weight loss longer.[3] True to the spirit that we influence those in our social circles, a person's intent on losing weight also impacts their spouse's weight. The spouse may subsequently and possibly unwittingly adjust their eating practices and benefit by losing weight as well![4]

WILLPOWER IS A BAD STRATEGY

I know I am not alone in seeking chocolate—and failing to resist the urge—when I am stressed. Willpower is a flawed strategy when it comes to making healthy choices. Many people eat regardless of whether they are hungry, and prompts for overeating abound.[5] For me, it's chocolate. For others, it's the Monday morning donuts placed in the center of the conference table. Our brain wrestles with itself. We know our intent and our goals and yet sometimes we can't resist the temptation.[6]

In my first job at Johns Hopkins, I worked in a corner suite with other physicians. Roughly in the middle of the collection of offices, there was a credenza that held documents and reference material. The surface was the perfect spot for leftover weekend treats, or a box of donuts purchased on the way to work or . . . chocolate. Instead of my peers supporting my desire to eat healthier, they were influencing me to eat more like them.

The challenge for me was to avoid the day's bounty. The goal was not so easy because when you walk through the entrance to the suite, straight ahead is this pedestal for snacks. It's as if I were Pavlov's dog, and despite my determination, it was difficult to not look at the area while walking to my office. Once my eye locked on to something, it had to be investigated. That was often the end of my willpower. My peers thought they were being nice by sharing a broad collection of goodies on a regular basis. Combined with the sitting that came with that job, I was concerned my "love handles" were going to return.

Fortunately, my office was on the side of the suite that had an alternative entrance. Given the layout of the floor, I rarely used it—until I decided I needed to enhance my willpower strategy. After weeks of entering and exiting the suite through this alternative route, the image of the credenza surface faded and my salivary reflex calmed down. Avoiding the extra sugar was no longer a struggle on my walk to the bathroom. That is, until some well-intentioned Hopkins employee, along my new path out of the physician suite, decided to put a small table outside her cubicle with a bowl of chocolate on top, with a sign, "Help Yourself," just to the side. The subculture of food within my team and those around me was quite evident, and my peers, unknowingly, were making it tough for me to reach my health goals.

BE YOUR BEST WITH A BUDDY

It's easier to be happy and feel well when we're with a buddy. Peer support is not only about helping our buddy build healthier habits (or get rid of unhealthy ones), but also about having a shoulder to lean on and a pair of ears to listen.

In the early onslaught of the COVID-19 pandemic, Massachusetts General Hospital faced conditions of high-stress, long hours, unpredictability, and trauma. In response, the hospital launched its MGH Buddy Program. Kerrie Palamara, who leads the hospital's Center for Physical Well-Being, helped create the program. "There was a sense of loneliness and disconnect between people and that people were really seeking human connection," she said. "So, the Buddy Program came from the desire to fill that need."[7]

Buddies can enhance a well-being culture. Two people are paired, get to know each other, and look out for each other's well-being in an "I have your back" way. According to the CDC, the buddy system is an effective method for staff members to share in the responsibility for their partners' safety and well-being.[8]

When the Wow Company, a UK firm of accountants, switched to remote working, co-founder Paul Bulpitt knew that the first step was to ensure their employees' well-being. Isolation is not part of the happiness recipe. This was no job for an app, so the company instituted a buddy system in which pairs of employees checked in with their buddy for half an hour every morning to ensure some human contact.[9]

Buddies in such a system get to know each other by talking about work, home life, hobbies, and family. They set up times to check in with each other and listen carefully to each other as they share experiences and feelings. They help each other and monitor workloads, stress, health, and, in short, make their buddy feel safe and supported.[10] Buddies can be used as early as onboarding to lower stress and to accelerate the newbie feeling like he or she is part of the team. When you started your current job, did the first day feel like you were back in grade school? Wondering with whom you'd sit at lunch?

Microsoft, one of the largest companies in America with over 180,000 employees, found that onboarding buddies provide context, making it easier to understand what's happening in the new workplace. The tech giant concluded that onboarding buddies boost productivity and increase new employee satisfaction (think retention!).[11]

Next, Microsoft set out to see how peer support might improve the job performance of its staff. The company had a feedback tool, but it was a bit clunky and without the option for employees to invite feedback from peers. Liz Friedman, the company's HR director of global performance and development, knew that people are more receptive to feedback when they ask for it. Ninety percent of their employees said giving and receiving feedback was valuable and important to personal growth. However, only 7 percent were receiving feedback on how to improve—something they wanted dearly.[12] So, the company decided to build a more effective tool based on peer support.

Working with David Rock (recall the SCARF model), Microsoft came up with Perspectives, a tool by which employees are invited to suggest things that their colleagues should "keep doing" and actions they should "rethink"—just a way of one person giving another their perspective.

Jay Clem, general manager of HR Resources IT in Microsoft Digital, had his team gather data from each employee's calendar, interactions, and document-sharing data to determine who they work with most closely on a regular basis. Through the interface, they were able to suggest a few people who an employee might want to ask to give feedback.

The innovation has been a success, and an employee getting feedback even has the chance to say thanks using Kudos, an app that makes it easy to share a little love with the fellow employee who took the time to provide feedback. Perspectives is not only a peer-support strategy; it is also helpful for creating a sense of community and a good social climate.

ALL ABOARD: PEER SUPPORT DRIVES SAFETY AT UNION PACIFIC

Sometimes, the work of peer support goes beyond helpful to absolutely critical. Take Union Pacific's (UP) culture of health, which, unsurprisingly, is heavily focused on safety. A railroad that hauls freight can see all sorts of injuries and accidents if everybody isn't paying attention, especially given that operations take place across many thousands of miles throughout the western United States. Consequently, UP relies heavily on peer support. First, their Total Safety Culture is employee-driven, not management driven. Second, every employee takes the following Courage to Care pledge:

> I have the courage to care. Worn with a lion's pride, it means those I work with will have my back, and I will have theirs. I pledge to shield myself and my team from harm. I will take action to keep them safe, by fixing an unsafe situation, addressing an unsafe behavior, or stopping the line. In turn, I will have the courage to accept the same actions from my coworkers, who care enough to correct my path. We wear this badge out of respect for each other and those who have gone before us. On my watch, we will all go home safe to our families every day.[13]

UP does more than ask for the pledge, though. They train employees on how to directly but positively address any behavior that seems unsafe with their peers and encourage employees to recognize their peers for high-safety behaviors. The result? Less than one injury for every 200,000 employee work hours.[14]

IF ONLY IT WERE A NORM OR PART OF THE SUBCULTURE

If I'm a nurse or work in food services, I'll be on my feet all day and I'll be sure to see my step count climb. However, the typical accountant, lawyer, business executive? No chance. Our professional subculture plays a huge role in the likelihood we'll get our movement in for the day and many other behaviors, for that matter. This is another way our peers can be helpful.

Peers can come from anywhere. They can be on our work team or a different one. They can be from the same profession or another. That's the power of peers. These are the people you connect with outside of the confines of the organizational structure, regardless of work location and job description. Obviously the more often you see and interact with your peer, the more helpful they can be in your quest to shape whatever behavior, belief, or attitude you choose. It's pretty easy to ask a co-worker to take a five-minute walking break.

For those of you working at companies where smoking is still a big problem, think about how to help groups of colleagues quit smoking, not just one at a time. Here's a subculture that often does not rely on a specific work team but, rather, is formed by behavior. In fact, friendships are often formed through the collective experience of smoking, which adds to the difficulty of stopping. Quitting smoking with a co-worker, friend, spouse, sibling—just about anyone—makes success more likely.[15] Consider ways for co-workers to quit together and provide an alternative way for peers to take a social break during the workday. The cost of a ping-pong table is much less expensive than a hospital admission for the employee who can't breathe.

―――

EXTEND YOUR REACH WITH CHAMPIONS

We have about 42,000 employees at JHM. Although our Office of Well-Being has support from marketing and communications and has colleagues in the departments of human resources, nursing, and medicine, there is no practical way that we're going to reach the ears and eyes of the entire workforce. We're certainly not going to be able to support them as individuals by ourselves. To make matters more challenging, we're across more than a dozen campuses. To encourage health and well-being as part of the workday, we needed a way to amplify our presence, deliver our message, and listen to our workforce. Enter the Healthy at Hopkins Champions.

Organizing employees with a passion for health and well-being allows them to make a meaningful contribution to the company. Not only does this improve their own well-being by contributing to their daily purpose, it can also play a substantial role in positively contributing to a well-being culture. Champions can facilitate change tailored to their own work-group, lunch friends, and other subcultures.

While it is critical to have leadership, paid health-promotion person-nel, marketing, and other infrastructure elements available for success-fully leading a well-being culture, it is equally important to have "boots on the ground." Your organization will not be successful with well-being culture building if it is perceived only as a top-down strategy. Equally important is to have peers spreading the message and lending support. Many people are uncomfortable talking about health issues in the work-place. When a trusted peer is involved, it makes it easier for health and well-being to be part of the discussion and the regular workday.

Beloved by the people of Texas, supermarket H-E-B has more than 70,000 employees across 350 stores and other facilities. H-E-B has nine regional wellness champions, with more than 500 champions assigned to specific sites. To keep this dispersed group rowing in the same direction, the company hosts monthly calls for the wellness leaders, sponsors train-ing webinars, and maintains an online wellness-resource center. They utilize their champions to educate, encourage, and mentor their peers, as well as promote local well-being events.

Hopkins Highlight

Caring for Caregivers After Traumatic Patient-Related Incidents

While champion programs might look similar across organizations, sometimes peer support programs need to be tailored to an industry, as with Union Pacific. At Johns Hopkins, the RISE (Resilience in Stressful Events) team provides confidential peer-to-peer support to employ-ees who have experienced a stressful, patient-related incident. An adverse patient event can have a profound impact on care providers, any of whom may become a "second victim" who is traumatized by the stressful situation. So it's not surprising that the RISE team went into overdrive during the height of the pandemic.

The RISE team provides trained responders—including physicians, nurses, respiratory therapists, social workers and chaplains—who can deliver emotional first aid to peers in a confidential, nonjudgmental environment. Every RISE responder has been trained in psychological

(*Continued*)

first aid and has demonstrated a high level of competence in assisting second victims.

Johns Hopkins employees, supervisors, and colleagues are encouraged to request the RISE team's services to help cope with any stress-producing patient-related events, including a patient injury, patient violence (yes, patients and visitors are unfortunately sometimes hostile to healthcare workers), and even a patient death.

CREATING PEERS THROUGH GROUP PROGRAMS

Finding a peer in the workplace who is interested in working on the same healthy habit together and who's ready at the same time can be challenging. It's not usually a natural conversation starter: "Hey, you want to lower our cholesterol together?"

Fortunately, there are a growing number of lifestyle medicine programs that can be delivered in the workplace that build in peer support. In fact, that's the secret sauce. Groups of employees with similar health goals, led by a qualified instructor, meet once or twice a week for two to three months and focus on new skills, problem solving, and building healthy habits. As participants get more comfortable with their colleagues, they begin to share more about their struggles. Allowing themselves to be vulnerable builds trust within the group. Their newfound peers offer advice about how they overcame those same struggles. Ultimately, it's their collective experience that results in the powerful results.[16]

You are likely familiar that diabetes is a common health problem. Not just in your community, but in your company. What you probably didn't know though is that one-third of American adults are at high risk for diabetes (they are prediabetic). If preventing diabetes were as easy as telling people to eat more fruits and vegetables, the disease would have been eradicated long ago. The National Diabetes Prevention Program, sponsored by the CDC, is a much more effective strategy. Over the course of 12 weeks and through 18 sessions, participants at risk for diabetes focus on meaningful changes, such as more movement, healthier food choices, and weight loss, with the goal of preventing diabetes. Participating in the program lowers the risk of developing diabetes by almost 60 percent,[17] which is why companies such as Dow Chemical, the University of Michigan, and law firm Latham & Watkins have all offered this program to their employees. A group of employees at risk for diabetes become peers for 12 weeks as they navigate the path to adopting healthier practices and thought patterns, which ultimately lead to a healthier and happier future.[18]

These longitudinal lifestyle programs don't need to be specific to a disease. In fact, Pivio (formerly the Complete Health Improvement Program, CHIP) is good for what ails you—heartburn, hypertension, and heart disease ("oh my").[19] Pivio addresses the usual suspects that contribute to disease—poor food choices, lack of exercise, too much stress, and not enough sleep. It's not a series of lectures. Sure, there is some education, but the participants interact. The curriculum prompts attendees to share specific challenges and solutions, fostering peer support along the way.

CHIP has been widely used, including at Cummins Corporation, a diesel and natural gas engine manufacturer. Not only did Cummins make this program available to its employees, but they also invited family members to participate! The architect of the lifestyle strategy at Cummins, Dexter Shurney, shared the same goal of this book—"to lower the disease burden of its employees and their families, helping them to achieve healthier, happier and more productive lives."[20]

Johns Hopkins has its own lifestyle medicine program, Keep Your Pressure Down. As part of our comprehensive strategy to highlight the benefits of healthy choices in order to address chronic illness, we offer a program with similar content and methods to DPP and CHIP, but focused on high blood pressure. Like these programs, it is group based, 12 weeks, successful in improving biometrics (like lowering blood pressure) and transformative for many of the participants.

Group programs don't have to be formulaic; there are other ways to provide support and to provide it for a variety of conditions. Johnson & Johnson created mental health employee resource groups as a means for allowing employees to share their struggles and find strength and comfort with colleagues having a shared experience. Google agrees that talking to co-workers has a different appeal than talking to a mental health provider. Googlers who complete a training program wear a blue dot on their work badge to signal that they are both available to talk and safe to talk with.[21]

I'M NOT SURE HOW TO LEND PEER SUPPORT

Had Mary, my bowl-of-chocolate friend from a previous workplace, been stationed on another floor, I probably would have visited less often and at least taken the stairs to burn off a few of those extra calories.

Mary is one example of a peer who, in her effort to be nice, thwarted my best intention for a healthy workday. Fortunately, our peers can also be a source of support. After helping Mary understand that willpower is not a strategy that works for me, she eventually removed the temptation!

Think about the number of times you've been given bad advice from a well-intended friend. Or more challenging, induced into abandoning your well-being goal at the sight of pizza. In our culture, most people lack the primary skills of how to give support. Not everyone is a blue-dot-toting Googler—the blue dot on their ID badge giving the approval that this employee completed mental health support training.

We have relegated these responsibilities to counselors, personal coaches, healthcare professionals, and trainers. However, their support is temporary at best and often based on a 50-minute session once a week. On the other hand, we need someone more qualified than Lucy van Pelt, a beloved Charlie Brown friend, and sometime curbside therapist—who, by the way, only charges five cents. What do we do in between? Our peers are there for us much more often, and employers can offer training to make meaningful support more available.

Imagine how our well-being could be shaped at work if we could deploy a tool like Perspectives to help us with our behaviors, attitudes, and beliefs—a process to lower our defenses and allow others to give us feedback. Union Pacific Railroad and H-E-B understood that not everyone knows how to be a good peer, so they trained their workforce. Whether it is through a webinar, a workshop, or a training offered to your champions, find a way to teach skills that allow us to be a more supportive and effective peer in the well-being journey. Consider having employees sign up in pairs. One more way of reinforcing the value of peer support.

Here are some skills that do not require a software program or a lot of advanced training.[22]

- Listening
- Helping set a goal
- Finding a good role model
- Helping eliminate barriers to a healthier and happier day
- Building trust
- Helping locate supportive environments
- Helping a peer work through a setback
- Celebrating success

Hopkins Highlight

Peer support at Johns Hopkins runs the gamut of disseminating information (champions), providing psychological first aid (RISE) and providing motivation and support (KYPD). While many employers offer well-being challenges, how many take peer support into account? At the time of publishing this book, we've offered our Race the Globe Steps Challenge, a program designed and executed with our partner, Labcorp Employer Services, six times. Each year we've attracted more participants (most recently more than 8,000 employees). In addition to tracking the steps for each of 11 Hopkins affiliates to show which part of our organization has the most steps, we also have teams of eight people vying for top place. These smaller teams allow peers to encourage each other to take more steps.

SOCIAL CONNECTEDNESS

At the risk of dating myself, let's talk about how poorly behaved students (not me, of course) were once instructed to stand in the corner of the classroom. It was a move that disconnected the individual from the rest of the class—and caused great embarrassment. Effectiveness aside, this behavioral consequence relied on our basic human need for social connection with our peers.

Social connectedness makes us feel cared for by others, culminating in a sense of belonging and being part of a community. Without social connectedness, people feel lonely, a contributor to depression. Social support groups improve our quality of life, lower our blood pressure, and significantly lower our risk of chronic diseases and their impact.[23]

Fostering a good social climate within your team will encourage peer support as the people on your team will feel closer to their teammates, creating trust and allowing them to disclose their health and well-being challenges and ambitions more comfortably. There are selfish reasons for employers to encourage social connectedness at work. We know that people with good social networks are more resilient and can handle crises more effectively.[24]

Gallup asks the question, "Do you have a best friend at work?" Employees who have a best friend at work are more likely to be engaged, perform well, and less likely to have an accident on the job. It makes sense, right? We are more likely to communicate and collaborate openly with our friends, giving us an opportunity to provide helpful candid feedback that can both positively impact our work as well as our well-being. Having more friends at work creates a sense of inclusion and promotes participation in social activities.[25]

The Wow Company agrees with Gallup: friendships among remote workers are crucial to avoid workplace isolation and maintain employee engagement. Gallup suggests looking for opportunities to bring employees together and encourage them to tell stories about themselves. We can even seek an understanding of what kind of friendships our employees are looking to make with the intent of helping to make a match.[26]

Hopkins Highlight

When Healthy at Hopkins started in 2007, like many other wellness programs from that time, it was a series of lunch and learns, walks and biometric screenings. There was no overt consideration of the social aspect of well-being, and it took concerted effort to right the ship.

There are many opportunities for employers to normalize relationships as part of well-being. It doesn't have to be complicated. We regularly post success stories of individuals (and sometimes teams) who have made progress in their health goals as a way of showing that the people around us are succeeding in their effort to achieve a better state of health and well-being. Seeing that a peer can succeed is more encouraging than reading about how a celebrity lost 50 pounds on a diet of only orange-colored foods (don't try this). Employers can be intentional with their messaging, which can help shape the attitudes and behaviors of the workforce that shows up every day. You know your program is working when impromptu efforts are made among employees to create opportunities to support each other.

Denise was a nurse on one of our campuses. She and her husband went line dancing every weekend. While she usually walked at lunchtime, the winter weather was too much for her to continue during these months. So she started line dancing in the fitness room. At first it was just a couple of people on her team and then when word spread, the whole room was filled.

(Continued)

Dancing is a fun way to move, and Denise taught everyone (including me) how to keep up. This was not a program that came from the executive suite or the Healthy at Hopkins planning team or any wellness committee. This was an impromptu effort of one employee seeking to keep moving during the cold weather and taking her peers along for the ride. Wouldn't you know that salsa and other dancing have popped up at our Suburban hospital in Bethesda, Maryland? If you know how to dance, consider teaching your peers!

THERE'S NO PLACE LIKE HOME

Our family is likely our most influential subculture. Organizations are wise to understand how they can include their employee's family as you create your strategy to support the well-being of your workforce.

Sometimes the thing we need most is to be with family during tough periods. That's not always possible if you're working. Intel expanded its paid leave to support employees through their rough times, beginning January 1, 2020. As Julie Ann Overcash, Intel vice president of Human Resources put it, "When our employees and their families are supported, they perform at their best." Intel's intent was to allow employees to focus on their families and loved ones in a time of need so they can return to work with the proper support.[27]

The importance of family time was at the forefront of several companies when they began hosting farmers markets to help employees get home without an extra stop at the supermarket. The Sidney & Lois Eskanazi Hospital in Indianapolis, Indiana, offers a farmer's market,[28] as does Adobe, Progressive Insurance, and Miami's Nicklaus Children's Hospital. "It's one of those things that promotes work–life balance," said Progressive spokesperson Ron Davis.[29,30]

U.S. Venture, a Wisconsin oil and energy company with 889 employees, boasts having a winner of the Virgin Pulse Life Changer award, with friends to thank. After a worksite health screening revealed Julie Ritzman was on a perilous path, she started making some changes. A co-worker encouraged her to join a bicycling challenge. Gradually, she built up her stamina. With the support of flexibility from her employer, she was able to take many of her bike rides with co-workers during the lunch hour. She led the U.S. Venture team with the most miles ridden. Every morning she was up at 4:30 a.m. for an hour-long bike ride. After biking for four years, along with healthier eating, Julie lost 90 pounds! Her husband lost 50 pounds, and their children began to exercise regularly, making well-being a family affair. She said, "I'm grateful to U.S. Venture for offering a well-structured wellness program that provides the tools and resources to make healthy choices."[31] A supportive peer at work and a flexible and supportive employer (U.S. Venture has a "Healthy Reimbursement" program that funded Julie's bike) contributed to Julie's happiness and health and, in turn, she did the same for her family.

While technology has been destructive to many aspects of our well-being, it's also brought us the opportunity to stay in touch more easily with our friends and family. If these are the people who support our emotional state and our health goals, why not make it easier for them to be part of the well-being culture you are building in your workplace?

Many employers use a portal to serve as a repository for information and communication around their well-being culture. Many wellness portals have features that help connect employees seeking to shape the same behavior. Consider making this portal available to your employees' friends and family. This can engage the employees' closest peers and allow them to be part of the well-being journey.

Purdue University added WellRight to its Healthy Boiler Wellness Program so registered employees and their spouses can log their activities and information as well as access health and wellness resources.[32] WellRight offers a flexible and customizable wellness program with over 400 creative activities that peers can choose to help reach their goals. Purdue offers cash incentives to not only the employees, but also their spouses and children.[33]

Tidelands Health, a four-hospital system in South Carolina, claims WellRight helped them with engagement struggles with their wellness program and in getting to know their employees and their families on a personal, individualized level.[34] Their multidimensional wellness program was especially helpful when the COVID-19 pandemic hit since they were able to provide tools around mental well-being to nurses and physicians, and their friends and families, during what became a heavier burnout period.

The West Ohio Conference of The United Methodist Church, with 200,000 members in 58 Ohio counties, eight satellite offices and three camping and retreat centers, uses the Virgin Pulse platform. Through it, the Conference is able to provide physical activity programs to all clergy and spouses as well as lay employees and spouses, getting them to "think outside the gym" and have fun with peer colleagues while getting active and fit.[35] The Virgin Pulse platform allows a user to invite up to five friends or family members to access the resource, so they can choose to work alongside the employee. The portal also has the capability of creating challenges in a variety of health and well-being areas for the employee to invite colleagues (and friends and family outside of the company) to participate. Used in this way, the Virgin Pulse platform allows an entire community to connect around well-being.

Shaping Your Team Subculture

Peer support is not the same as teaching. Although sharing knowledge may be helpful, it isn't necessary. Remember, most people already know what is healthy and what isn't! Peer support is different from a therapist or counselor. There is no attempt to psychoanalyze or get to deep-rooted issues. Peer support works best when both parties are equals, where there is no real or perceived power differential. For this reason, it's unlikely that a manager can successfully serve as a peer to a subordinate.

There are several things, though, that a manager can do to foster peer support on the team.

- Choose someone on your team to be a well-being champion. It will be easy if there is an apparent health buff. Plan on giving your champion time on your weekly team meeting agenda to share a health message of the week, make the team aware of any programs or resources, upcoming events, or new policies that impact well-being.
- If you've ever built a healthy habit or gotten rid of an unhealthy one with the help of a peer, share your story. By telling your team how having a peer helped you, it serves as an endorsement for them to find their own peer to address their own health and well-being goals and challenges.
- You might unknowingly serve as a peer by modeling healthy behaviors and attitudes. We tend to learn vicariously through watching others, which primes us to imitate these behaviors later.[36]
- When you learn that two people on your team are supporting each other to create and sustain healthier habits, praise their collective effort at a team meeting (assuming they've given you permission). This will not only reinforce the behavior for the two persons high-

(Continued)

lighted, but also plant the seed for others on the team to join their efforts. A pat on the back from the manager tends to reinforce behavior.
- Be a messenger! When your organization posts programs or resources that highlight a peer support strategy, call it out!
- Keep your ears open. If you find out that someone on your team is trying to achieve a new behavior or get rid of an old one, you might play matchmaker if you know of someone in a similar situation.
- When you know two people on your team are trying to achieve the same health or well-being goal together, remove barriers for them! For example, arrange the schedule so they can take their breaks at the same time. That gives them time they likely need.
- Celebrate success! When peers on your team have worked together to improve their well-being, celebrate the effort and the outcome, just as you would an accomplishment with a team project.

The health and well-being of your team is an essential part of being successful, so treat it as though it deserves special attention, because it does! When other people on the team see how much you value colleagues working together to get to a better state of mind and body, they give the same approach more thought.

HOW I HELP HOPKINS GET HEALTHY

Sometimes it's difficult to ask for help. Maybe you're not comfortable asking because you were raised to figure things out yourself. Maybe you're surrounded at work by braggarts and weekend warriors who run marathons throughout the year, making your goal of walking 7,000 steps every day seem trivial. Perhaps you're embarrassed about an unhealthy behavior you're trying to shake, and you really don't want others to know. For me, I found it difficult to figure out how to let people know that their intention of being nice by offering me chocolate was really making it hard to stay on my path of healthy eating. My peers were being nice, after all!

It got me thinking that I must not be the only one who was struggling on how to express their peer support needs comfortably, without offending others around them or being embarrassed. How are we to get the peer support we need if we can't even talk about it? One simple tool was to let a white board do the talking for us. For less than three dollars, we procured Healthy at Hopkins branded, 8 x 11 whiteboards. A double-backed Velcro fastener was added so the boards could be secured on the side of a workstation or on an office door such that anyone walking by could see that employee's message. "Please Support My Health By . . ." on the top of the board prompted the addition of that person's need. Common responses were . . . "Ask me to walk at lunch" and "remind me to drink water." Despite the occasional "out of office" hijacking of the board, by and large, they fueled conversation and action around needed support.

Put Your Own Mask on First

Consider taking advantage of the power of peer support by any one or more of the following:

- If you are trying to build a healthy habit, find a work colleague whom either already has the habit or is also striving for the same goal. Either way, your chance of success is improved.
- If you are trying to overcome an unhealthy habit, join a support group through the workplace. If the problem you're addressing doesn't currently have a support group in place, be the person to work with human resources to organize the resource and get a front row seat.
- Consider getting trained in psychological first aid. Not only will you be helping others when their time of need comes, it will also boost your self-confidence and add fulfillment to your life when you can support your peer after a stressful event.
- Who is your best friend at work? If you don't have one, make a concerted effort to create and foster this relationship.
- Is there someone at home you can connect with during the workday to support your health goals? Your emotional needs?

THAT'S A WRAP!

Peer support is assistance provided by family, friends, and co-workers. Without such support, many people will be unable to achieve their personal well-being goals. Peer support is unique in that it is based on a trusted relationship, is ongoing, and is grounded in a familiarity with day-to-day circumstances. Helping someone achieve a healthy lifestyle goal is a great way to show we care.

Those giving peer support also benefit substantially from their altruistic efforts. Offering peer support raises self-esteem and reinforces positive practices. Helping peers creates a more supportive social network for healthy behavior, and they will likely be supportive in return. It is often reported that it is the teachers and support group leaders and not the students that are most likely to maintain their healthy behavior. Increasing peer support is a useful strategy for giving more people the benefits of the helping role.

Consider which steps you can take toward using peer support to lead your company to becoming a healthier, happier, and more resilient organization:

- Assess your company or organization's unique aspects and particular needs so you can tailor peer support. It's hard to find an effective off-the-shelf solution that fits every industry.
- Will you assign (mandate) buddies or encourage them?
- Can an IT solution support your effort?
- Consider peer support groups for specific health challenges or ones that focus on lifestyle choices.
- How will you integrate family and friends from outside of work into your strategy?
- What are you doing for your remote workers?

Leaders play an important role in mobilizing effective peer support within their workgroups. It all begins by encouraging people to seek out peer support through buddy systems, support groups, or reaching out to co-workers, family, and friends. We're happier when we're socially connected, and it's easier to achieve our health goals with supportive co-workers, friends, and family. Encouraging peer support is one way leaders can support a well-being culture. There is a whole chapter's worth of other ideas for leaders, starting on the next page.

8

How to Be the Best Boss

Lead with Well-Being

LEADERS HAVE THE SAME CHALLENGES as everyone else, including the need to attend to the health of a family member. Ellen Derrick, a managing partner at Deloitte Management Consulting, makes a concerted effort to focus on her own well-being as she supports her daughter Kate, who has cystic fibrosis and diabetes. When Kate had to be hospitalized, Ellen shared, on social media, her own well-being plan that helped her cope with the circumstances. Ellen recognized the need to take care of herself, and that meant finding joy through friends, music, and comedy. Ellen tried to keep her schedule as normal as possible, and at the same time, learn to give herself permission to lower the expectations of herself during this period.[1]

Similar to Mark Bertolini, Aetna's CEO, who divulged his own mental health challenges, thereby making it easier for others at Aetna to share their struggles, Ellen received an outpouring of support.

In addition to setting the expectations for an organization, a leader also needs to be unafraid to be vulnerable. This makes it easier for the rest of the workforce to not only seek help, but to also tighten relationships over similar struggles.

You don't have to be at the top of your organization, like Ellen and Mark, to make a difference in the health and well-being of the people you lead. There is leadership across all levels and all parts of the organization that, when applied, will create the energy needed to allow a culture of health to flourish.

Leaders play a role in supporting all the well-being culture building blocks and in addition, have special responsibilities such as:

- Setting well-being as a priority
- Managing with well-being skills
- Serving as a role model
- Leading change

If we leave the responsibility of building a well-being culture only to executives like Ellen and Mark, momentum will never build, and the message will fall short of penetrating the fabric of the organization. The challenge then, is to harness the plethora of leaders (including you) that exist within your organization to exert their positive influence on health and well-being.

MAKING WELL-BEING A PRIORITY

Former Starbucks CEO and president Kevin Johnson faced the early days of the COVID-19 pandemic head on with a March 22, 2020 message to employees that "No partner should be asked to choose between work and their health." He asked Starbucks leaders and franchises to care for their employees, and in April he again stressed the company's commitment to "prioritizing the health and well-being of our partners and customers."[2] Kevin proceeded to pay every retail employee in the United States and Canada for 30 days, immediately relieving the anxiety many people were feeling at the time of whether they would continue to get a paycheck as stores began to close. In doing so, he set the tone for the company's approach to COVID-19.

Kevin made well-being a priority. Unfortunately, many leaders have a long laundry list of priorities. This makes knowing where to start really challenging. Karen Martin, author of *The Outstanding Organization*, captures it succinctly: "When everything is a priority, nothing is a priority." When you start with well-being as the priority, it makes it possible for all of the other priorities to be fulfilled. Without a healthy and well team, it will be tough to excel.

As a leader, you are in a position to positively impact the health and well-being of dozens, hundreds, maybe even thousands of people.

If you do your job well, you'll have healthier, happier, and more resilient employees and you'll help keep our hospitals empty. Intentionally aligning your business ambitions with well-being will make it easier for your workforce to appreciate the importance of their own well-being.

Dell Technologies declared health a priority for their employees and their customers. Dell has the moonshot goal to "advance health, education, and economic opportunity initiatives to deliver enduring results for one billion people by 2030."[3] Dell started with their own employees in 2004 when they launched "Well with Dell" aiming to create a culture of well-being that supports the healthy lifestyle of their employees and their families.[4] With 165,000 worldwide employees, they are on their way to reaching their moonshot goal.

Similarly, Labcorp's mission is to improve health and improve lives.[5] This is good news for their 70,000 employees. As gyms started closing when COVID-19 settled in, Labcorp offered employees a generous allowance for home exercise equipment.[6] To ease the omnipresent stress during that period, Labcorp supported laughing through comedy sessions.[7] Labcorp, as well as Dell, have both been named Platinum-level winners of "Best Employers: Excellence in Health & Well-Being" awards by the Business Group on Health.[8]

Here are three ways to show that well-being is a priority on your team and in your company.

Put Well-Being on the Agenda

If it's not on the agenda, it doesn't get discussed. Just like finance, customer service, and quality improvement have regular updates, so should employee health and well-being. It might only consume a minute one week, but the next week it could be 10. There is no shortage of content that can be shared and discussed. Your agenda time can be used for more than just regurgitating upcoming events and programs. For example, you could lead a gratitude exercise in which each person at the table shares one thing they're grateful for related to their work or with whom they work. When there is a standing space for health, it forces the meeting leader to consider the content for that week or month.

Every leader can put well-being on the agenda if you include it as a business goal. That means starting at the top and holding every manager accountable for addressing well-being in either a prescribed message that permeates the workforce or by allowing the flexibility required to address the well-being needs of the team subculture. Given that your leaders may not be comfortable with the topic or understand the substance, tie your "agenda" strategy to your culture connection point of training. Provide leaders with the training they need to understand the full spectrum of well-being, from work boundaries to respecting family time, to mindfulness as a tool to manage stress. Help your managers learn to communicate with respect to the individual well-being journey each person on the team is taking.

Incorporate Well-Being into Annual Events and Other Customs

Promoting and participating in organization well-being programs, events, and traditions are a meaningful way to express your ongoing commitment to the well-being culture. You could take the initiative to lead an event yourself. This effort can be as simple as organizing a spring walk attended by your immediate team or a more ambitious undertaking, such as including the departments around yours or the entire building. Maybe you want to focus on healthy eating. Why not start "Fruit Friday" and bring in a selection of fruits to pass around to your team? Scale it up and push a "Friday Fruit" cart through the facility, handing out a fruit of choice to the workforce, while receiving feedback on the well-being culture strategy and answering questions. Can you imagine what your team might be thinking the first time they see you handing out fruit?

You don't have to lead the effort to show that well-being is a priority. Skip the email and invite each member of your team personally to participate. Add your own twist to your team's participation. Maybe giving each member of your team red, white, and blue socks before the company July 4th walking event will enhance your team cohesiveness.

If you're not comfortable with such overt acts, recruit the champion on the team and give explicit permission to rally everyone. Another option is to invite someone from the company health-promotion team to lead a well-being exercise on specific occasions. Even someone on the more social side of your group can instigate a birthday celebration or work anniversary with a well-being activity as a way of honoring a team member, with a custom that is aligned with health rather than something covered in frosting.

Whatever strategy you choose for getting yourself and other leaders involved with the workforce in a meaningful way, the consistency of a healthy practice led by organizational leaders becomes ingrained throughout the organization and reflects it values. Time spent participating in annual events and well-being customs indicates that well-being is the utmost of company priorities.

Address Institutional Barriers to Success

I once fell off a bike (well, actually many times) going over a speed bump. There I was, exercising and trying to live my healthy lifestyle, plastered to the pavement. It probably wasn't the best idea to be biking before the sun rose, but with three young kids, I did some crazy things to fit exercise into my day. The speed bump did its job and I wasn't able to exercise for some time as I healed.

It can be frustrating (and maybe even painful) for your employees to keep hitting speed bumps in their efforts to participate in company well-being programs. They need to understand that you see their participation as worthwhile, so try to reduce barriers to participation. Perhaps a flexible schedule or some other arrangement can be made so that employees can participate without detracting from their work. Maybe a frank conversation about what parts of their job are interfering with their well-being is in order.

Is it possible that you're the speed bump? If you're sending emails at night, what message are you also sending along to your team? If they are looking at their phones to be responsive, then they are not relaxing, recharging, and getting the rest they need in order to be at their best the next day. More than half of office-based workers have checked their email at least once after 11 p.m. when they should be sleeping![9]

The expectations at Johnson & Johnson illustrate how managers support employees as opposed to hindering their efforts. At J&J, managers are held accountable for the health and well-being of their team members, which is why you will see them in the free and convenient gyms leading by example by exercising alongside team members, who are encouraged to be physically active and visit the gym on company time.[10]

It's common for someone in a large organization to be asked to pursue a well-culture, only to learn that not everyone got the same message. Leaders need to help clear the way; be sure others are assisting and not thwarting progress, and that can be hard when not everyone is working toward the same goal. Giving the orders to create a well-being culture and then washing one's hands of being involved is a sure way to demoralize your team. As with other company initiatives, as a manager, you need to support the plan and your team!

Dan, an IT leader at one of our Hopkins' affiliates, is leading by example and removing barriers to success. Dan's been an avid runner for a long time. When he came to Hopkins, he made it a point to continue his habit of running at lunchtime. There are showers and lockers in his building, which made it easier to keep this habit going. He noticed his team wasn't moving as much during the day, because they were always tied to their computers. In *West Wing* style, he started walking meetings with individuals. He started team meetings with stretching and encouraging colleagues to stand during part or all of the meetings.

Hopkins Highlight

Shortly after introducing his first five-year strategic priorities, which included employee health and well-being, Paul Rothman, former dean of the School of Medicine, chose to use his monthly column in our institution's newspaper to focus on "So Long, Soda." His column supported the creation of a healthy beverage culture that had been underway for more than a year. Paul articulated the irony of treating our patients with sound nutritional recommendations but not heeding our own advice. In addition, he cited the conclusions of research pointing toward the perils of drinking unhealthy beverages, an example of tying a message back to an organization's priorities. He referenced the part of the strategic plan that directly relates to offering more healthy beverages. He went on to articulate the healthy beverage strategy, so that our workforce understood what changes were coming. In one article, Paul conveyed well-being as a priority by aligning this institutional well-being transformation with our mission and our goals.

BE A WELL-BEING ROLE MODEL

Several years ago, I met with one of our School of Public Health faculty members about our employee health and well-being program. After adjourning, we walked out of the room together. We both needed to leave the seventh floor and exit the building. While I took for granted our walk was headed for the stairwell, I was informed "the elevators are over there." I knew where the elevators were. I just always use the stairs and I figured my colleague did the same, given we just spent an hour discussing employee health! In a well-being culture, you don't need to wait for a steps challenge to take the steps.

Often what we do speaks louder than what we say. People pay attention to those who influence the company, their team, and their workday. The employees are watching you! Whether we realize it or not, our behaviors as leaders greatly influence those we lead.

It seems using the elevator instead of the stairs is a particularly common practice that runs counter to a healthy culture. For someone in a leadership position, barring a physical impairment, using the stairs is an easy 'step' to being a role model. Of course, walking upstairs (versus down) takes a little more exertion for someone who's out of practice.

This example of my colleague reflexively pushing the elevator button as opposed to heading toward the stairs is just one example of how difficult it can be to overcome norms and create new habits. Good leaders are more than just their title. Good leaders are role models. This section on being a role model could read as a greatest hits collection of this book. Everything that it takes to create a great social climate involves you! Have fun, be kind, listen, and the list goes on. Don't hide your well-being practices. If they aren't visible, tell them to your team—it's not likely you're meditating in the middle of the hall. When the topic of stress or insomnia comes up, tell your team about your mindfulness practice. Participate visibly in organization well-being programs. It's a nonverbal way of giving your team permission to participate as well.

Go one step further and make it easier for well-being practices to surface on your team. Have a walking meeting or take a break to stand during your meetings and stretch. Maybe a 90-second breathing exercise is all it will take for everyone to decompress—yes, we can learn breathing patterns to lower our stress level. Knowing that the team leader supports healthy behaviors makes it much more likely for the team to engage. There are many ways you can be an effective well-being role model, and none of them require that you become a super athlete, meditation guru, or a vegan.

Hopkins Highlight

How We Highlight the Well-Being of Leaders at Hopkins

With six hospitals, a medical school, a primary care network, an insurance company, and more, there are hundreds of leaders at Johns Hopkins Medicine. Here are some of the ways we highlight their well-being efforts:

- We regularly publish a story in our *Wellness Weekly* newsletter on how our leaders take care of their own well-being.

(Continued)

- When we have programs, like our annual step competition, we not only feature our leaders participating, but we have a special category for our leaders to compete against each other. We also include the leaders in the award process for the top steppers. It's a great feeling for our employees to be recognized by their leadership for taking healthy steps!
- A picture is worth a thousand words. That's why we take pictures of our leaders participating in our different programs or using our well-being resources. These pictures are used in marketing material, alongside articles about the well-being program, and in presentations.

MANAGE WITH WELL-BEING SKILLS

Everyone has a boss or manager and possibly more than one. For those who have had many managers over the years, we know that one may stand out as a "good" boss and another as a "bad" boss. Why? Simply stated, the good manager made us feel good and the bad manager made us feel bad.

It's not that complicated. Unfortunately, most leaders are promoted into their positions because of previous success and not because of their leadership skills. It's certainly unlikely that part of the decision process for earning the promotion was consideration of how the leader would impact their team's well-being. And offering training to lead with well-being skills? In honor of my family's Brooklyn roots, "fuhgeddaboudit."

What We Say Matters

After a particularly challenging day, have you ever played back in your mind, over and over again at night, what your boss said to you? Or come home in a good mood because you had a great day at work, partly because of how you were treated by your manager? Leaders are in a position to be supportive—or not—and their words can leave a lasting impression. Be very intentional and specific with your words so you aren't misunderstood.

No one wants to work for a nitpicker. While many leaders are looking to address problems, you can be the one looking for standout job performance. By providing regular positive feedback, your teammates will be more likely to accept constructive criticism in the spirit intended. Most importantly, avoid only giving positive feedback when negative feedback is going to follow. By using this sequence, your employee will quickly learn that if their supervisor is giving them praise, they will soon be on the receiving end of criticism. As a result, your employee will never have the opportunity to bask in some well-earned compliments.

The very basic question, "How are you doing today?" can go a long way and listening to what's on you co-worker's mind is a fundamental way to connect. Demonstrating that you care improves trust and eases some of the formalities that come with the workplace. Ultimately, your demonstration of caring helps your colleagues' well-being.

Make it a practice to share your own challenges. Once again, Mark Bertolini pops into mind. The challenges he faced while recovering from his accident almost led him to end his own life. Making yourself vulnerable and showing your human side levels the playing field and makes it easier for others to follow suit. It gives permission to the team to acknowledge that sometimes we come to work with personal issues on our mind and we all need understanding. Mark's outreach garnered over a hundred thankful responses from employees sharing their own stories. By decreasing the stigma and offering resources, Aetna was able to foster an environment in which employees felt comfortable seeking assistance and in which mental health was not stigmatized.

Use positive language. Yes, things can get tough, and we've all felt like cursing when we've stubbed our toe. However, setbacks should be expected and one of your roles as the leader is to reassure the team and rally to assess the situation and move forward. If you choose words that paint a frustrated or pessimistic tone, you will only compound the emotions that members of your team may already feel.

Your tone and your body language matter just as much as your words. Speak the way you want to be spoken to. The art and science of communicating is more complicated than most people realize. There is no shame in asking for help. In fact, investing some of your own time in improving your communication skills will not only help you support the health and well-being of your team, but it will also likely improve your own health as you'll enjoy fewer misunderstandings and conflicts.

One of the most helpful things I learned about communication from one of my mentors was that we learn a lot more by listening than by talking. You don't always have to speak. Sometimes the best thing you can do for someone is just listen.

Management Style Matters

Your management style influences the social climate and, in turn, the health of your teams, not to mention their effectiveness! Paying attention to how your management style impacts the health of those you manage will enable you to improve the team's efforts and accomplish your goals. What you say and what you do are important parts of how we are perceived as managers. But there is more.

Sure, people work to earn a living. Yet, most people are seeking more than a paycheck. They want to work in an area that they find interesting, with people they enjoy, and on programs, projects, and other assignments that bring fulfillment. These positive attributes of the job are much easier to attain when working with a supervisor who envelopes best management practices.

Give your team some latitude. Let them be involved with as much decision-making as you can. Groups are more likely to embrace change when they are part of the decision-making process. No one likes to be micromanaged. Employees benefit from having some autonomy.[11] It allows them to take a more vested interest. It also allows them to bring their own creativity, experience, and education to the table. Be sure, however, to set some guidelines and expectations. It can be frustrating to finish a project, only to find out the result wasn't what your boss expected or to feel like the goalposts moved. Check in periodically to make sure you're on the same page. Allowing a degree of independence is a necessary part of personal and professional growth. Allowing your employees to be heard builds their sense of self-worth—definitely an ingredient of well-being. Managers who create fulfilling opportunities win respect and enhance their relationships.

Be sure to regularly assess the amount and complexity of work you are assigning. This is necessary to ensure that you are not overwhelming (nor underwhelming) the employee. People generally want to be challenged. They need a purpose and to feel as though they are contributing. This practice of assessing the workload is also necessary to be sure that each member of the team feels they are being treated fairly and that work is being evenly distributed.

Give credit where credit is due. Many people do good work, and they deserve to be acknowledged. Don't just tell the individual. Tell the team. Let the person who is getting the accolades be the one who gets to present their project to the larger group. Don't take credit for their work. Be a humble leader and recognize that you can surround yourself with good people who can make meaningful contributions.

The lack of adequate resources necessary to perform one's job functions can be frustrating. Imagine you are asked to assemble and bind 25 large packets of information for a meeting. You must hand punch all these papers because there is either no automated feature on the copier or you're not allowed to purchase a three-hole punch tool. You're stuck punching one hole at a time. (Not to mention trying to pick up those little round pieces that seem to have magically been applied with glue as they floated to the ground). Preposterous I know, but I bet you can find real examples in your workplace. Feeling like your time isn't being utilized well due to a lack of appropriate resources is a source of contention—one that can create bitterness if it happens too often.

Encourage work–life flexibility. In other words, understand that most people have things going on outside of their workplace that periodically may overlap—a sick child that can't go to school, an elderly parent that needs help arranging a doctor's appointment, an oil leak from the car that, if not fixed soon, will keep your employee from getting to work. Life happens, and if you encourage your team to speak up when they need flexibility in their workday to address their challenges, you'll decrease stress levels and increase good will.

In this same context, encourage work–life balance. The number of hours your workers devote to your organization versus the number of hours that remain for their personal life is of paramount consideration. For many employees, it's no longer a balance when work has infiltrated home life. About one out of three Americans, with traditional five-day-a-week jobs is working on the weekends.[12] Not only is this taking away from much-needed rest and recovery, but it impacts families as well. The negative impact of overworking on well-being is compounded by its potentially detrimental effect on marriages and relationships with children.[13] Insist that members of your team take vacation time. Unfortunately, 7 out of 10 employees in the United States don't use all their vacation days.[14] Your team member will be much happier, engaged, and productive if they are well rested. Take this advice yourself. What's the point of working most of your adult life if you're too ill to enjoy your retirement?

One last tip that always works. Apologize when you are wrong. No one is perfect. You will make a mistake or two when you manage. In my case, more than two (way more than two). You can't always be right and your employee always wrong! Apologizing demonstrates humility, builds trust, and shows respect—all contributions to building a positive work climate. Your team will appreciate your candor, feel better themselves, and be more forthcoming to admit when they are wrong.

There are so many different strategies for being an effective manager. In fact, hundreds if not thousands of books have been written on being a good manager. It is rare, however, to find one focused on the way in which being a good manager positively impacts the health of your team. When you read any management resource, think about how what you're reading impacts the well-being of your team. If you were on the receiving end of these management strategies, how would it impact your own well-being?

Well-Being Training Matters

The prospect of becoming a manager or a leader at a different level can be exciting. It's a vote of confidence that someone thinks you've got the right stuff. But you may find yourself in that role and realize that maybe you have some of the right stuff—but not all the stuff. Leading can be challenging and most people don't take a class on leadership. Training is important to give leaders the tools they need to be successful. Many companies already have training programs to learn new payroll systems and software and understand appropriate conduct in the workplace. So why not training programs on happiness, health, and resilience?

Managers, champions, and other leaders need to be trained for their role in supporting a culture of health in the workplace. Role playing, case studies, and other methods of interaction can be valuable methods for skill building.

There are many ways leaders can support and show commitment to a workplace well-being culture. The more of these strategies leaders learn and deploy, the quicker a culture of health will take root and the more likely it is to grow. If your organization doesn't have the resources to train every leader, pay particular attention to managers with high staff turnover. Given that the most common reason employees leave their job is because of their manager, this may be the group on which you focus your efforts. Training is worth the investment because when employees stay on the job, the organization succeeds through the benefit of an experienced pool of committed employees (as well as lower costs for recruitment).

BE A FORCE OF CHANGE

Whether you lead six people or 600, you can be the change agent who creates a well-being culture on your team that contributes to the happiness, health, and resilience of your colleagues. What a tremendous privilege!

But remember, old habits die hard, and not everyone will want to participate in creating a well-being culture. Praise, practice, and push-back are all necessary to move a well-being culture from a good idea to a lasting one.[15] You may have to remind yourself every morning that being a change agent requires some attention and intention.

One important job leaders have is to promote, advocate, and defend the importance of employee health and well-being. There are very few areas of business that are scrutinized as much as employee health and well-being. When an employee needs a computer to get work done, seldom is there a question about whether that resource is valuable or what the return on investment is. When the person using that computer though, suffers from daily headaches caused by a stressful workplace environment, some may want to overlook that problem. That's short-sighted, because if an employee can't perform their job well under these conditions, they are more likely to call out of work and maybe even leave their job! Then you have no one to use the computer that you just bought.

Right now, your organization could be at any stage in the journey of creating a well-being culture. Your company might be just starting or perhaps reassessing your existing strategy. Perhaps you have a workplace-wellness program that no one uses, and it looks like it is on the chopping block for the next budget year. Whatever the situation, you need to be prepared to articulate the reasons why health and well-being are important to your team. Our American culture has created an invisible fence between our workplace and our health and tearing down the wall will take time, persuasion, and repetition. All leaders play a role in change. Whether for your own team, your peers, your own manager, or the C-suite, you can be the difference between plans on a document and plans coming to fruition.

Praise and Persistence

You're never too old to have your behaviors, attitudes, and beliefs reinforced. Your responsibility is far from over after communicating the well-being vision and the plans to reach your goals. It takes a long time to shape a well-being culture. Look at this as a marathon and not a sprint. Human beings are complicated, and putting a bunch of them together on your team makes for quite the social experiment. You might read the social climate chapter a few times before the content starts to become part of your fabric. How long you've been leading your team will influence how long it will take to shift its well-being culture. Good or bad, your reputation precedes your effort to lead this culture shift.

Informal (or natural) leaders play an important role in swaying their colleagues on opinions and behaviors. These informal leaders can be helpful or harmful to your team and your organization. It's highly likely you have an informal leader on your team. Involving your champions will make shaping your well-being culture much easier.

Pushback

Even once every well-being culture building block is in place, not everyone will join the effort willingly. Yes, there is often a gap between the plan and the execution. Expect that you will see both subtle neglect and overt defiance in response to the well-being culture building effort. Prepare to nip these counterculture behaviors and attitudes in the bud. Letting them pass without addressing them only lets the weed roots grow deeper.

We often think of pushback in terms of how we will stop people from doing the wrong thing. For example, a sexual harassment policy is a way to confront unsavory behavior. However, sometimes we need to speak up when someone is doing something right! It's not uncommon for someone who has a healthy practice to be on the receiving end of a few jabs, and as the manager, you might have to intervene. For example, someone who meditates at work might have been the subject of gossip that included the word "flake" (although meditating is becoming a norm at Hopkins!). Someone who exercises during the workday may not be perceived as a "hard worker," and the person who chooses to eat a vegan diet may be perceived as a "worrywart." If you hear one of your team members being mocked, shut down that behavior. If you don't, it could get worse, and others on the team who aim to make healthy choices may be discouraged. Don't be surprised if the negative comments are coming from the person who is in greatest need of health improvement.

You can reduce the level of ridicule thrust on positive practices if you praise healthy practices. You can further reinforce this action by rewarding and recognizing employees for adopting healthy lifestyle practices. Communication and rewards are both culture connection points! Be blatant. Communicate that being critical of healthy practices is not acceptable in this place of work.

COMMUNICATE OFTEN AND VARY THE MESSENGER

Jimmy Carter, the 39th president of the United States, popularized the peanut. Ronald Reagan, the president who followed, did the same for jelly beans. Whether or not we like the person or the food, there's no denying that leaders send a very powerful message with their words and their actions.

Leadership at all levels needs to communicate the well-being vision and current efforts at regular intervals. The frequency of communication might vary based on the role the leader plays within the organization. For example, the president might be featured quarterly demonstrating some part of that individual's routine that keeps him or her healthy, or a photo of that person participating in a company-sponsored well-being program with accompanying story could be placed in the organizational newsletter.

Although it would be helpful for you to spend a couple of minutes each week during the team meeting sharing that week's newsletter, events, and other health messages, you don't have to be the only communicator. If your organization has a champion network, make sure someone on your team is participating. Your champion can oversee providing regular updates to the team.

Executive messages are also important at key times or in meaningful situations. For example, if there is an annual presentation on the state of the organization, including employee health and well-being will be crucial if it is to hold the same stature as other topics. The culture of health should also be featured in any annual report, giving the year's summary of what was accomplished. The branded health and well-being program can also be included in annual benefits information. Despite all the resources the organization might be providing, they may not all be apparent, so providing them in one place can make it easier for everyone.

When your team has a well-being achievement, share the news! Make a request to put it in the company social media channel or newsletter. It's a great way to enhance your team spirit and it could provide the motivation for another team to strive for the same accomplishment.

Shaping Your Team Subculture

Whether you are the CEO or a frontline manager, you play the same leadership role in creating a well-being culture on your team. Which of the following are you already doing, and which need improvement?

- Making it clear that well-being is a priority
- Putting well-being on the agenda

(Continued)

- Including well-being in annual events
- Removing barriers to make it easier to have a healthy day
- Being a well-being role model
- Using positive words and giving positive feedback
- Encouraging self-care

HOW I HELP HOPKINS GET HEALTHY

When I first arrived at Hopkins, I spent a lot of time observing my surroundings and the work culture. I was struck many times by the irony of the messages delivered from a healthcare organization. One stood out as particularly egregious: a bake sale to raise money for the American Diabetes Association (ADA). While Hopkins has a rich history of raising funds for worthy causes, we hadn't always been mindful of the mixed messages that might be sent in the process.

I couldn't be complicit any longer. Knowing that pushback was needed in this instance, I drafted a letter to my boss and his boss (the president of Johns Hopkins HealthCare). Granted, I was nervous about sending it up the ladder, especially as a new employee. However, leaders need to have the courage to take risks and act. I knew that selling unhealthy baked goods did not align with the core values of Johns Hopkins as a premier healthcare institution, and my gut was telling me that raising my concern was not a risk at all.

The letter highlighted the irony between helping the ADA, while simultaneously making diabetes worse for those who ate the food we were selling! Traditional baked goods are inherently full of sugar, refined flour, and butter. Fortunately, the letter was enough to convince the leaders of Johns Hopkins HealthCare that we needed to change tactics on our fundraising. JHM no longer turns to food (especially unhealthy choices) to raise money for charity.

Put Your Own Mask on First

When you're a kid, the biggest concern about getting into bed might be whether you can run and then jump far enough to reach the mattress without any monsters underneath the bed grabbing your feet. As an

(Continued)

adult, getting into bed might be scarier when you're going through periods of not sleeping well (like when you are writing a book) and you're not sure if insomnia will strike again that night. This has been one of my intermittent well-being challenges for much of the past two decades. I'm in good company, though, with 1 in 4 Americans having insomnia every year.[16] If you are a team of 12, that means 3 people on your team are probably coming to work tired. Are you one of them?

There is an intimate relationship between the stress from our work and the social support we receive in the workplace with our sleep quality and quantity.[17] When we don't sleep well, it makes it more difficult for us to work well the next day and handle stress appropriately. For example, we might snap at someone on our team or choose to eat a third donut in the break room; these behaviors can, in turn, interfere with that night's sleep, and so on. Whether we're tired, hungry, or in pain, how we feel inside will influence how we lead.

Stress impacts the way we carry our bodies and the way we talk. We're different people when we're stressed. It's quite likely you've been around someone who is under a great deal of stress. You feel it inside yourself. You may find your muscles tense. It's also possible you find yourself getting quieter around this person at the times they are showing signs of stress, so as not to provoke any unwelcome response. Most Americans experience stress on a regular basis, citing work as the number-one source. Is it possible you are a source of stress for your team?

As a leader, it's important you address your own well-being if you expect to be a source of positivity and not a source of stress for your team. How much you exercise, what you eat and drink, and whether you're distracted play roles in your ability to be fully engaged while at work. We are complicated creatures. Our health habits (or lack thereof) and our emotional state are intertwined. Every piece of your well-being counts. How you show up to work and how you feel inside greatly impacts the well-being of those you lead. Put your own oxygen mask on first.

THAT'S A WRAP

It's a lot of work to create a well-being culture. Shaping a good social climate and living the company's shared values are fundamental to the culture shift. You play a pivotal role in both of those initial steps.

However, if you don't want your progress to stall, you'll have to support well-being as part of your daily responsibilities.

While the human resources department likely has a plethora of benefits to address the perceived needs for the people on your team, you are the primary person, the front line if you will, in terms of creating a happy, healthy, and resilient team. Ideally, you will have created a social climate such that your team is forthcoming with their well-being needs, opinions, and questions. However, it's more likely your colleagues are not going to express their feelings, struggles, or pain in an email or write it on their foreheads. Part of your job is to know when something has changed. Pay attention to things such as missing deadlines, facial expressions, late arrivals, and nodding off. You can be the difference between your employee having a "well day" or finding yourself with a vacancy on your team. If you lead with well-being, you may quickly become someone's (or the whole team's) favorite boss.

When you create a good social climate and build trust on your team, it will be easier for well-being to flourish. For example, I once took my blood pressure during a Zoom meeting only to find it was quite a bit higher than desirable. My muscle tension hadn't failed me as a warning sign. I felt comfortable enough to send a private chat to my supervisor in the meeting to let her know I was stepping away for a few minutes (a cup of tea was in order) because my blood pressure was elevated. Another manager may not have been so understanding or frankly wondered why I was taking my blood pressure during a meeting! I trusted that my supervisor would know that I wouldn't have stepped away if it wasn't something important, and I was also confident that had I shared my blood pressure reading, she would agree that it was time for me to take a break for self-care.

There are a lot of speed bumps on the path toward a healthier, happier, and more resilient team and organization. Organizational change is difficult under any circumstance. When you consider changing strongly rooted behaviors and attitudes of dozens, hundreds, or thousands of people, you can anticipate there will be a few bumps along the way. Some are easier to see, and others are a surprise because in some ways, we're riding in the dark. The big speed bumps, the culture killers, are worth our attention.

9

Culture Killers
Watch Out for the Speed Bumps

I'M NOT MUCH OF AN artist. But I can recall a time in middle school art class when our teacher gave us a hunk of clay and instructed us to make something to go in the kiln. The final product would be a Mother's Day gift. My first thought was that my gift would end up being one more thing for my mom to politely guffaw over before placing it in the basement when I wasn't looking.

When beginning to build a culture of health, it can sometimes feel like you've been handed a hunk of clay. You know you are supposed to create something beautiful, maybe even meaningful, and yet the task at hand is intimidating, and figuring out where to start is challenging. And like my middle school project, it can also be a little messy.

Many companies have made failed attempts at improving their organization's collective well-being. That's a lot of failed art projects in the basement. But these failures aren't because you don't have a $5 billion-dollar park-like campus, like Apple in Cupertino, California (although it doesn't hurt to have beautiful surroundings).[1] You can still get fresh air and trees elsewhere and even bring them inside if needed. Yes, plants, fishponds, all kinds of natural elements have been connected to well-being at work. But nature is only one piece of an intricate web of ingredients.

It's understandable that, with so many possible ways to support well-being, you may have previously struggled to make a plan, stay focused, and show progress. While putting a comprehensive plan in place may feel complicated, you now have all the building blocks you need.

Whether you lead a team of 6, 60, or 60,000, arriving at a well-being shared value, shaping your social climate so that it supports healthy norms, and is reinforced by peer support and culture connection points, is achievable. Organizations are always changing to meet the competition, latest technology, and economic circumstances. When was the last time you sat down to address changing the organization to support a well-being culture? Or will this be the first time?

Getting it right isn't easy, as Amazon found out. Its WorkingWell initiative was intended to improve employee health at the company's fulfillment centers. This included AmaZen Booths—mindful practice rooms—where employees could experience calm and access mental health resources. But critics of the company pounced on the news as being in stark contrast with Amazon's increase in revenues, profits, and stock prices during the pandemic, while its 1.3 million employees experienced higher than average workplace injuries and strenuous working conditions, all of which cast a shadow over any well-being initiative.[2] Here's an example in which the shared value of well-being wasn't first integrated into the organization's work practices and, instead, a culture connection point was applied like a Band-Aid to a much bigger wound than it could cover.

Organizational change has been studied and practiced for many years. Maybe you're lucky enough to have someone within your company who is an organizational change expert! Yes, it's a thing—one that comes with a degree. If you do have such a person, they are obviously a key player on your team. However, most of us won't be so lucky.

Change can be hard, yet having a framework and plan in place will make it easier. While I can't make you an expert in organizational change in the remaining three chapters, there are some fundamental pieces that shouldn't be ignored.

You could start building a well-being culture with any of the building blocks, especially if you already know which building block needs the greatest attention. But bear in mind, as the figure in Chapter 1 shows, it's hard to separate the building blocks, and you may need to address several of them as you're planning, to see significant progress. Here's a quick refresher that might be helpful as you read the well-being culture-building warnings in this chapter:

- Shared Values: The organizational priorities that align with employee priorities

- Social Climate: The collective feeling of inclusivity, positivity, and shared vision
- Norms: The commonly accepted (and expected) behaviors of the group
- Culture Connection Points: The levers the employer can use to influence the behaviors, attitudes, and beliefs of the employees
- Peer Support: The support that one receives from a co-worker that is helpful for lifting our mood or building healthy habits
- Leadership Engagement: The many roles leaders play in shaping the well-being culture

If your project plan isn't already drawing on multiple building blocks, then reconsider. Seeking a norm change without having a good social climate or using enough culture connection points will not likely achieve the results you are seeking. Planning on a top-down-only strategy, without garnering enthusiasm from a portion of the workforce that you can rely on to serve as engaged peers, is likely to fall short.

While it's certainly helpful to have an organization-wide effort, don't be intimidated to start shaping a well-being culture on your team without broader support. In fact, if you plan and deliver, your success might be the inspiration your company needs to make well-being a shared value.

Even when you're following a well-being culture framework, it's likely you'll still hit a few speed bumps. You may even be thrown off your bike. Here's what to look out for as you pedal your way down this well-being path.

CULTURE KILLER #1—ALL TALK, NO ACTION

You likely agree that your own health and well-being are important. It's also not a big leap to believe that you care about the happiness, health, and resilience of the people in your organization as well. You are reading this book, after all. Why is it then that your colleagues nod their heads "yes," but their calendars say "no"? There's no time to address the well-being culture. There are too many other priorities.

Getting your leaders to care is a step past getting them to agree that well-being is important. While statistics are important, numbers don't evoke the same familiarity as knowing the personal challenges of the people on your team. Whether you are a team leader or you are leading the entire well-being effort at your organization, to get people inside your organization to care about well-being, you may need to create an emotional reaction.

Stories (a culture connection point) are an excellent way to make the issue of creating a well-being culture both real and important.[3] Start with yourself, by being vulnerable to help others know that you, the advocate, the change agent, are not exempt from struggling. Vulnerability also helps create a good social climate. Be sure to choose stories that will resonate with your audience. While Mark Bertolini's story may have resonated with some employees, it's quite likely that there are many employees who've never skied and their biggest well-being challenges are keeping their kids safe, doing their homework, and getting their bills paid. To Mark's credit, he was one of the earliest executives to lift the minimum wage, recognizing that financial security goes hand-in-hand with well-being.[4] However, stories don't have to be personal. You can highlight any irony between your company's mission and the well-being effort—for instance, the "fire truck" parked under the emergency room sign.

Still, *caring* doesn't mean acting will follow. Most people have plenty of options on where to focus their attention. Your team and your colleagues need to be inspired and need to feel there is urgency in the call to action.[5] Urgency is the first of John Kotter's eight stages of organizational change. Stories can play a role here as well.[6] Sharing a story of how an individual, a team, or another company (maybe even a competitor) overcame a well-being challenge to arrive at a better place will help your audience imagine the possibilities. Ideally, the story chosen would allow the listeners to see themselves succeeding. In addition to the personal health benefits, a story can include inspirational anecdotes of how a team improved its social climate and stemmed the number of resignations or another pertinent achievement. Remember, well-being challenges are not just about the individual. They affect the team and the entire organization.

"No time" doesn't just apply to those responsible for planning and delivering. It applies to each person on the team embracing the opportunity to include well-being during their workday. One common misconception is that you need to attend a program. The well-being culture allows you to flow through the day immersed in gestures, words, and skills that allow you to practice and experience well-being while working. Still not convinced?

Everyone needs to go to the bathroom at some point during their shift. Why not make listening to or singing a song while walking to the bathroom a norm? Choose something calming if you've been scurrying around for hours, or something upbeat if you've been tied to your desk. Maybe you'll find yourself playing the air guitar in the process and giving everyone else a chuckle along the way. You've helped yourself and the well-being of the people you work with, all in a matter of minutes.

"No action" includes no budget. You or the well-being person on your team may want a budget (although air guitars are pretty cheap these days). If you are in the position of hiring a well-being leader, it's not fair to bring them on board, give them an assignment, and then tie their hands behind their backs. Let's face it, your company is spending thousands of dollars on every employee for health and disability insurance as well as worker's compensation claims. There is money that can be allocated. It's really a matter of prioritizing a well-being culture.

Leaders play an essential role in determining how financial resources are committed. It wouldn't be a surprise if the first image that popped into your mind at this point were an exercise facility. While that would certainly make a statement, you don't have to start with this high-ticket item. Good fitness as part of the company culture doesn't have to be expensive to be effective.

The Chief Wellness Fool, Sam Whiteside, loves to encourage mixing up the well-being routines to keep everyone fresh at the Motley Fool offices. He might pull different "Fools" from various departments to collaborate in a spontaneous fitness class. The company's monthly health newsletter *The Flex* proposes new challenges to get staffers moving. That may vary from pushups during a meeting or walking around the building. It's always best, he thinks, to do something new around the office.[7]

For the price of paint and paintbrushes, you can spruce up your stairwells and make them more inviting, creating a welcome environment to choose over the elevator. You can even have a message in the elevator suggesting the rider take the stairs next time! George Washington University created the "Take the Stairs, See the Stars" campaign. Stairwells were painted to feature portraits and quotations from famous alumni, such as Colin Powell and Jacqueline Kennedy Onassis.[8] A little money to creatively promote taking the stairs is an ongoing way to show your commitment to physical well-being.

CULTURE KILLER #2—LACK OF ACCOUNTABILITY

You've asked someone on your team to be the well-being champion or your company has hired a well-being culture leader, assembled a wellness committee, and rolled out the plan to the institutional leadership. The launch is a smashing success, and the employees are excited.

And then crickets. Once thought to be supportive, the people on your team or the other leaders in your organization are now "too busy." You've come up against culture killer #1, no action. What happens next determines whether you stall or go forward.

To ensure success, it's paramount that your plans to build a well-being culture are not only written into the job description of key players in the broadest view, but also that the effort is written into annual business goals and performance evaluations. Well-being needs to be treated like any other work responsibility. Do your job and be accountable.

Of course, accountability applies to everyone. If you have an employee who smokes in front of the "No Smoking" sign and you don't say anything, neither one of you is doing your part to enhance the culture of health. It's your job to be a role model and to push back against behaviors that run counter to the norms that are being sought and the social climate that is being shaped. That means negative attitudes and hostile body language can no longer go unchecked.

People are watching. When a manager is allowed to speak condescendingly, or a co-worker is allowed to bully, people notice. When the responsibility of communicating well-being messages and resources is dismissed, the void is filled with the "real" priorities. When the job responsibility of delivering well-being is shirked and no follow-up is forthcoming, it sends a message that maybe well-being isn't important after all; that even though we made plans, we weren't serious. The lack of accountability can really damage the social climate.

CULTURE KILLER #3—THE ANTAGONIST

Even after all the planning, you can't predict how different people will react within your organization. Well, you can a little bit if you've worked with these people previously. You can spot some folks who are wildly enthusiastic from a mile away. Then there are others who "don't believe in it" and will say so with a sour face during meetings. Fortunately, there is a typical pattern of reactions that makes addressing them manageable.

Not all individuals in your group will adopt the idea of a well-being culture of health within the workplace at the same time. Instead, your leaders will adopt in a predictable pattern, and can be classified into adopter categories based upon how long it takes for them to begin participating in a well-being culture strategy. Practically speaking, it's very useful for a change agent (which includes you) to be able to identify which category stakeholders belong to, since the goal of change agents is to facilitate the adoption of the well-being culture. Mainly, interpersonal relationships and social networks influence the adoption of new ideas. If the initial adopter of an innovation discusses it with two members of a given social system, and these two become adopters who each pass the innovation along to two peers, and so on, support for well-being will grow quickly.

The Diffusion of Innovation theory purports there are five categories of persons when it comes to adopting new ideas: innovators, early adopters, early majority, late majority, and laggards.[9]

Innovators lead the charge. Innovators put themselves out in front and often have the passion needed to persist through the many challenges involved in leading an organization in their health and well-being efforts. Innovators are eager to try new ideas, to the point where they take pride being out in front. If reading this book was your own idea, you may be an innovator.

If your manager or human resource department gave you this book, perhaps the expectation is that you will become an *early adopter*. People in the early adopter category are opinion leaders and socially connected. Change agents will seek out early adopters to help speed the culture building process. Early adopters are usually respected by their peers and have a reputation for success. Early adopters make great partners in building a culture of health and well-being.

Members of the *early majority* category will adopt new ideas just before the tide changes and the entire group or organization starts to fall in line. The early majority has many peers. You likely have an informal leader (or two) on your team that cooperates quickly with change. This step of expanding the base of adopters is akin to moving from kindling to logs when creating a campfire. Your best approach is to help them see how they can make a difference in the team well-being culture through their own actions. They may make excellent well-being champions.

The *late majority* is a reluctant group, adopting new ideas later than most, sometimes out of fear of change, fear of failure, or simply inertia. Along with the entire organization, this group should be assured this effort is not about making people behave a certain way; it's about making it easier to have a healthy day for those who choose that path.

Laggards are most comfortable conducting business the same way as it has always been done. They will be the last to engage in new efforts, including supporting your effort to build a well-being culture on the team. More concerning though, these are the folks who are most likely to be vocal opponents of a healthy-culture strategy. Simply stated, there may be an antagonist on your team and most certainly at least one within your organization. They are the ones likely to express that "it won't work" and "we have other priorities that need to be addressed first." Your goal with the active opposition is to make them less inclined to work against your well-being efforts, not to make them advocates.

This wouldn't be the first area of change they oppose. The people who make up this group are more likely to find problems than see opportunities. These are the people who see the cup half empty. They are detractors from the social climate. Laggards may never actually participate in healthy-culture building and may only respond if held accountable. Laggards can be culture killers.

It is important not to provoke laggards. If they become more vocal, they can chip away support from early adopters and cast doubt among decision makers. Here are some steps you can take to limit the impact of antagonists:

- Swiftly address their concerns—Assure them that there is minimal effort needed.
- Show empathy—You could offer information that addresses some of their concerns or, at least, that balances these concerns against well-being benefits.
- Listen—One strategy with this group is to acknowledge their concerns, express your conviction that they have a right to disagree, and let them have their say.
- Be patient—Do not spend a great deal of energy on this group, as your efforts may serve only to further antagonize them. Let a shift in the broader culture do the work for you. If your efforts are successful, the antagonists will become less vocal.

CULTURE KILLER #4—THE ARROGANT

Joe Cassano, former president of American International Group's (AIG) financial products unit, may have been the single biggest reason behind the company's collapse in the Great Recession. He had a temper, belittled others, and had no tolerance for dissent. His behavior was counter to creating a good social climate. Instead, it created a toxic workplace. And Joe's arrogance landed AIG in hot water when his strategy of credit-default swap contracts fell apart.[10]

Arrogance can kill your attempt at creating a well-being culture in many ways and it may turn up in protests such as "This doesn't apply to me. I'm already healthy" or "It's not my job." There is a failure to recognize that everyone is needed to create a well-being culture, and your colleague likely doesn't understand the full scope of what it means to be healthy.

When the arrogant ask, "Why can't everyone just make better choices?" they are showing a lack of empathy. A lack of an ability to understand that our colleagues all face different circumstances and carry the baggage of their childhoods, current home lives, and communities to work every day.

Arrogance is a deterrent itself to a strong social climate and a culture killer. Arrogance disrupts the sense of camaraderie that is an essential ingredient for a cohesive, successful team.[11] On the contrary, humility, knowing the challenges of living a healthy and well life, as well as the limitations of creating a well-being culture at work without addressing the culture at home and in the community, is likely to foster resilience and growth.[12]

CULTURE KILLER #5—LOSING FOCUS (OR NEVER HAVING IT TO START WITH)

When I was growing up, we'd drive from Buffalo to Brooklyn for family holidays. We didn't have a GPS back then, so we used a paper map. Yes, a good old map. Most of the time we did just fine. However, there were times we'd drive to Brooklyn after dad got off work. Not a great time to start an eight-hour drive. A tired driver is a sure recipe for getting lost. Following the path of creating a well-being culture can be similarly tricky. Here are some ways to avoid making a wrong turn.

- Don't lose sight of the reasons you are focusing on a happier, healthier, and more resilient team. On very busy days or during stressful situations, it can be difficult to step back and look at the bigger picture. Creating a well-being culture on your team will help ease the stress and make working through the challenging times less burdensome.
- Don't skip well-being, and that includes for yourself. Put your own oxygen mask on first. If you begin to neglect self-care, you will bring your whole team down with you. Christakis and Fowler, authors of *Connected*, distilled reams of research into 300 pages of example after example of how we not only influence the people we work with in our immediate teams, but also their work colleagues,

and so on.[13] Organizations are a big social network, and everyone's well-being counts, including yours.

- Avoid too many chefs in the kitchen. While addressing a single team can be straightforward in terms of who is responsible and what roles colleagues play, it can get more complicated when the entire organization is cooking. This is possible in large organizations with many well-intended people.

- Galvanize the team or workforce around a central message. Having a theme or tagline can make it easier to keep them engaged. How can you get your employees to metaphorically touch the doorframe of your workplace before entering, like Southwest pilots touch the heart on the side of the plane before boarding for takeoff? Create a sense of belonging and a shared vision. If only Nike could flip "Just Do It" to something like "How Are You Doing It?" to their employees! To create the greatest sense of community, you only need one brand and one vision. More than one will only confuse your workforce and dilute your overall effectiveness.

- Manage well-being culture building like any other business imperative. Assign a project manager (or champion if we're talking about your team), set deliverables, and provide regular updates in executive or team meetings, depending on the audience.[14]

CULTURE KILLER #6—FASTER IS NOT BETTER

Almost 20 years ago plans were in place to build a bridge from Ketchikan, an Alaskan island with a population of less than 9,000 people, to another island of 50 people, at a projected cost of more than $400 million. Seen as a colossal waste of federal funds, objectors aptly named the project the "Bridge to Nowhere."

If you're given a budget, resources, or both, don't let them go to waste. Your team needs time to plan, design, and establish an infrastructure in order to effectively implement your well-being culture.[15] Sometimes, in the excitement to do something—anything—there is a rush to start building before the necessary planning is completed. Be forewarned, you may end up with a bridge that very few people will cross. For employee health, too often programs are created and aren't attended.

If you are responsible for a small team, perhaps your planning will only need to be a series of informal discussions. However, if you're responsible for a larger part of your company or the organization-wide strategy, then an employee needs assessment, culture assessment, or focus group can be helpful places to start.

In a race to prove worthiness, a well-being team might skip the discovery phase and be apt to create and deliver a plethora of programs or other culture connection points. Programs are helpful to some employees, but have limited impact if they are not situated in a well-being culture. Programs are culture connection points. Do not forget that you have five other building blocks and lots of other types of culture connection points to leverage if you want to create meaningful support for well-being. For most people, their mental health and lifestyle habit goals require a more sophisticated approach than one program can provide. One reason workplace wellness hasn't delivered the fruits that were expected is because a major amount of energy has been expended only on programs.

Failure to adequately plan or leaning too heavily on one approach is likely to result in falling short of your long-term goals, which might garner a snarky "I told you so" from the laggard.

CULTURE KILLER #7—IGNORING THE ACTUAL WORK

I continue to be surprised by how many organizational leaders are flabbergasted by why their employees aren't so well when there are so many wellness programs in place. Overreliance on programs without addressing the impact of the actual work on well-being is a common problem.

Humans have some basic needs beyond food, shelter, and safety. Three that are at the interface between work and well-being are autonomy, proficiency, and purpose. Daniel Pink, author of five *New York Times* best-selling books, refers to them as type I (intrinsic) behavior. While these three desires are positioned as motivators in his book *Drive*, they are also part of our well-being needs. We want to have some control over what we do, and any perceived lack of control is a major contributor to burnout.[16] Adults don't want to be micromanaged. We derive pleasure from being good at what we do. It brings us confidence and pride. Finding meaning in our jobs beyond a paycheck is not only good for engagement; it's also associated with better health.[17]

It's no wonder Apple is a success. It's not just their products. It's their people. If you've ever shopped in an Apple store, you know what I'm talking about. Employees are trained to provide a personal experience to the shopper.[18] That means employees need a high degree of autonomy as well as a proficiency in meeting the variety of needs that walk through the door. It's not just the customer who leaves smiling. Apple enjoys an impressive employee retention rate, in part due to the intentional effort to empower their employees.[19]

Goldilocks was on to something when she was looking for just the right temperature of her porridge. When your work is too difficult or there is too much, the stress is palpable. When the work is too easy, you may need to start drinking coffee to stay awake. An important part of our well-being is to have just the right balance of challenge.[20] Ideally, each of us would find most of our time in a state of flow while working. Flow is a state in which we need no conscious prompts to move from one action to the next; the steps in our work come naturally and without interruption from distractions.

You probably have experienced flow without realizing it carries a name. Perhaps it came in the form of playing basketball, knitting, or reading a book. Yes, it's also possible you experienced flow at work. Recall a project you enjoyed where the process unfolded in a manner that felt both challenging, yet pleasurable. You remained engrossed in the effort and lost track of time.

Your employees are more likely to find flow and enjoy their work when they experience:[21]

- Clarity of goals and feedback
- Immersion in the work
- Deep concentration
- Lack of self-consciousness (think sense of community and trust)
- Loss of the sense of time
- A balance between skill and challenge
- Intrinsic reward
- A transcendence of self (think helping the team, the organization, the greater good)

Ideally, Goldilocks would have rolled up her sleeves and made her own porridge, but management, historically, has more or less dictated job content without input from employees. However, in recent years, employers are finding enhanced engagement and effectiveness—not to mention improved employee well-being—when staff are included in crafting and defining their positions.[22,23] Not only would the porridge temperature have been just right, but Goldilocks likely would have enjoyed it more.

Hopkins Highlight

Clinician burnout is a huge problem in America, and we should all be concerned. Doctors and nurses are leaving the profession at a pace that if not quelled, threatens to result in a grave shortage (beyond the current scarcity). About half of nurses and physicians have some symptoms of burnout: emotional exhaustion, cynicism, and a low sense of personal accomplishment from work.[24]

In 2018, Johns Hopkins Medicine established the Office of Well-Being to address burnout and its causes. Among the imperatives of the office is addressing workplace inefficiencies that lead to long days at a frenetic pace. Burnout is an organizational problem, not just an individual's struggle. Be sure to avoid Culture Killer #7: Ignoring the Actual Work.

CULTURE KILLER #8—PASSION WITHOUT A FOUNDATION

In addition to your own effort to build a well-being culture on your team, you'll want to advocate for an organization-wide culture change. No matter the size of your company, you want the most qualified person possible to get a culture-driven well-being program up and running. Just because I became adept at *Space Invaders* as a kid didn't mean my next step was to lead the IT department at George Washington University. I was great at playing the game, but I had no idea how the game was built or why I was hooked every day after school. You will find that there are many people in your organization who are passionate about health. Make sure they have a strong foundation in well-being and leading change before handing them the keys to the car.

If you want to successfully build a culture of health, hire the most qualified person possible to lead the charge or be sure to sponsor training for those already in place to lead the effort. Someone with a degree in health promotion is a great place to start but doesn't need to be the only avenue. There are programs in community health and social psychology that can also provide a good foundation. Of course, if you are part of a smaller organization, where change can happen more quickly, and information is exchanged more efficiently, perhaps a part-time employee can fill the need. The notion of hiring someone whose sole job is addressing the health and well-being of the workforce is a very real challenge for many organizations.

It's one thing to make well-being part of someone's job at a small company. However, at a larger company, adding well-being into someone's job description can be a mistake. Can you imagine if the bookkeeper is also asked to operate the forklift? This position is an investment, not a cost.

Organizations that are truly committed to enhancing their culture of health will create a highly visible position, with an appropriate title, reporting to a top executive, perhaps even the CEO. Health and well-being are core components of a successful organization. Given that well-being permeates all parts of the mission and company objectives, it makes sense that it should receive the same attention as quality control or payroll.

Outsourcing your employee health and well-being strategy to a vendor may be as easy as writing a check, but that consultant or company will never know your organization the way someone on the inside of your walls will. This is an important difference because a good understanding of the company is needed for:

- Navigating the resources and appropriate people
- Understanding the current culture and what's possible for creating a future well-being and health culture
- Establishing relationships at all levels of the organization for collaboration and to help get approvals and buy in

Vendors can be very helpful with many of the well-being culture building blocks, such as creating culture connection points, building social climate, and establishing a champion network. However, it's challenging for a third party to take the lead in optimizing the well-being culture. You need to be in the culture to know the culture best.

Building an organizational well-being culture requires a leader. Whether *you* are that person (you are the one reading this book, after all) or you will be playing a supporting role, make sure appropriate consideration is given when filling this position.

CULTURE KILLER #9—WHEN YOUR GOAL IS RETURN ON INVESTMENT (ROI)

I can't tell you how many times I've been asked over the years, "What is the return on investment?" This always causes a flood of answers to rush into my head. What is the return on investment of your computer? Your desk? Your chair? Humans need basic tools in order to do our jobs, such as a computer, desk, chair, *and* our health and well-being. The wake of the COVID-19 wave has taught us many things, including employees are seeking better jobs and employers, ones that are supportive of their well-being.

Many of us are familiar with "No Margin, No Mission." This phrase emphasizes the importance of being profitable to stay in business. It's also been used as a quick retort to shut down budget requests to keep the margin alive. Well-being is not an expense, it is an investment and without it, you'll end up with "No People, No Profit."

The evolution of well-being has made a healthy and welcome change for most organizations away from ROI. The motivation for many companies is about caring for employees as people and that is the reason why companies are successful (or not). If the bottom line or the company's return on investment (ROI) is the primary reason for a well-being program, then it is going to be well-near impossible to embrace an active well-being culture that thrives in the hearts and minds of your workforce.

Do not overlook the cost of recruitment, retention, presenteeism, disability, and many other factors. A well-being culture brings improved morale, more collaboration, better health, greater resilience, and creativity—all of which are tied to lower costs and organizational success.

There are so many inherent flaws with measuring ROI. This is the topic of many journal articles and even the book *Why Nobody Believes the Numbers*.[25] Measuring ROI is possible in some circumstances, particularly when a health insurance company collaborates, but it's not likely your request will be granted with a quick phone call. Questioning the ROI is a reliable method to derail a discussion on building a well-being culture. Make note of the persons who ask for a ROI. They are likely to be among your laggards.

THE SPEED OF CHANGE

Building a healthy workplace culture will not be a straight path. It's likely the process will start slowly, but when positive changes become visible, this success will build on itself and individuals will start to embrace the quest more vigorously. One of the most rewarding parts of building a healthy culture is when you start to see grassroots efforts—employees engaging in health and well-being on their own volition. You might even witness groups of co-workers organizing to support each other on their health journeys.

In addition to avoiding the culture killers, there are five variables that will influence how quickly your culture of health initiative will take root, spread across the organization, and become engrained within the workplace.

1. The greater the **perceived benefit** to the individuals on your team and the larger organization, the more quickly the process will move. The more benefits you can articulate, the more likely you will offer one that resonates with a broad audience. It is helpful to anticipate which benefits your audience will want to hear and then tailor your message. I often find myself feeling like my second and third jobs are marketing and sales. You may want to read Daniel Pink's *To Sell Is Human*. Most of us are selling something. You may as well get good at it.

2. When the healthy-culture initiative **supports the values, beliefs, or history** of the organization, it is likely to be more quickly adopted.

3. The **simpler the transformation proposed**, the more easily it will be accepted. Complicated plans are intimidating and allow more opportunities to find fault. Even if you have grand schemes of sweeping changes, perhaps only introduce one at a time, so as not to overwhelm your team or the decision makers and early adopters.

4. If you are able to test the plan on a small scale, it will be more readily accepted. Sometimes this is referred to as a **pilot**. Especially when you are working within a large organization, showing that it can work on your team or your building or campus will build confidence that the strategy can be successfully deployed across the organization.

5. When the culture change process is highly **visible**, it makes it easier for members of the organization to contribute and participate. It's in your best interest to communicate in multiple ways to increase the likelihood the message is being received by all members of your team.

Shaping Your Team Subculture

Here are some ideas on how you can avoid seeing the well-being culture of your team take a wrong turn:

- Be sure to follow through on decisions the team made for improving the well-being culture. You don't want to be seen as the leader who says the right things but doesn't follow through.

(Continued)

- Nip pessimism in the bud. If someone on the team is derailing the enthusiasm, take your teammate to the side and try to discern what is feeding their attitude. Perhaps they've been part of previous similar attempts that have failed. Address their concern and conclude by making it clear that having a negative attitude isn't good for their own health or acceptable for the well-being culture being pursued.
- Build a strong sense of community so that everyone on the team understands that each of us has our own well-being struggles. Foster empathy so that the team is more forthcoming with support for their peers.
- Regularly schedule updates on the team effort to create a well-being culture.
- It's great to build well-being practices into the day, but if the strain of the work is overbearing, it's difficult to feel well. Periodically review assignments to see where team members need help. What resources are missing that would make completing assignments less difficult? Have you made the priorities clear and stopped programs, procedures, and projects that are ineffective and time consuming?
- Be sure that each member of the team is contributing to the well-being culture as planned. If the desirable norm is to not send emails after work, then hold each person and yourself accountable. It's easy to slip back into unhealthy habits.
- Celebrate success. Acknowledging even small steps on your team's journey to creating a more well and healthy culture will help maintain and likely accelerate your transformation.

Put Your Own Mask on First

Choose three quick ways to inject well-being into your workday so that you never use "no time" as an excuse for skipping self-care. These should only take seconds to minutes. These are my favorites:

- Focusing on my breath (I like the 4-7-8 breathing exercise)
- Listening to an upbeat song (and singing along in my head)
- Looking out the window (on good days I get outside for 15 minutes)

Identify those that are antagonistic and arrogant on your team and in your organization. Choose one and picture that person's face. How

(Continued)

does this person's image make you feel inside? Relaxed or stressed? Happy or irritated? If the image of this person conjures up a negative feeling, learn how to avoid allowing this feeling to permeate within so as to not harm your own well-being. Identifying your emotional response to different people in your organization is a step on your well-being journey.

How will you keep focus on your own well-being? Some people use tracking devices. Others establish routines. I place sticky notes on the border of my computer monitor. One reads "Smile."

Plan ahead. What is getting in the way of having a healthy workday? Pack your lunch the night before work. Keep a pair of sneakers in your backpack or work drawer. Address your well-being culture killers.

What can you say no to on your to-do list that will allow you more time to focus on the parts of your job that bring you joy—the responsibilities that don't feel so much like work because you derive satisfaction when engaged in this area.

THAT'S A WRAP!

The good news for each of these culture killers is that they can be overcome. These are not just C-suite problems. These are organization-wide problems. Leaders at all levels and personnel in all areas can contribute to or weaken a well-being culture.

Companies that fail to evolve are at risk for joining companies like Kodak, Xerox, and my beloved Atari.[26] If your organization doesn't develop a well-being culture, employees will find greener pastures and engagement will continue to stagnate. Address your culture killers.

While Amazon likely encountered many culture killers in their attempt to help their employees' distress, there are two in particular that I can see, looking from the outside. Amazon fell into Culture Killer #6 and rushed to do something to address the stress of their warehouse employees. There was good intention behind AmaZen, but the timing was poor. Simultaneously, Amazon was in the news for having a track record of on-the-job injuries. The National Council on Occupational Safety and Health cited Amazon as one of the most dangerous places to work.[27]

Amazon would have fared better had they addressed the actual work first (Culture Killer #7). Workplace injuries bring more than physical suffering. They break trust and eat away at the social climate. While Amazon simultaneously made announcements about how they would address workplace accidents, it would have been more effective to have shown improvements in this area prior to rolling out AmaZen.

Amazon was indeed addressing safety to the tune of $300 million in 2021 alone.[28] With astonishing worker turnover and record injuries compared to other companies, there is a lot of work ahead. Employee retention and workplace injuries are two barometers of employee health and well-being, but they are not a replacement for measuring your well-being culture.

10

Counting Culture
Assessing Your Progress

—

FACED WITH NEGATIVE PUBLICITY IN the 1990s that its products were created in sweatshops across the globe and that its workplace was unfair to women, Nike had to commit to and measure its changes in response to the accusations about the well-being of its employees as well as the environment. When two female employees filed a class action suit, Mark Parker, CEO at the time in 2018, issued a mass apology for the toxic culture. The company subsequently began reconciling promotions and salaries of female employees.[1]

To work with its wide array of suppliers to incorporate worker engagement and well-being processes in their overall HR approach, Nike developed its own Engagement and Wellbeing Survey (EWB). The survey aims to paint a comprehensive picture of the state of well-being and engagement at each facility. By the end of 2020, the survey included 64 factories in 13 countries, with 385,000 workers.[2]

The company states that "each employee shapes Nike's culture through behaviors and practices." The company solicits employee feedback through its EWB survey program, which allows each of the company's employees worldwide the opportunity to give confidential feedback. The survey measures employees' emotional commitment to the company, including satisfaction with their managers. The tool provides employees a path to speak up if they experience anything that doesn't align with the company's values or workplace policies. All of this is addressed in Nike's annual report.[3]

But culture surveys can be used for more than damage control. This form of measurement is an important step for organizations seeking better well-being for their employees. Do you have a system in place? As a manager, you will want to know the results specific to your team as well as to the company.

Whether it's culture surveys or another methodology, you must know where you are beginning to know if you are moving forward. In other words, you need a baseline. Measurement is not limited to the beginning or end of your effort. It is part of the journey. You need data throughout your culture transformation to track progress or possibly setbacks. It's the regular monitoring of data that will allow you to make adjustments that will improve your strategy. It's a challenge that needs to be tackled if you expect your team and your leaders to stay engaged and continue to support the efforts.

There are many ways to demonstrate the progress you are making and the value your effort brings to your team and your organization. You'll likely need to think long and hard about which measurement method is needed for the different parts of your strategy and the different stakeholders you are addressing. The chief financial officer would clearly like to see that you are saving money. However, the human resource department would be thrilled to know that you have decreased turnover or increased engagement scores. Brainstorm with your team to determine how you can best measure their actions and perceptions. Remember, being inclusive in the workplace is a well-being strategy in itself!

YOUR OPINION MATTERS

What if an automobile factory failed to track the price of its cars or the quantity it manufactured? If that were the case, someone could just drive off from the factory in a car and it wouldn't be missed. Now, this idea sounds ridiculous because there are systems in place to track this information. I'm the first to admit that tracking dollars and cars is much easier than measuring culture. Behaviors and attitudes are less quantifiable and more varied.

Measuring culture doesn't have to be complicated. Sometimes employers default to drawing blood and scrutinizing numbers when simply asking employees for their opinion would not only be less expensive but also more meaningful. Opinions matter. When asked to self-report the quality of our health, those that report poor health have a one and a half to three times higher chance of dying compared to those who report excellent health.[4] A blood test can't tell us whether or not our peers and manager are supportive, whether our workplace creates a positive and supportive social climate, and how easy or difficult it is to build and maintain healthy habits.

The information you collect when measuring culture serves as a barometer of whether your strategy is impacting the behaviors, beliefs, and attitudes of your team or workforce. The collective opinions of your team ultimately determine whether your strategy is working. Your team and your workforce are your customer and judge. You may uncover some optimistic information that you can leverage, or alarming feedback that needs to be addressed before you can possibly make substantial strides forward.

Ron Friedman is a researcher in the human motivation space, and his work has been featured on National Public Radio, and in *The New York Times*, *The Washington Post*, and the *Boston Globe*. In his book the *Best Place to Work*, Ron concludes there are three keys to creating an extraordinary workplace:[5]

1. Psychological needs are at the heart of employee engagement.
2. Organizations are more successful when they address the limits of the mind and body.
3. Integrating work and family life improves the quality of both.

Isn't it interesting that Ron's three keys are all related to having a well-being culture? With that in mind, could we make the leap that those companies that are deemed to be "the best place to work" are also those with the best well-being cultures?

Several organizations have captured which companies are great places to work, through the power of employee opinion. Each quarter, Comparably, a company founded on the mission of making workplaces transparent for both employees and employers, honors companies with Best Places to Work Awards as rated by their own employees.[6] Workplace culture is measured from questions in nearly 20 categories, including leadership, work environment, co-workers to professional development opportunities, work–life balance, perks and benefits, and outlook. Microsoft was ranked number 1 in 2022 for "Best Global Company Culture."[7]

Fortune magazine's number 1 Best Company to Work For in 2022 was repeat-winner Cisco, with 98% of survey respondents stating they were proud to tell everyone they worked at Cisco. The company embraces every well-being culture building block. Cisco employee Mollie Pinckney, Raleigh, North Carolina, said, "Cisco doesn't just talk. They listen, learn, and innovate. There's a reason they're one of the best places to work, and I see it in action every day."[8]

To name its Best Places to Work For, *Forbes* magazine partners with research company Statista to measure up the leading employers around the country and the world by input from the companies' workers.[9] Their independent survey samples approximately 60,000 American employees and their willingness to recommend their own employers to friends and family.[10]

Comparably, *Fortune* and *Forbes* include a large number of employees, afford them an opportunity for anonymity, and ask for their opinions about their workplace and employer, not their cholesterol and their body weight.

If you are responsible for a large group of employees and administering your own survey, format the process so that the scores from members of various subcultures (i.e., different departments) can be determined. Additionally, questions could be added to determine if demographic factors (such as gender or age) or group identification (such as job classification, professional role, workgroup, and campus location) are important.

I'm sure you'd love to be employed at a "best place to work." You can start by creating a "best team to work on" by focusing on your team's subculture.

HOW IS THE SUBCULTURE OF MY TEAM?

We measure a lot of things related to our team. We measure sales, the number of widgets built, and how quickly the phones are answered. How are we measuring whether our effort to create a well-being culture to support the people who are making the sales, building the widgets, and answering the phone is working?

What matters most are the perceptions of the people on your team. What other way is there to know whether your team feels like the shared behaviors, beliefs, and attitudes are all favoring well-being? You can choose questions that allow your employees to provide feedback on leadership engagement, workplace norms, the social climate, and the rest of the culture building blocks.

What follows are examples of what you can ask to learn whether your well-being-culture building efforts are working. Using a question set with a five-point scale to reflect how well your employee agrees with the statement can be a simple way to understand the pulse of your team. Following are three sets of questions that will be helpful to your effort. Answering a 1 means strongly disagree, 2 disagree, 3 neither agree or disagree, 4 agree, and 5 strongly agree. Provide an anonymous platform for the following questions so that your team is more inclined to answer authentically. Keep in mind that these are sample sets of questions that you can modify to suit your needs.

Is the Social Climate on My Team Improving?

We all want to be happy arriving at work. Feeling like we belong, that there is an upbeat attitude, and a collective effort are not yes-or-no questions. Your team's social climate runs along a spectrum. Asking your team a set of questions will provide a general sense of where the social climate rests.

1. There is an upbeat attitude on my team.	1 2 3 4 5
2. My teammates trust each other.	1 2 3 4 5
3. People on my team talk about things other than work.	1 2 3 4 5
4. People on my team help each other complete assignments.	1 2 3 4 5
5. I feel like our team is working toward the same goal.	1 2 3 4 5

How Is My Team Doing on Creating Norms That Support Health and Well-Being?

We spend most of our waking hours working. It's important that we are surrounded by an intention to support healthy habits and positive emotions.

1. Our team has discussed which healthy habits we want to achieve.	1 2 3 4 5
2. Our team has agreed on specific ways to support a well workday.	1 2 3 4 5
3. Our team takes specific steps to balance work and home.	1 2 3 4 5
4. Our team has received resources and support from the organization to reach our healthy norm goals.	1 2 3 4 5
5. My teammates support my effort to create or maintain healthy habits.	1 2 3 4 5

How Is My Manager Doing Creating a Team Well-Being Culture?

You play a critical role in shaping the well-being culture on your team and it's helpful to reflect and understand your progress with this responsibility. While it will be helpful for you to ponder the following statements, it's more important that you know how your team perceives your effort. Is there a way to administer these questions to your team anonymously so that you receive feedback?

1. My manager is a role model of health and well-being.	1 2 3 4 5
2. My manager removes barriers to a well workday.	1 2 3 4 5
3. My manager communicates company well-being programs and resources.	1 2 3 4 5
4. My manager cares about my well-being.	1 2 3 4 5
5. My manager celebrates when someone on the team shares an improvement in their health or well-being.	1 2 3 4 5

For each of these question sets, if your team scored an average total of:

5–10: You need help. Consider getting support from your organizational development team since you are facing a daunting challenge. You might also want to participate in a well-being culture training program.

11–19: You're off to a good start. Continue to reference the chapters in this book that the assessments have identified as needing the most help. Enroll in a well-being-culture training program. Be sure to look at your own well-being. It's possible that if you're on the wrong path, that it's spilling over to your team.

20–25: You are on a great path. However, don't take your hands off of the steering wheel. People on your team and the organization itself experience constant change, new babies in the family, growing competition in the industry, and maybe even an unfavorable diagnosis from the doctor. Your well-being is a journey and always changing.

———

A BIGGER PICTURE

If you are in a position to influence the organization in its entirety, you'll want to assess all of the well-being culture building blocks. Using a six-question survey based on a five-point scale to reflect how well your employee agrees with the statements can be a simple way to understand the pulse of your workforce. There are many ways to ask about each part of the culture framework. Following is one set of questions similar to what we ask at Hopkins, and the building blocks they represent. Answering a 1 means strongly disagree, 2 disagree, 3 neither agree or disagree, 4 agree, and 5 strongly agree.

Leadership

1. My manager encourages me to take care of myself.   1 2 3 4 5

Norm

2. Generally speaking, the people I work with try to make   1 2 3 4 5
   healthy choices during the workday and treat each
   other well.

Social Climate

3. There is an upbeat attitude on my team.   1 2 3 4 5

Shared Values

4. Employee well-being is a top priority.   1 2 3 4 5

Culture Connection Points

5. The workplace is designed to make it easy to have a healthy   1 2 3 4 5
   and well day.

Peer Support

6. My co-workers support my health and well-being goals.   1 2 3 4 5

Ideally when reporting the results, your organization will be able to provide the aggregate as well as the outcome for specific departments, such as finance, sales, and customer service. Providing department- (or even team-) level data makes it much more useful to adjust and improve. Remember, start with a baseline, and assess your team's perception at some regular schedule.

It's quick and easy for employees to choose a number or rank strengths and weaknesses. However, these types of quantitative surveys don't tell the whole story. Qualitative data provides more insight from employees.

What's on Your Mind?

Think about a favorite sport. How many times has a game ended with you feeling like the score doesn't tell the whole story? The same is true with the numbers from surveys. If you are able, give your team a chance to provide feedback in a more unstructured manner. A more nuanced approach of ascertaining your employees' perceptions will likely prove helpful in shaping your culture-building strategy. There are several ways to obtain more personal feedback.

Writing

You might choose to create a feedback form with open-ended questions. As with the survey strategy, you could choose one or two questions to reflect each part of the culture-building framework. This might prompt your employees to provide more meaningful answers as the opportunity to speak freely (assuming the questionnaire is anonymous and confidential). Open-ended questions allow for more colorful information to flow.

However, it is also possible that your employees won't like to write much, especially if what they have to say is critical and they don't feel safe sharing (which will be true in a culture that hasn't fostered trust). This format of counting culture may feel like more work than choosing a number and result in fewer participants. You must weigh the value of receiving more detailed feedback against the likelihood of lower participation in the process.

Individual Interview

Individual interviews can bear helpful information and provide a meaningful option to employees who aren't comfortable putting their thoughts down on paper. You may want to ask someone from your human resources department to administer the process (without you in the room), so that employees can speak more freely. A set of standard questions asked of many employees from different parts of the organization can provide a well-rounded view of your company's overall effort. Of course, there are challenges with this approach. The number of employees that participate may be much lower than a survey, making it difficult to get the full picture. It's usually not feasible to interview everyone.

Group Interviews

One way to get more participants while minimizing your investment of time is to interview a group of employees about their perception of the well-being culture. You could interview five or six employees at a time. Too many people at one time may discourage participation from all persons.

Sample Interview Questions
- What would be most helpful to support your well-being?
- In what ways could your manager be more supportive of your well-being?
- What obstacles stand in your way of having a well workday?
- How can we better support your work–life balance?

Those being interviewed could share ideas on how to improve the problems identified in the interview.

I shared three different ways to obtain qualitative data. Each has their advantages and drawbacks. You don't have to limit your approach to just one. You could use a combination of two styles of the data collection mentioned and even all three strategies if you are ambitious!

Am I Doing My Part to Create a Well-Being Culture?

Sometimes the most useful information comes from within. We each play a role in our own and our co-workers' happiness, health, and resilience. Take time to reflect on how well you are contributing to the well-being culture.

Place a check in the box that best describes your contribution.

Attribute	Needs Improvement	Doing Well	I'm a Role Model
Putting well-being on the team meeting agenda			
Offering to help a colleague with their project			
Expressing appreciation to a team member			
Celebrating someone else's accomplishment			
Remaining optimistic during challenging days			
Supporting a team member who is trying to develop a healthy habit			
Speaking up when someone isn't acting appropriately			
Sharing things about yourself that are not work related			
Taking care of yourself so you can better take care of those around you			

Use the results to plan how you can contribute more to the well-being culture.

MEASURING THE EFFECT OF WELL-BEING PROGRAMS

Because many companies emphasize programs, programs, programs, only one of the culture connection points, it's worth spending a little time thinking about how you can measure whether or not these programs, programs, programs, are worthwhile. After all, the idea is to create a well-being culture at work so that everyone can feel happier, be more resilient, *and* be more successful in maintaining and creating healthier habits. Sometimes, healthier lifestyles get a boost through programs.

The Pragmatism of Participation

One of the great things about having a healthy culture is that you don't have to sign up. But you do have to sign up for CHIP (Complete Health Improvement Program; now known as Pivio). Recall Dexter Shurney and his successful effort to implement CHIP at Cummins (discussed in Chapter 7).

Prior to working at Cummins, Dexter was employed at Vanderbilt University. At the time, Vanderbilt's assets included a university, a medical center, and its own health plan that insured tens of thousands of people. To address the rising number of insured members developing diabetes, and the high cost of treating these members (more than three times compared to those members without diabetes), Vanderbilt offered the CHIP program. Vanderbilt had the luxury of comparing the participants in the program to other nonparticipating employees who also have diabetes, because of the access to health plan data. Dexter implemented CHIP at Vanderbilt University, and he also measured its impact.

Not only did employees sign up, but they also showed up. Seventy percent of the CHIP participants stayed in the program until the end. That's not an easy feat considering there were 14 classes over the course of two months. If Vanderbilt employees didn't show up for the CHIP sessions, they might as well have stopped offering the program. There's no point in allocating resources for something that's not being used. For some parts of your culture-building strategy, measuring participation is a must. For many employees though, participation in a worksite program is not on their agenda.

One common fallacy is to measure the success of a health and well-being effort based on attendance alone. Ninety-one percent of American adults have a health and well-being goal.[11] This doesn't mean they are necessarily working on it during the workday.

WW (formerly known as Weight Watchers) provides the strategies and knowledge, along with a peer support group to help participants lose weight. For many people, excess body weight is a painful or embarrassing topic. It's reasonable to think that they don't want to share this challenge with their co-workers.

Just because employees don't sign up for a program doesn't mean they aren't interested or already engaged in the same lifestyle being addressed by that program. Think of all the different options one might have instead of a weight loss program at work:

- Support from their primary care doctor
- Support groups in their community, like WW
- Online programs, like Noom
- Meal replacement programs, such as Optavia (formerly MediFast) and NutriSystem
- Books, podcasts, and online content

Showing up for a program and signing in might denote your presence. However, it's not the same as the person being engaged. We've all attended a presentation at which we are nodding off or checking our text messages. Staying alert and paying attention is hard if the program isn't well done or if the speaker isn't engaging. That's really what we're seeking right? Engagement?

While participation and engagement aren't the best measurements to show success, they do have their place. For example, company wellness challenges have mixed results for their participants. However, they can have benefits beyond the specific focus of the challenge. When planned to have employees work together in pairs or teams, these programs can prove meaningful to create peer support and build a good social climate. The experience might create a sense of community in which peers can count on each other to support their health goals. However, a challenge may not be the program that everyone wants to join. Take the swimmer who can't get "steps" for time in the pool. If you have a lot of swimmers in your company and your employees aren't participating in a steps challenge, then maybe it's not worth your time and energy to offer the challenge in the first place.

Another area where participation counts is receiving feedback. Well-being culture surveys can help you know where to focus. However, if you only get a few employees to respond, what good is the survey? Ideally, when you are seeking employee input, your participation will be at least 70 percent to feel confident that you have good representation from your team or workforce.

Feedback includes giving information back to the employee. If you are trying to address elevated (slightly above normal) and high blood pressure (at or above 130/80) in the workforce, how can your employees know if their lifestyle adjustments are working if they don't get their blood pressure measured? The same is true for your entire blood pressure strategy. If very few of your employees agree to either have their blood pressure taken at work or have their doctor submit it to a secure platform, you won't know if your program is working.

There is a place for participation; just understand the benefits and challenges of using participation as a metric before you make the decision.

Results—When the Dust Settles

When pharmaceutical companies are trying to move a new medication from the laboratory to pharmacy shelves, they need to prove that the medicine works and it's safe. They do this through studies in which some participants get the medicine and others (the control group) get a placebo. You can take a similar approach in measuring the outcomes of participants in your programs. In the case at Vanderbilt, the participants in the CHIP program were compared to a group of employees who had diabetes but were not enrolled in CHIP (the control group—akin to a placebo).

Dexter used data from the health plan to see differences between the two groups of employees. CHIP participants decreased their doctor visits by up to 25 percent. In addition, 24 percent of the participants eliminated one or more of their medications! The participants were more likely to eliminate one or more of their diabetes medicines, and they were also able to stop cholesterol and gastrointestinal medicines.

Even though tying your well-being culture strategy to ROI (return on investment) is a culture killer, there are times when it's fitting. Dexter focused on a small group of employees and had access to health plan claims. He was able to compare the medical and pharmacy costs of the CHIP participants with the control group. The results were impressive. For every dollar spent, $1.38 was saved. This didn't come as a surprise given that the health of participants improved, resulting in fewer medicines and doctor visits.

If you are charged with the honor of being a steward of health and well-being for your whole workforce, then utilization data from a health plan can be appealing. However, if you are a manager, using health plan data isn't practical. Even if you could access health plan data, it would not be provided for your team only. It's aggregated for the whole company. Can you obtain aggregate health-assessment data for your team? Knowing the common health conditions your team faces and the habits for which they need support building can make it easier to direct your energy.

A WELL-BEING CULTURE IS AN INVESTMENT, NOT A COST

The e-commerce company Next Jump, which handles loyalty programs for Dell, AARP, Intel, and Hilton, may be a smaller company than some previous examples shared, but nonetheless embraces health and wellness as a shared value. Measurement for Next Jump is not about savings, but about earnings. Next Jump offered better breaks so employees can re-energize. Employees are offered a wide range of physical activities and encouraged to engage in them for 20 minutes at least twice a week. Psychological and emotional coaching is offered as well as free healthy snacks. With that well-being push to help employees with their energy and wellness, founder and CEO, Charlie Kim, proudly touts Next Jump's fourfold increase in its annual sales growth, from 30 percent to 120 percent, confirming by that simple measurement—that if you take care of your people, they will take care of your business.[12,13]

Unfortunately, many employers do not see employee health and well-being as an investment, but rather only a cost. When you make your budget request, you may need to help your boss imagine paying more upfront in order to pay less later. For a fraction of the cost of treating a disease, you can help either prevent it or address it without immersing your employees in expensive medical care solutions. Let's look at hypertension.

Nearly half of Americans have hypertension and more are at risk.[14] That's a lot of people who can go on to develop complications such as heart attacks, stroke, and kidney failure. What is the cost of a home blood pressure monitor? You can get a good one for less than $50. What is the cost of a hospital admission for a stroke? A heart attack? Dialysis? $20,000 is a modest estimate, considering the number doesn't include the long-term costs of medications, disability, and more.[15,16] Pursuing a blood pressure strategy is a bargain!

Perhaps from your team culture survey results, you know you need to first work on creating a positive social climate before getting into specific health issues. How can you rationalize a team experience of cooking or line dancing lessons? Both types of lessons are clearly connected to health (nutrition and movement, respectively) and they can result in improved relationships within the team and a boost to employee morale.

Not every company will be able to tie its efforts as directly to business success as Next Jump. It's easier however, to look at value. Value is the relative worth or importance of a resource or strategy. Value explains what the organization will get for their investment without promising hard dollars back in the bank. When requesting money to support your team well-being culture, you may want to explain what value your plan will yield. If stress is causing arguments among teammates, what will it take to lower the temperature and improve collegiality? If hypertension is very common within your workforce, what is the cost of your plan to lower blood pressure compared to the cost of the medicines needed to treat the condition? It's possible that the cost of a program can be paid for by just one employee succeeding, as determined by being able to stop a prescription medicine. You might have to sharpen your pencil to demonstrate that your plan is an investment and not a cost.

You may already be spending time and money on a health-related strategy that can be extended. If your company is ripe with back injuries, you might be focused on proper lifting techniques. While back pain is often precipitated by straining your muscles, stress is commonly a contributor. Why not extend the plan to include yoga? Not only will you be treating the muscles, but you'll also be treating the mind. Think this is a crazy idea for a workforce of mostly men? *Real Men Do Yoga* features how male athletes use yoga to win (busting a culture myth that yoga is only for women) and is only $16 a copy, far less than the thousands of dollars it can cost for treatment and lost productivity.

Don't forget that some of the best strategies to build a well-being culture are free. Smiles are free. Appreciation is free. Fun can be free. Get the point? But how do you measure smiles, appreciation, and fun? These and other free strategies are measured in your culture surveys.

YOUR MEASUREMENT PARTNERS

You are not alone in your interest in shaping and measuring a well-being culture. There are other people in your organization who have a vested interest in seeing that health, happiness, and resilience are improving.

The following table highlights the many human resource and occupational health benefits of a healthy culture, as well as their measurement challenges.

Benefit of a healthy culture	Reason to consider this metric	Challenge of using this metric
Lower absenteeism	Healthy employees are more likely to show up to work.	• Authenticity of reason for being absent. • Data collection system to accurately record reason for being absent.
Increased employee retention	A workplace culture of well-being increases job satisfaction and therefore employee retention.	Employees may stay in their job for other benefits, such as the salary, health insurance, and retirement benefits (all culture connection points—not the whole culture).
Lower disability claims	Healthy and well employees are less likely to be impacted by a health challenge. The same condition in two employees, one who has a high level of well-being and one who doesn't, can have very different experiences coping.	• Reasons for disability, such as car accidents, pregnancy complications, and cancer diagnosis are often outside of the influence of the culture of health approach. • A cause of disability is often difficult to attribute or not attribute to the culture of health. For example, if the employee was not wearing a seat belt when in the car accident, that represents a failure in the healthy-culture strategy. However, it's also possible the other driver was intoxicated, and the impact of the accident was no fault of your employee.

(Continued)

Benefit of a healthy culture	Reason to consider this metric	Challenge of using this metric
Lower worker's compensation claims	Healthy and well employees are less likely to have accidents in the workplace, and when they do occur, the seriousness of the incident is mitigated.	Unless you are a leader with a need to know, it's not likely you'll get access to this data. Health information is private.
Increased employee morale	Positive social climates, peer support, and other aspects of health culture lead to high morale.	• Morale is self-reported and subjective. • If the company is failing, even the best healthy-culture strategy can fall short of raising morale.
Increased productivity	• When employees are well, it is easier to focus and give more effort to the task at hand. • A good climate makes it easier to introduce work innovations. Employees are even likely to contribute new strategies for enhancing productivity. • In many organizations, productivity and service go hand-in-hand. In a healthy culture, fast service with a smile is possible.	• For many jobs, measuring productivity is difficult. Is it the number of words typed in a minute? Number of good ideas generated in a day? • Productivity is influenced by tools and resources available to do the job. For example, no matter how well one is feeling, a critical machine may work at one speed and therefore throughput remains constant. • If a new resource is provided, like faster computers, that cannot be attributed to a well-being culture (although one might say that having the resources needed to one's job does contribute to a positive social climate).

HOW I HELP HOPKINS GET HEALTHY

When you mix health and well-being with the workplace, you might ignite very passionate responses on both ends of this spectrum, supportive and contemptuous. Our beverage work evoked this rainbow of responses. Although two of our nonhospital campuses had made some progress, most affiliates hadn't even started. This was discouraging, but it wasn't time to give up. I knew we had to take a different approach.

We needed to highlight the success of those small campuses and goad the hospitals off the sideline and onto the playing field. It was time to start showcasing the progress across the enterprise with our JHM leadership, thus allowing them to find their voice in the discussion. We developed a method for measuring progress. We created a dashboard that listed each of our JHM affiliates along with the four different beverage exposure points on campus: vending machines, cafeterias, retails spots (i.e., gift shops, restaurants), and company meetings and events. We then assigned a color: green for having completed the conversion in that category, yellow for making progress, and red for not having started to address that culture connection points.

The first version of the dashboard was pretty much "red" all over the place, with the exception of these small campuses mentioned above. Imagine you are the president of one of our affiliates and you come to learn that your affiliate is "red," while this much smaller part of Hopkins is "green." The first dashboard certainly got the discussion started. I really poked the sleeping bears! Finance and food services were alarmed by the impact this would have on their revenue. Then there were the personal concerns about someone getting their preferred soda! Yes, personal preferences are always part of the discussion, whether overtly or simmering in the background.

Some supportive JHM leaders couldn't understand why more progress hadn't been made. This was the conversation I was trying to provoke. These were the conversations that helped us get down to some root problems. This transformed into a supply chain effort and a new vending machine contract that saved money. The vendor operating our cafeteria (at the time we outsourced) was dragging their feet to change the beverage offerings. This led to a finance discussion and ultimately a decision by Ron Peterson, the Johns Hopkins Health System president (the president of all the hospital and other affiliate presidents) to pursue the healthy beverage strategy despite the possibility of lower revenue (a real leadership statement!).

The innovators stepped up and shared why they supported the plan and how they were able to make changes. Before long, we were underway. Transformation didn't happen overnight, but at least the log jam had been broken. Early adopters already had completed some steps. The dashboard started to change colors. One group after another, the early, then late majority, changed their beverage choices, prices, product placement, and marketing. The dashboard left the laggards standing out in red, and they too came around.

Organizational Assessment Tools

Ron Peterson liked where we were going with creating a healthy beverage norm and he wanted to know what was coming next. Ron wanted to know the bigger picture and how it would be measured.

Historically, employers have pointed the finger at employees as being responsible for achieving health and well-being. Sure, employers may provide a lunch-and-learn on healthy eating. However, if this is followed up by donuts in the middle of the table at the team meeting later that day, our colleagues don't stand a chance of keeping their New Year's resolution. Using an organizational assessment tool is one way to measure the company effort to support and promote well-being. Keep in mind, however, this reflects the *effort* to support a healthy workplace culture, not a measurement of the culture itself.

The CDC Worksite Health ScoreCard (WHSC) is one organizational assessment tool. The CDC WHSC is comprised of 18 health and well-being categories (more than 150 questions), spanning from mental health (depression, stress) to prevention (vaccines, nutrition) and chronic disease (diabetes, high blood pressure).[17] The tool reflects the presence of policies, benefits, programs, and environmental supports (culture connection points) that make it easier for employees to be enveloped in a well workplace.

There are several attractive features of this tool, including:

- Few resources are needed to complete the assessment.
- It's scientifically based (all the questions in the scorecard have references).
- You can compare the results of your organization to others who are of similar size and in the same industry.
- You can compare year-over-year results to track progress.
- It's free!

A tool that assesses the organization's commitment to health promotion forces that organization to look at itself in the mirror. It's one thing to want a healthy and well workforce; it's another thing to apply the resources and effort needed to support a culture of health. Are you doing your part or are you just pointing your finger at your employees? Since Hopkins started using the CDC ScoreCard in 2015 to the time this book was published, our scores have improved and now far exceed the benchmarks.[18]

Other organizational assessment tools for you to consider include the Health Enhancement Research Organization ScoreCard, the Worker Well-being Questionnaire, WellBQ (sponsored by the National Institute for Occupational Safety and Health), and the CEO Cancer Gold Standard.

THAT'S A WRAP

When I drove my daughter to preschool years ago, one of her favorite songs to listen to in the car was "Seasons of Love." This song, featured in the musical *Rent*, begs the question, "How do you measure a year?" and proceeds to give a litany of possibilities. The same can be said of measuring a well-being culture, although I don't have the talent to create the lyrics nor sing publicly.

Measurement takes a bit of effort, and you'll want to invest some time and energy up front getting help so that you arrive at meaningful information.

Measurement comes with challenges:

- Survey fatigue is real and perhaps your situation dictates that your assessments are administered once a year.
- We don't all have access to health plan claims, human resource, and occupational health data. Our options as a team leader can feel limited.
- While there are free measurement options, some will cost a little to a lot of money.
- Numbers don't tell the whole story. Even though the CHIP program at Vanderbilt had 70 percent participation, there were only 30 people registered. Vanderbilt employs thousands of people.

As for Nike's use of measurement in repairing its public image, the steps mentioned at the beginning of the chapter were gradually making a difference. Nike's investment in national and local partnerships is making a significant positive change for kids and communities around the world. The company's 2022 impact report says it reached 600,000 kids worldwide, 55 percent of them girls, through its collective efforts. Nike also shared its best practices and tools with more than 24,000 coaches to teach the fun and fundamentals to make sports more accessible and approachable.[19]

By October 2019, John Donahoe was named CEO at Nike and immediately began to work on the company's culture. The planet- and animal-friendly rating service, Good On You, rated the company based on hundreds of issues and said the signs of positive change are there and gave the company an "It's a Start" rating by 2020.[20] Two years later, Comparably's survey of Nike employees showed 78 percent of the reviews were positive.[21]

11

Dinner Is Served

WHEN I WAS GROWING UP in Buffalo, my mom and dad would throw us into the back of our station wagon on Thanksgiving Day and magically eight hours later we'd show up at our grandparents' house in Brooklyn, ready to have a huge feast with our aunts, uncle, and cousins. Those holiday feasts hold great memories for me, and as an adult, they provide me a new appreciation for the work that unknowingly went into making those childhood memories come to fruition.

I didn't know what it meant to work all day, pack for four young kids, and then very early the next morning, drive eight hours across the New York State Thruway to arrive by lunch. As much or more work was going on at the receiving end: planning a menu for close to 20, creating the shopping list, looking for volunteers to do some of the food preparation, setting the table, and later keeping the glasses full and the food warm as the holiday unfolded.

Now that we have Thanksgiving at our home, I understand that the production starts weeks in advance and the recovery lingers long after the guests are gone. Nonetheless, I wouldn't trade it.

Building a well-being culture on your team and in your organization is much like Thanksgiving dinner. It will take time to plan. It's necessary to get many "family" members to pitch in. A pie may fall on the floor (yes, this really happened one year)—mistakes happen. Most of the guests and your teammates will never know how much work it took for each dish to land on the table, and how many hours went into the whole production being orchestrated. Even though the holiday meal took only a short while to enjoy, the tradition and customs created a lasting warm feeling that contributed to our family culture.

Your teammates each bring their favorite "dish," their own family's subculture, to work with them every day. These collective "ways of doing business" influence the subculture of your work team, most often a contribution to the well-being of the team, but sometimes a distraction.

_____

THE BEST COMPANY TO WORK FOR . . . TWICE

You now have the prescription to shape a healthy, happy, and more resilient team culture. Many companies have put pieces of this road map in place, but few have done it as well and as consistently as Cisco Systems.

Cisco, an international IT company based in San Jose, California, with nearly 80,000 employees, is routinely ranked at the top *of Fortune* magazine's Best Companies to Work For, including the top spot in 2021 and 2022.[1] Cisco used every one of the culture building blocks to achieve this prestigious recognition. The company considers its culture its greatest asset and strives for a "Conscious Culture" that focuses on:

- Environment—diversity and inclusion
- Characteristics—unique beliefs, behaviors, and principles
- Experience—everyday interactions people have with their leaders and colleagues

Collectively, these elements contribute to a good *social climate*. The Ethics Office provides a space for employees to speak up and identify what's working (and what's not) and suggest ways to improve. By reporting the collective feedback and then communicating the action resulting from the concerns submitted, Cisco amplifies the well-being culture through the simple concepts of "opinions counting" and "action taken." The *culture connection point* of communicating back to the organization is an important piece.[2]

Cisco is serious about diversity and inclusion (*sense of community*). Cisco's The Multiplier Effect (TME) is a concerted effort to improve opportunities for all. According to Dev Stahlkopf, Cisco's Executive Vice President and Chief Legal Officer, "The company asks every one of our leaders to sponsor one or more individuals who differ from them in some aspect, whether it be gender, race, culture, generation, orientation, or ethnicity. TME requires those who participate in the program to be advocates and actively seek ways to increase the sponsees' exposure and access to other leaders."[3]

Count Cisco's CEO Chuck Robbins as another prominent *leader* communicating the importance of speaking openly about mental health. In 2018 Chuck sent an email to all Cisco employees sharing his concern for any employee struggling and letting them know they didn't need to go it alone.[4] In a "no shame, no stigma" effort, the company made it a priority to end the taboo against talking about mental health, and to encourage people to ask for help. When you see the word *priority*, think *shared value*—something the organization is focused on and is important to the employees as well.[5] By coordinating efforts to end the stigma of talking about mental health, Cisco is striving to end an unhealthy *norm* (silence) and replace it with a healthy *norm*—conversation. Cisco is using the *culture connection points* of benefits, information, training, and stories to shape the desired behavior—seeking help. *Leaders* were trained to recognize signs of mental illness and in the *subculture* of Cisco's United Kingdom workforce, mental health "first aiders" lend *peer support* to help access resources.

During the height of the COVID-19 pandemic, Fran Katsoudas, Cisco's Chief People, Policy & Purpose Officer, announced a "Day for Me" event in May of 2020 when Cisco employees could take a day away from work to focus on their mental health. Cisco felt well-being should always come first and employees needed a day to unplug from stress.[6] You have to love (think stuffing and gravy) a company that fosters *peer support* to find solutions to well-being speed bumps.

Reija and her friend Nora were among the many Cisco employees heading back to work after maternity leave. But they were far from fresh. Reija said, "We decided to do something to help our fellow Cisco colleagues. We started an Inclusion & Collaboration employee network called 'Back to Business (B2B)' with the goal of creating a safe environment to share experiences and get support from colleagues who have gone through similar circumstances. We wanted to encourage employees and their managers to start having honest discussions when preparing for leave—to include how the employee might want to be contacted while away, and how they'd like to return to work once ready (full-time, part-time, etc.). Whether it's welcoming a new child, dealing with a family illness, or some other life situation, we should be helping each other ease back into work."[7]

There's no place like home. In the early days of the pandemic, Cisco shifted to a mandatory work-from-home *policy* for its main San Jose office and several other US offices for the safety and well-being of its employees.[8] When the pandemic showed signs of easing, the company opted out of a return to the offices in favor of the employees and teams choosing how they would continue working. Cisco had for years been building a hybrid work model.[9] Fran has given the implications of hybrid work some consideration. "In the hybrid world, leaders are going to have to be more empathetic and flexible, but also get to know the individuals on their teams (*sense of community*) in a more intimate way. The best *leaders* will be those who are closest to their teams—understanding what works best for individuals, deciding when and how their team will come together, and incorporating team *rituals* to endure a strong sense of culture."

"Home" is not just where we sleep. Cisco recognizes that current events in communities and the country impact their employees' well-being. Topics for company check-ins have expanded to include racism, bigotry, and injustice. In fact, Cisco has a team to address systems and support for families and communities. Always progressive, shortly after the pandemic settled in, Cisco employees in the United States were able to share a crisis and support line (*culture connection point*) with friends and family who did not have access to such resources, at no charge.[10] International companies face adversity wherever they have a presence. Cisco offered to assist those employees living in Ukraine with evacuation as the invasion by Russia appeared imminent. Health and well-being can literally mean life and death decisions.[11]

Cisco is not only focusing on their well-being culture; they also continue to upgrade their Webex product to support the well-being culture of teams outside the company and entire organizations for that matter. With virtual meetings here to stay, Cisco enhanced Webex with People Insights to guide individuals and teams toward better work–life integration and more and better collaboration. Cisco is also leveraging the platform to help individuals, teams, and companies foster more meaningful workplace relationships, even when your colleague isn't sitting next to you. Meetings are too often a well-being drain, ineffective and time sucking. Worse, they sometimes bleed into family or me time. The platform provides insight into how often meetings start and end late and other nuggets that may help teams and organizations find more meaningful use of their time.[12]

There you have it. Cisco cooked up an awesome meal. The collective well-being culture experience of Cisco employees is an important contributor to Cisco's success. You don't have to be a huge IT company though to put the pieces of a well-being culture in place. You just need a genuine interest, commitment and the six well-being culture building blocks.

———————

THE COST OF BEING FRUGAL

The former CEO and co-founder of Gravity Payments in Seattle realized his entry-level employees and friends were sometimes struggling from paycheck-to-paycheck while he was making over a million dollars a year. He realized that instead of caring for the well-being of his employees, the salary he was offering wasn't enough to meet their basic needs, let alone optimize their well-being.

How he responded would rock the way many organizations dealt with the disparity that had made their employee's lives stressful. He began with 20 percent annual raises and then leapt to a $70,000 minimum wage while cutting his own salary from $1.1million to $70,000 to make that happen. He said he acted out of a moral imperative rather than a business strategy, yet the company prospered. In fact, with a more motivated workforce and increased engagement, profits exploded, and Gravity continues to thrive.[13]

Aligning with Abraham Maslow's hierarchy of human needs, Gravity Payments leadership recognized the basic physical requirements of food, water, shelter, clothing, sleep, warmth, and safety as chief motivators for people.[14] Without them, it's hard to embrace a *positive outlook*. Employees will be distracted until these needs are met, so the likelihood of creating an ideal social climate at work or adopting healthy habits will be weak until these other issues are addressed.

Some employers have already been taking steps to support financial well-being. While using an opt-out strategy is a clever way to get employees to contribute to their retirement plan, it's not going to help those without enough money to pay their utility bills. It's also not a strategy for helping your employees navigate a complicated financial world and keep them from being taken advantage of. Financial literacy reduces stress, which in turn supports better mental and physical health.[15]

It's not enough to give raises if your employees don't know how to use their money wisely. Learning how to manage and control money lowers our risk of dying.[16] Not a bad goal, right? It's not a far leap to see the connection of having money, being able to buy healthy food, pay a heating bill, and purchase sneakers—generally being able to live a healthier lifestyle.[17] Being in a state of financial strain makes getting a good night's sleep challenging.[18] The next day you are too tired to be fully present with your job and yet the heavy weight of your financial burdens still exists.

Seriously consider providing a livable wage to your employees and supporting financial literacy skills, because you will pay one way or the other. Yes, your payroll will increase (not necessarily to Gravity's minimum wage). However, for those underpaid employees, you're already paying for mental health visits, diabetes, heart disease, and cancer. Financial hardship brings stress, less healthy choices, and ultimately illness. Financial distress can lead to bleak health outcomes, such as heart disease and depression.[19,20]

The Great Resignation, a period of high employee turnover following the arrival of the COVID-19 pandemic, caused organizations to ring in the great pay raise. In 2021, Costco announced it was raising starting wages to $17 per hour. CEO W. Craig Jelinek said the raise was "good business," since livable wages reduce turnover and enhance the company's reputation as a good place to work and one where workers tend to stay for years.[21] Target, another company wanting to do "good business," chose to also raise their wage, and retail workers can now earn up to $24 an hour.

Great leadership can quickly be undone by unethical behavior. Although the former CEO of Gravity Payments was previously lauded in the press for raising the salary of the employees, now the press is holding him accountable for allegations related to his personal behavior. He recently resigned to address the growing number of accusations and his legal challenges.

———

A JOB IS MORE THAN A PAYCHECK

Purpose gives meaning to life. While money is needed to buy seed and fertilizer, purpose provides the sunshine needed for us to grow. A study at the University of California, San Diego found that people who "felt they had meaning in their lives were more likely to feel physically and mentally healthy, while those who were 'searching' for meaning were less likely to feel that way."[22] A sense of purpose can be anchored in family, community, a social cause, or your job.

If you ask around at work, you may discover that many of your colleagues are there for more than a paycheck. Sometimes our jobs help us in our search for life's meaning, a concept made more broadly appreciated by Viktor Frankl, Austrian psychiatrist, and Holocaust survivor. Victor observed horrendous atrocities committed around him while held captive in a concentration camp. During that time, he hypothesized that those imprisoned who had meaning in their life were more likely to survive. He himself spent numerous hours trying to recreate his work, a manuscript he had been writing at the time of his imprisonment.[23]

Subsequent to Viktor's liberation from captivity, his work gave rise to research in the field of purpose. Consequently, the Purpose in Life scale was developed to measure the self-reported perception of whether one's life is purposeful and meaningful.[24] Adults that score higher on the Purpose in Life Scale live longer, have fewer illnesses, and recover more quickly when they have a purpose.[25] Purpose is associated with stronger immune function as well as success with alcohol and other substance abuse treatment programs.

The benefits of purpose extend beyond health. When your employee has a sense of purpose in her or his job, morale, teamwork, performance, and customer satisfaction all improve. Of course, these all contribute to profitability.[26] There is a strong association between employees who are engaged and those who find purpose in their job. When you are fully engaged, you are more likely to be attentive, connected with others, seek out similar goals and have a sense that your contribution matters. Perhaps most important for the organization, you are willing and interested to focus, and commit the time and energy needed for success in your job.

In 2014, Gallup performed a global poll of "purpose well-being," which exists when people like what they do each day and are motivated to achieve their goals.[27] Among the findings was that employees with high well-being tend to be highly engaged in their work and are emotionally invested in the values of what they do. Unfortunately, only 37 percent of the respondents living in the Americas reported a strong level of purpose well-being. Imagine that. It's possible that only about one out of three members of your team or employees in your organization really like what they do each day at work! Among the statements participants in the survey were asked to rate included the following:

- You like what you do every day.
- You learn or do something interesting every day.
- Your friends and family give you positive energy every day.
- You have enough money to do everything you want.
- Where you live is a perfect place for you.
- Your physical health is nearly perfect.[28]

IBM has a long history of embracing employee health (it's in the mission statement) and they cite "Purpose" as one of their five dimensions.[29] Perhaps you should address purpose with your team as well. What follows is a list of the strategies you can use to help your employees find purpose in their jobs. You're likely doing many of these already but hadn't realized their contribution in helping your employee find purpose. Some of these will be familiar to you as basic management techniques and yet, knowing that these strategies are helping your employees with their purpose may spur a new sense of urgency that they are applied more regularly. As you learn the nuances of each employee, the strategies you choose will vary to best meet the needs of that individual.

- Connect individual contributions to the product.
- Provide regular feedback.
- Encourage peer recognition.
- Provide opportunities for input on decisions.
- Set challenging goals.
- Support professional development.
- Integrate disruptive events into purpose.
- Return to the mission, vision, and core values of the organization.
- Support creative expression.

Purpose is only one of many ingredients that help build resilience.

IS YOUR ORGANIZATION READY FOR THE NEXT CHALLENGE?

Greensboro, North Carolina, was once a blue-collar town whose economy relied heavily on textiles. The success of Vicks VapoRub, the home remedy for the common cold, keeps Greensboro on the global map today, even as the textile business has all but dried up. The family that developed and owned Vicks VapoRub set up the Smith Richardson Foundation, which ultimately funded the creation of the Center for Creative Leadership (CCL) in 1970. CCL is located in Greensboro.

Since its inception, the CCL has conducted programs in more than 160 countries and has supported two-thirds of the Fortune 1000 companies. The CCL has graduated more than a million leaders.[30] I am one of them. The CCL says, "Building a resilient organization requires collective teams of individuals who rally for a common goal, are open and responsive to the challenges placed before them, and work tirelessly through ambiguity and uncertainty."[31]

Nothing said uncertainty more in our lifetimes than the arrival of COVID-19. The pandemic brought in new norms of masks, social distancing, remote working, and an abundance of uncertainty. The degree to which your team and organization was able to respond and recover from this public health crisis depended on your well-being culture. All the ingredients for a resilient individual and team are in the building blocks.

The prescription for resiliency is skewed toward the social climate building block. The combination of feeling like one belongs (and is supported), having a positive outlook, and a shared vision all align with greater resilience capacity. Helping employees appreciate their contribution to their team and organization (purpose) bolsters the capacity to withstand bad news and challenging circumstances.

It's unfortunate that so many of our colleagues are struggling. The cure for burnout exists. There is a prescription available, but it won't work as quickly as swallowing a pill. Some companies are providing individual counseling services or group programs, which I consider just a start. Companies would be wise to understand that burnout is largely the result of having an unwell workplace culture, including failure to recognize "the limits of the mind and body" (thank you, Ron Friedman). Burnout is an organizational problem with individual casualties. Investing in a well-being culture will not only decrease the number of employees experiencing burnout and the intensity of the symptoms, but it will also lead to organizational success.

MAKING LIFESTYLE MEDICINE A NORM

I was pretty excited when I finished my family medicine residency training program and became a full-fledged family doctor. My long journey had finally culminated in a job with a reputable family practice in a suburban community.

Having studied nutrition in college and building on that education throughout my medical training, I knew that more than 80 percent of the patients I was seeing could have avoided a visit to the doctor's office if they were able to make better lifestyle choices.

In 2004, about 40 physicians gathered at Skamania Lodge, on the southern border of Washington state, far away from the hubbub of Seattle. Half of the attendees were speakers in what became the first American College of Lifestyle Medicine conference. We believed that the field of medicine could do better if it gave credence to the power of healthy choices not only in preventing disease but also as a treatment option. In 2021, in a virtual format, more than 2,500 professionals of all sorts (i.e., nurses, pharmacists, dieticians, doctors) attended. Practitioners and patients want a better path to health and well-being.

Lifestyle Medicine is a medical specialty that uses the power of healthy lifestyles (i.e., movement, social connectedness, sleep, and nutrition) to prevent and treat chronic disease. Not only does living a healthy lifestyle improve our health but it also enhances our well-being. People with healthy lifestyles are more energetic, optimistic, and happy. It's easier to adopt and maintain healthy habits when living and working in well-being cultures. Healthy lifestyles and well-being are interdependent.

Lifestyle medicine is the exception to the rising cost of healthcare. As we've learned more about the interdependence of our behaviors and moods, as well as effective methods for building the skills needed to stay on a healthy path, the prescription of lifestyle medicine has gotten more effective. With success comes fewer doctor visits, prescriptions, and lost days of work. We even had one of our employees come off her sleep apnea machine by the conclusion of our Keep Your Pressure Down program (a Hopkins lifestyle medicine group program focused on lowering blood pressure).[32]

Still, choosing lifestyle as a treatment option is not broadly adopted. However, you can change this within your organization. Make sure there are board certified lifestyle medicine practitioners in your health insurance network. If not, insist that your insurance carrier provide at least one such practice. Here are other ways to bring lifestyle medicine to your employees.

- Contract directly with a certified lifestyle medicine practitioner to serve your employees on or near your campus.
- Sponsor a lifestyle medicine program on your campus, such as the Diabetes Prevention Program or Pivio (aka CHIP). Maybe even adopt Keep Your (Blood) Pressure Down.
- Promote the lifestyle medicine benefit at open enrollment, when your employees sign up for health insurance (assuming that you indeed were successful with either the first or second preceding bullet).

- Communicate success stories of employees who were able to decrease their medication or avoid surgery by adopting healthy lifestyle practices.
- Tie workplace norm strategies (i.e., consumption of healthy beverages) to avoidance or treatment of certain disease states (i.e., diabetes) to help employees make the connection between wise choices and health.
- Make a reward or recognition strategy to include sponsorship of a lifestyle medicine consult, retreat, or other lifestyle medicine professional intervention.

A lot has changed in healthcare since Alexander Fleming discovered penicillin in 1928. Research has resulted in many more medicines coming to market, tests making it easier to diagnose, and surgical techniques to relieve pain and save lives. Throughout these advancements though, the simple act of making healthy choices every day and all day has fallen off the priority list. Building a well-being culture at work makes it easier to make healthy choices both intentionally and subconsciously. A well-being culture makes it more likely for lifestyle medicine to succeed.

HOW I HELP HOPKINS GET HEALTHY

It was a daunting task to convince Hopkins to create a healthy beverage culture. I knew the process worked at other hospitals. I just had to figure out how to show the transformation could work and then the rest of the pieces would fall into place if I skillfully navigated the organizational change. Recall this was the first major step on our journey to shape a well-being culture at Hopkins, so a huge amount of time was spent planning and executing. Like learning to ride a bike or any other new skill, it took time and we fell off the bike more than once. However, we followed a path that proved valuable. By utilizing the well-being culture building blocks, avoiding the culture killers, and paying attention to the various constituents based on their place in the diffusion of innovation model, we succeeded.

The image of Hopkins was at stake; or at least that's the story I used to evoke an emotional response. How could a health system of our stature rightfully continue supporting a practice that has been clearly documented to contribute to obesity, diabetes, and other diseases? It helped that employee well-being was a *shared value*; part of our five-year strategic plan.

- I worked to create trust among a diverse work group comprised of human resources, facilities, food services, faculty, and marketing. By creating an inclusive social climate in which everyone's opinion counted and creativity and ownership were encouraged, our *social climate* made it easier to advance.
- The *norm* of choosing healthy beverages was influenced using several *culture connection points*:
  - Communication—We used a wide variety of marketing tools including posters, tabletop tents in the cafeteria, emails, and screen savers. For our subculture of home visiting nurses, we created a card to attach to their car's sun visor that served as a quick reference for the amount of sugar in popular drinks in case there was a stop during their day for something to drink.
  - Symbols—We placed a green sticker in front of the healthy drink choices and a red one in front of the unhealthy choices, leaving yellow for the next best option.
  - Rewards—Water costs less! Before we started our healthy beverage culture shift, water cost more.
  - Learning—Most of our employees didn't understand how much sugar was actually in soda, so we created visuals comparing the number of sugar cubes in a can of soda with a donut and other obviously poor nutrition choices. Most people also didn't recognize the impact of sugar on different health conditions and generally how it made them feel.
  - Stories—We ran success stories of employees who reduced or stopped drinking unhealthy beverages and how that improved their health. These employees served as inspiration for their *peers*.
- *Leaders* were critical in making supportive decisions. Our school of medicine dean dedicated his monthly column to the detriments of sugary beverages.
- We started the transformation at one of our smaller affiliates. Johns Hopkins HealthCare (JHHC) didn't have a cafeteria or any onsite retail partners. Change only needed to occur in the vending machines and at company meetings and events. With an *innovator* leading that affiliate, we were able to trial our marketing campaign and iron out our other processes before taking it to the broader Hopkins community.

- To make the pilot at JHHC visible, we created a dashboard that was shared at health and well-being meetings. Not only did this provide the benefit of seeing JHHC advance, but it also served to prompt the *laggards* to act.

Taking the five variables that influence the speed of culture change into account, we were able to plant a flag in the ground and methodically move the project forward until the entire organization adopted the healthy beverage strategy. Honestly, creating a healthy beverage culture took about three years. This was much longer than I anticipated. However, now our culture-enhancing strategies can be as quick as six months to a year from conception to implementation.

Put Your Own Mask on First

A few months before my wife and I got married, I was stopped at a traffic signal. Something caused me to look in my rearview mirror. I saw a van traveling at a speed that was way too fast to be able to stop in time. The impact left me with low back pain. Some pre-ceremony acupuncture and a few celebratory drinks were my solution to get me on the dance floor at our wedding. The long-term answer for me though was yoga.

My yoga practice helped relieve my pain. What I learned over the years was that it also helped me sense the muscles throughout my body, not just my low back. As a result, I now recognize when my muscles are tightening. I recognize this as a sign of stress and potentially that my blood pressure is high. My well-being journey extended to learning breathing techniques and progressive muscle relaxation. Combined, these skills have helped me relax my muscles, breathe more deeply, fall asleep more quickly, and lower my blood pressure.

Self-care comes in many forms and hopefully you don't need a car accident to prompt you to find your path. Here are my last few self-care tips:

- Take inventory of your financial well-being. While a financial counselor may cost you up front, you'll likely save that amount and more by avoiding costly mistakes. You'll also sleep better.

(Continued)

- Talk to your manager or qualified career coach if you're uncertain about your purpose within the organization.
- Participate in a lifestyle medicine program or see a lifestyle medicine practitioner. Go to lifestylemedicine.org to find a credentialed provider.
- Read a book on ways to increase your happiness.
- Try a vegan "turkey" at Thanksgiving this year! Just look at the sodium (salt) on the food label first.

THAT'S A WRAP (FOR REAL THIS TIME)

It's likely that reading this book was not the first time you gave thought to your own health and well-being or that of those around you. It won't be the last time either. I hope reading this book has given you pause and made you think about the failed "willpower" approach. I also hope that you now know there are many influences around us that collectively shape our attitudes, beliefs, and behaviors. Your health and well-being are greatly influenced by the culture in which you spend your days. You now possess the roadmap to shape your culture and the culture of your workplace to be more supportive of health and well-being.

Beyond the basic needs of survival, your job and your workplace profoundly impact your health and well-being, which in turn greatly influence those around you and the success of your organization. Just as human behavior is complex, so is workplace culture. Anything short of a comprehensive approach will not provide the results you are seeking.

For more than two decades, I've sat in meetings where the conversation stalled on a debate over which well-being domains should be included in the organization plan: physical, social, financial, spiritual, you know the drill. I've had a similar experience at conferences where a presenter is making the case that a specific aspect of well-being is most important. In my opinion, we need to stop trying to compartmentalize well-being. Well-being is a continuum, a journey, the sum of our thoughts, experiences, and behaviors, with innumerable influencers. When you build a well-being culture, each person can find their own well-being journey supported, without having it fit neatly in a column. Providing a well-being culture allows your employees the opportunity to see their definition of well-being supported by their workplace.

Many companies have cultures of inclusion and cultures of safety, and many are starting to reconcile that well-being is as much about culture as it is an individual endeavor. In fact, most employers want a culture of health.[33] Most have concluded that this is an essential ingredient for success. Following the prescription articulated in this book will be very important if you expect to succeed. While I provided a comprehensive plan, I am sure you will uncover more nuances as you build a well-being culture with your team.

Well-being is not a program, policy, or portal, although they may contribute. As Lydia Campbell, MD, Chief Medical Officer at IBM, put it, "A culture of health requires a fundamental commitment to its possibility—not just through a policy, but in every decision we make."[34]

Jen Fisher and Anh Phillips came to a similar conclusion in their book *Work Better Together*. This Deloitte duo explored the impact that the information technology boom has taken on our well-being. "We've seen well-being efforts fail when companies throw a lot of money at well-being tools, resources, and programs without a full development strategy. We've shown that the most successful programs drive well-being into the flow of work."[35]

Regardless of where you are positioned as a manager in the organization, reading this book makes you much better equipped to "drive well-being into the flow of work" by shaping a well-being culture on your team. However, you can't succeed if you do this work alone. Well-being is a team sport.™ Start having the discussion with your team and your colleagues. How are we going to steer this ship? How are we going to shape a culture of health in our workplace so that everyone benefits?

When every team is on a well-being journey, the entire organization will see gains. Customer service, food services, and housekeeping staff have very different stressors from your finance and human resource departments. Respect the differences in the subcultures and accommodate the nuances. When employees are well, organizations thrive.

While Hopkins has made a great deal of progress on building a well-being culture and prioritizing our own health and well-being, like most every other healthcare organization, the COVID-19 pandemic has taken a great toll. The impact has not been uniform, however. Some hospitals are bouncing back more quickly; some teams have a more positive outlook. The well-being culture foundation influences team resilience, which in turn impacts the speed of recovery.

There will always be market and community challenges (maybe even a natural disaster) that will test the resilience of your team and organization. Even when things feel quieter, there will be a hum of employees joining and leaving your team. Each small pebble in the pond will add or challenge your well-being culture. The intention to shape your circumstances needs to be ongoing.

A Cure for the Common Company provides a road map for your organization's journey. You may take a wrong turn, but if you come back to this prescription, you will reach your destination. There will be joy and laughter waiting for you at the other end of the New York State Thruway.

That's a wrap.

NOTES

INTRODUCTION

1. "Why Wellbeing Is the Unspoken Key to Future of Work." (2019). Accenture, November 15. https://www.salesforce.com/blog/df-sponsor-accenture/.
2. Thorburn, E. (2021). "4 Ways to Attract New PT Staff When the Workforce Is Dropping Like Flies." WebPT, October 28. https://www.webpt.com/blog/4-ways-to-attract-new-pt-staff-when-the-workforce-is-dropping-like-flies/.
3. Dill, K. (2014). "Survey: 42% of Employees Have Changed Jobs Due to Stress." *Forbes*, April 18. https://www.forbes.com/sites/kathryndill/2014/04/18/survey-42-of-employees-have-changed-jobs-due-to-stress/?sh=667bc9c23380. Last accessed August 2, 2022.
4. "Survey Shows Workers Often Go to Work Sick." (2016). *Cision PR Newswire*, January 12. 2016, www.prnewswire.com/news-releases/survey-shows-workers-often-go-to-work-sick-300202979.html.
5. "2021 Employer Health Benefits Survey." (2021). Kaiser Family Foundation. https://www.kff.org/report-section/ehbs-2021-summary-of-findings/.

6. Ray, J. (2019). "Americans Stress, Worry and Anger Intensified in 2018." Gallup.com, April 25. https://news.gallup.com/poll/249098/americans-stress-worry-anger-intensified-2018.aspx.

7. Reilly, C. (2020). "The Rise of the Chief Wellbeing Officer," *Forbes*, July 7. www.forbes.com/sites/colleenreilly/2020/07/07/the-rise-of-the-chief-wellbeing-officer/.

8. "Working Well: A Global Survey of Workforce Wellbeing Strategies." (2018). Buck, December. https://content.buck.com/hubfs/Downloads/Surveys/Buck%202018%20GWS%20Executive%20Summary_final.pdf.

9. "Unlocking the Power of Company Caring: Workplace Wellness Study 2016." (2018). Everyday Health and the Global Wellness Institute. https://globalwellnessinstitute.org/wp-content/uploads/2018/06/EverydayHealth_GWI_Company_Caring_Workplace_Wellness_Study_Final.pdf.

10. Ibid.

11. Ibid.

CHAPTER 1: INSPIRATION FROM A FIRE TRUCK: THE CASE FOR BUILDING A WORKPLACE WELL-BEING CULTURE

1. "Thinking of Changing Your Behavior in 2017? Try Moving First." (2017). Press release, SPSP, January 13. https://spsp.org/news-center/press-releases/resolution-habits.

2. Halvorson, H. (2011). *Succeed: How We Can Reach Our Goals*. New York: Penguin Group.

3. "FastStats—Exercise or Physical Activity." https://www.cdc.gov/nchs/fastats/exercise.htm

4. Golden, S. D., McLeroy, K. R., Green, L. W., Earp, J. L., and Lieberman, L. D. (2015). "Upending the Social Ecological Model to Guide Health Promotion Efforts Toward Policy and Environmental Change." *Health Education & Behavior*, 42 (1 Suppl): 8S–14S.

5. Wright, T. (2010). "The Role of Psychological Well-Being in Job Performance, Employee Retention and Cardiovascular Health." *Organizational Dynamics*, 39 (1): 13–23.

6. Mowll, C. (2016). "75% of Employees Leave Their Jobs Due to Their Bosses: How to Fix It." LinkedIn, June 14. https://www.linkedin.com/pulse/75-employees-leave-jobs-due-bosses-how-fix-craig-mowll/.

7. Edington, D. W., and Pitts, J. S. (2016). *Shared Values, Shared Results: Positive Organizational Health as a Win-Win Philosophy*. Ann Arbor, MI: Edington Associates.

8. Mattke, S., Liu, H., Caloyeras, J., Huang, C. Y., Van Busum, K. R., Khodyakov, D., and Shier, V. (2013). "Workplace Wellness Programs Study: Final Report." *Rand Health Quarterly*, 3 (2): 7.

9. Lewis A., Khanna V., and Montrose S. (2014). "Workplace Wellness Produces No Savings." *Health Affairs* (blog), November 25. https://www.healthaffairs.org/do/10.1377/hblog20141125.042926/listitem/.

10. Misselbrook, D. (2014). "W Is for Wellbeing and the WHO Definition of Health." *British Journal of General Practice*, 64 (628): 582.

11. Dunn, Halbert L. (1959). "High-Level Wellness for Man and Society." *American Journal of Public Health and the Nation's Health*, 49 (6): 786–792.

12. "Leading the Way in Health Insurance." BlueCross BlueShield. https://www.bcbs.com/about-us/industry-pioneer. Last accessed August 1, 2022.

13. OPM. "Policy, Data, Oversight: Overview of Work-Life." US Office of Personnel Management. https://www.opm.gov/policy-data-oversight/work-life/employee-assistance-programs/. Last accessed July 26, 2022.

14. Owens, D. M. (2006). "EAPs for a Diverse World: Employers That Provide Culturally Competent Employee Assistance Programs Show Employees That They Care." *HR Magazine*, 51 (10): 91–96.

15. Reardon, J. (1998). "The History and Impact of Worksite Wellness." *Nursing Economics*, 16 (3): 117–121.

16. Hettler, B. (1976). "The Six Dimensions of Wellness Model." National Wellness Institute, 1–2.

17. Pencak, M. (1991). "Workplace Health Promotion Programs: An Overview." *Nursing Clinics of North America,* 26 (1), 233–240.

18. Lewis, A. (2012). *Why Nobody Believes the Numbers: Distinguishing Fact from Fiction in Population Health Management*. Hoboken, NJ: Wiley.

19. Safeer, R., and Allen, J. (2019). "Defining a Culture of Health in the Workplace." *JOEM*, 61 (11): 863–867.

20. https://globalwellnessinstitute.org/press-room/statistics-and-facts/.

21. https://www.nimh.nih.gov/health/statistics/major-depression.

22. https://www.apa.org/news/press/releases/stress/2020/report-october.

23. Safeer and Allen, "Defining a Culture of Health in the Workplace."

24. Goetzel, R. Z., Shechter, D., Ozminkowski, R. J., Marmet, P. F., Tabrizi, M. J., and Roemer, E. C. (2007). "Promising Practices in Employer Health and Productivity Management Efforts: Findings from a Benchmarking Study." *JOEM*, 49 (2): 111–130.

CHAPTER 2: GETTING PERSONAL: HOW OUR SUBCULTURES INFLUENCE OUR WELL-BEING

1. Kaplan, S. (2016). "What a Year of Working the Graveyard Shift Taught Me About Sleep." *Washington Post*, April 20. https://www.washingtonpost.com/news/speaking-of-science/wp/2016/04/20/what-a-year-of-working-the-graveyard-shift-taught-me-about-sleep/.
2. Griffin, R. (2010). "The Health Risks of Shift Work." *WebMD*, March 25. https://www.webmd.com/sleep-disorders/features/shift-work.
3. https://urbanhealth.org.uk/partnerships/current-partnerships/engaging-with-employers-to-protect-the-health-of-night-shift-workers.
4. Reina C. S., Rogers, S., Peterson, S. J., Byron, K., and Hom, P. W. (2018). "Quitting the Boss? The Role of the Manager Influence Tactics and Employee Emotional Engagement in Voluntary Turnover." *Journal of Leadership & Organizational Studies*, 25 (1): 5–18.
5. Amaya, M., Battista, L., and Melnyk, B. (2018). "The Ohio State University's Strategic Approach to Improving Total Population Health." *American Journal of Health Promotion,* 32 (8): 1823–1826.
6. Di Bronzolo, M. (2020). "Why You Need to Train Managers as Part of Your Mental Health Strategy." *TrainingZone*, November 20. https://www.trainingzone.co.uk/lead/culture/why-you-need-to-train-managers-and-leaders-as-part-of-your-mental-health-strategy.
7. "Stress in America™ 2020: A National Mental Health Crisis." (2020). American Psychological Association, October. http://apa.org/news/press/releases/stress/2020/report-october.
8. Frye, K. (2022). "Employees Who Smoke Can Cost You: So How About Doing Something? *Corporate Wellness Magazine.* Accessed January 4. http://corporate wellnessmagazine.com/employees-smoke-can-cost-something.
9. World Health Organization. (2019). "WHO Report on the Global Tobacco Epidemic, 2019: Offer Help to Quit Tobacco Use." WHO, July 25. https://www.who.int/publications/i/item/9789241516204.
10. Fischer, J. (2022). "One Size Doesn't Fit All as Global Companies Empower Employees to Reach Health Goals." 3M. https://www.3m.com/3M/en_US/particles/all-articles/article-detail/~/workplace-health-wellness-center-live-well-culture-3m-medical-director/?storyid=c80ee9aa-b4d7-49ae-b387-50b9b4539c16.
11. Kushner, J. (2019). "China Is Leading the Next Step in Fighting Malaria in Africa." *The Atlantic*, July 4. http://the atlantic.com/international/archive/2019/07/china-tackles-malaria-kenya/592414/.

12. 3M. (2020). "3M to Invest $50 Million over 5 Years to Address Racial Opportunity Gaps." 3M News Center, September 14. https://news.3m.com/3M-to-invest-50-million-over-5-years-to address-racial-opportunity-gaps.
13. Napier, A. D., Depledge, M., Knipper, M., Lovell, R., Ponarin, E., Sanabria, E., and Thomas, F. (2017). "Culture Matters: Using a Cultural Contexts of Health Approach to Enhance Policy-making." World Health Organization policy brief no. 1. https://apps.who.int/iris/bitstream/handle/10665/344101/9789289052337-eng.pdf?sequence=1&isAllowed=y.
14. Pyrillis, R. (2016). "Minorities and Wellness." Worceforce.com, July 29. https://workforce.com/news/minorities-and-wellness.
15. Munnell, A., Hou, W., and Sanzenbacher, G. T. (2018). "Trends in Retirement Security by Race/Ethnicity." Center for Retirement Research at Boston College, IB#18-21 (p. 4).
16. "Black and Hispanic Households Face Retirement Challenges." (2018). Prudential Insights, December 21. http://prudential.com/corporate-insights-/black-and-Hispanic-households-face-retirement-challenges.
17. "Why Employers Should Care About Caregiving." (2021). Prudential Insights, October 7. http://prudential.com/corporate-insights/why-employers-should-care-about-caregiving.
18. Freeman, M. (2021). "Prudential Adds Wellthy, a Service for Caregivers, to Its Financial Wellness Portfolio." Bloomberg, February 16. http://bloomberg.com/press-releases/2021-02-16/prudential-adds-wellthy-a-service-for-caregivers-to-its-financial-wellness-portfolio.
19. Allen, A. (2018). "The Role of Subcultures in Wellness Initatives." *American Journal of Health Promotion*, 32 (8): 1815–1816.

CHAPTER 3: BEST COMPANIES VALUE WELL-BEING: SHARED VALUES

1. Heathfield, S. M. (2021). "Find Out How Zaboos Reinforces Its Company Culture." The Balance Careers, February 17. https://www.thebalancecareers.com/zappos-company-culture-1918813.
2. Dewar, C., and Doucette, R. (2018). "Culture: 4 Keys to Why It Matters." McKinsey Organization blog, March 27. https://www.mckinsey.com/business-functions/people-and-organizational-performance/our-insights/the-organization-blog/culture-4-keys-to-why-it-matters.
3. Barrett, R. (2017). *The Values-Driven Organization, Cultural Health and Employee Well-Being as a Pathway to Sustainable Performance*, 2nd ed. New York: Routledge.

4. Bruce, S. (2015). "EVP—Enron's Was Chiseled in Marble." *HR Daily Advisor*, April 2. https://hrdailyadvisor.blr.com/2015/04/02/evp-enrons-was-chiseled-in-marble/.

5. Elliott, G., and Corey, D. (2018). *Build It: The Rebel Playbook for World-Class Employee Engagement*. Hoboken, NJ: Wiley.

6. Fraunheim, E. (2020). "How Target Creates a Great Workplace for Millennials." *Fortune*, August 6. https://fortune.com/2020/08/06/target-best-workplaces-millennials-company-culture-melissa-kremer/.

7. Richards, D. (2010). "At Zappos, Culture Pays." *Strategy+Business*, August 24. https://www.strategy-business.com/article/10311.

8. Gorsky, A. (2018). "The Past, Present and Future of Our Credo: A Conversation with Wharton's Adam Grant." LinkedIn, December 13. https://www.linkedin.com/pulse/past-present-future-our-credo-conversation-whartons-adam-alex-gorsky/.

9. "REI Co-op Makes Fortune 100 Best Companies to Work For List for 21st Consecutive Year." (2018). REI Co-op Newsroom, February 15. https://www.rei.com/newsroom/article/rei-co-op-makes-fortune-100-best-companies-to-work-for-list-for-21st-consecutive-year.

10. Lyman, A., and Adler, H. (2011). *The Trustworthy Leader: Leveraging the Power to Trust to Transform Your Organization*. San Francisco: Jossey-Bass.

11. "REI Mission, Vision & Values." (2022). Comparably. http://comparably.com/companies/rei/mission.

12. Lyman, A. (2009). "REI—Working Together for a Better World: Best Company for 25 Years." Great Place to Work Institute. http://rei.com/pdf/jobs/2009-Best-Company-for-25-Years-REI-for-REI.pdf.

13. http://hubinternational.com/about-us/

14. Edington, D., and Reupert, O. (2022). "Caring as a Shared Value: Caring for the Employees and for the Organization," *Corporate Wellness Magazine*. https://www.corporatewellnessmagazine.com/article/caring-shared-value.

15. Ibid.

16. IBM. (2013). "Employee Well-Being." 2013 Corporate Responsibility Report.http://ibm.com/ibm/responsibility/2013/ibmer/employee-well-being.html.

17. Dvorak, N., and Patel, N. (2018). "It's Time for a Core Values Audit." Gallup: Workplace, October 5. http://gallup.com/workplace/243434/time-core-values-audit.aspx.

18. "Zappos 10 Core Values." https://www.zapposinsights.com/about/core-values. Last accessed June 9, 2022.

19. "History Timeline: Post-It® Notes." https://www.post-it.com/3M/en_US/post-it/contact-us/about-us/. Last accessed June 11, 2022.

20. Edington, D., and Pitts, J. (2016). *Shared Values Shared Results: Positive Organizational Health as a Win-Win Philosophy*, p. 144. Ann Arbor, MI: Edington Associates.

21. White, G., and Levin, M. (1996). "Target Stores to Stop Selling Cigarettes." *Los Angeles Times*, August 29.

22. Berman, J. (2017). "Wegmans Improves Its Bottom Line By Helping Emplooyees Shrink Their Waistlines." *Huffpost*, December 6. https://www.huffpost.com/entry/wegmans-wellness_n_3696411.

23. http://nestle-cwa.com/en/about us.

24. http://nestle.com/default/files/2021-06/nestle-purpose-values-en.pdf.

25. L. Gettler, L. (2016). "Why Should Companies and Employees Have Shared Values?" *Acuity*, December 20. http://acuitymag.com/business/why-should-companies-and-employees-have-shared-values.

26. http://careers.southwestair.com.

CHAPTER 4: OH, THE WEATHER OUTSIDE IS FRIGHTFUL: SOCIAL CLIMATE

1. Moos, R. (1973). "Conceptualizations of Human Environments." *American Psychologist*, 28 (8): 652–665.

2. O'Neill, K. (2020). "Steps You Can Take to Build a Resilient Organization." Center for Creative Leadership, September 16. https://www.ccl.org/articles/leading-effectively-articles/steps-you-can-take-to-build-a-resilient-organization/.

3. Cohen, D., and Prusak, L. (2001). *In Good Company: How Social Capital Makes Organizations Work*. Boston: Harvard Business Press.

4. MIT Media Laboratory. (2008). "Every Move You Make." *The Economist*, August 20. www.economist.com/science/tm/displaystory.cfm?story_id=11957553.

5. Rath, T. (2006). *Vital Friends: The People You Can't Afford to Live Without*. New York: Gallup Press.

6. Boden-Albala, B., Litwak, E., Elkind, M.S.V., and Sacco, R. L. (2005). "Social Isolation and Outcomes Post Stroke." *Neurology*, 64 (11): 1888–1892.

7. J. Holt-Lunstad, Smith, T., Baker, M., Harris, T., and Stephenson, D. (2015). "Loneliness and Social Isolation as Risk Factors for Mortality: A Meta-Analytic Review." *Perspectives in Psychological Science,* 10 (2): 227–237.

8. Gale, C., Westbury, L., and Cooper, C. (2018). "Social Isolation and Loneliness as Risk Factors for the Progression of Frailty: The English Longitudinal Study of Aging." *Oxford Academic*, December 22. http://academic.oup.com/article/47/3/392/4772155.

9. Murthy, V. (2017). "Connecting at Work," *Harvard Business Review,* September. https://dondcruz.com/wp-content/uploads/2021/08/Connecting-At-Work.pdf.

10. Dol, Q. (2020). "Inside HQ1: The Coolest Features at Seattle's Headquarters," *Built in Sea,* February 5. http://builtinseattle.com/2019/03/08/coolest-features-amazon-seattle-headquarters.

11. https://www.npr.org/2022/01/22/1073975824/architect-behind-googleplex-now-says-its-dangerous-to-work-at-such-a-posh-office.

12. https://www.shrm.org/hr-today/news/hr-magazine/pages/0615-great-places-to-work.aspx.

13. Boxer, E. (2018). "Aetna's CEO Narrowly Escaped Death and Learned This Secret to Success." *Inc.*, June 11. http://inc.com/elisa-boxer/aetna-ceo-says-what-saved-him-from-suicide-can-make-you-a-more-compassionate-leader.html.

14. Reina, D., and Reina, M. (2015). *Trust and Betrayal in the Workplace: Building Effective Relationships in Your Organization*, p. 91. Oakland, CA: Berrett-Koehler Publishers.

15. https://www.fearlessculture.design/blog-posts/southwest-airlines-culture-design-canvas;https://www.businessinsider.com/southwest-airlines-puts-employees-first-2015-7.

16. https://www.businessinsider.com/southwest-airlines-puts-employees-first-2015-7.

17. Oden-Hall, K. (2017). "Benefits of Fun in the Workplace." *Forbes*, February 9. https://www.forbes.com/sites/paycom/2017/02/09/benefits-of-fun-in-the-workplace/?sh=197b2f8678b1.

18. http://glassdoor.com/10-companies-with unique-volunteer-opportunities.

19. http://colgatepalmolive.com/en-us/oral-health-education/dental-volunteers.

20. "12 Companies with Amazing Community Support Programs." (2020). Comparably, December 3. http://comparably.com/news/12-companies-with-amazing-community-support-programs.

21. https://www.greatplacetowork.com/certified-company/1000289.

22. Lucas, K. (2022). "What Is an Egalitarian-Style Company?" *AZCentral*. https://yourbusiness.azcentral.com/egalitarianstyle-company-27614.html.

23. http://garyhamel.com/video/natural-leadership-wl-gore-associates.

24. Youssef, C. M., and Luthans F. (2007). "Positive Organizational Behavior in the Workplace: The Impact of Hope, Optimism, and Resilience." *Journal of Management,* 33 (5): 774–800.

25. "The 10 Factors That Fuel a Resilient Workforce." (2021). *The One Brief*, March 24. https://theonebrief.com/the-10-factors-that-fuel-a-resilient-workforce/.

26. Fredrickson, B. L., and Levenson, R. W. (1998). "Positive Emotions Speed Recovery from Cardiovascular Sequalae of Negative Emotions. *Cognition and Emotion,* 12: 191–220.

27. Fredrickson, B. L. (2003). "The Value of Positive Emotions: The Emerging Science of Positive Psychology Is Coming to Understand Why It's Good to Feel Good." *American Scientist* 91 (4): 330–335.

28. J. Fowler, and Christakis, N. (2008). "Dynamic Spread of Happiness in a Large Social Network: Longitudinal Analysis over 20 Years in the Framingham Heart Study." *British Medical Journal,* 337 (a2338), doi:10.1136.

29. Zenger, J., and Folkman, J. (2013). "The Ideal Praise-to-Criticism Ratio." *Harvard Business Review,* March 15. https://hbr.org/2013/03/the-ideal-praise-to-criticism.

30. https://www.prnewswire.com/news-releases/survey-90-of-ceos-claim-to-lead-with-gratitude-while-only-37-of-employees-are-satisfied-with-the-appreciation-they-receive-300785710.html.

31. Smalley, A. (2019). "How These Companies Celebrate the Holidays." Power to Fly, December 20. https://blog.powertofly.com/how-companies-celebrate-the-holidays?rebelltitem=2#rebelltitem2.

32. https://richardsafeer.com/2021/11/one-simple-way-to-improve-wellbeing-at-work-smile/.

33. Wilson, A. (2019). "10 Companies Getting Workplace Wellbeing Right," Workstars, November 20. https://www.workstars.com/recognition-and-engagement-blog/2019/11/20/10-companies-getting-workplace-wellbeing-right/.

34. "The Importance of Shared Vision." (2021). Future State, April 20. http://futurestatecoo.com/blog/shared-vision.

35. Adams, C. (2014). "What We Can Learn from the Miracle 1980 U.S. Olympic Hockey Team." hottytoddy.com, July 15. http://hottytoddy.com/2014/07/15/what-we-can-learn-from-the-miracle-1980-u-s-olympic-hockey-team/.

36. https://www.maciverprojectservices.co.uk/2010/kotters-leading-change-step-3-creating-a-vision/#:~:text=According%20to%20Kotter%20the%20vision,the%20direction%20of%20the%20change.

37. Nordli, B. (2018). "Why Zoom Video Communications Built a Team Dedicated to Happiness." Built in Colorado, July 27. http://builtincolorado.com/2018/07/27/spotlight-working-at-zoom-video-communications-culture.

38. Ibid.

39. Martins, A. (2021). "The Best Dog-Friendly Companies of 2022." *Business News Daily*, December 20. http://businessnewsdaily/15108-best-dog-friendlycompanies.html.

40. http://salesforceben.com/why-is-salesforce-one-of-the-best-places-to-work/.

41. http://runsignup.com/Tace/TX/SanAntonio/FiestaFitFest.

42. http://endeavors.or/partner-spotlight/6-ways-heb-goes-beyond-groceries-to-serve-communities/.

43. Ibid.

44. https://m.facebook.com/southtexasfoodbank/videos/766325940855224/?locale=fi_FI&_rdr.

45. https://www.fox7austin.com/news/h-e-b-goes-mobile-again-for-feast-of-sharing-celebrations.

46. https://www.glassdoor.com/Award/Best-Places-to-Work-Dallas-LST_KQ0,19_IL.20,26_IM218.htm.

47. Stefano, R. (2018). "HubSpot Named the #1 Best Company for Employee Happiness by Comparably." *HubSpot Company News*, October 4. http://hubspot.com/company-news/hubspot-named-a-best-place-to-work-for-employee-happiness-benefits-perks-and-compensation-by comparably.

48. Pfeffer, J. (2018). *Dying for a Paycheck*, pp. 36–64. New York: HarperCollins.

49. https://www.cdc.gov/nchs/fastats/leading-causes-of-death.htm.

50. Collins, J. (2011). *Good to Great*, pp. 41–64. New York: HarperCollins.

CHAPTER 5: ALL THE COOL KIDS ARE DOING IT (OR THINKING IT): NORMS

1. Tylor, E. (2016). *Primitive Culture, Volume I*. (Dover ed.; orig. ed. 1871).

2. Van Leeuwen, E .J. C., and Haun, D. (2013). "Conformity in Nonhuman Primates: Fad or Fact?" *Evolution and Human Behavior,* 34: 1–7.

3. Huan, D., and Tomasello, M. (2011). "Conformity to Peer Pressure in Preschool Children." *Child Development,* 82 (6): 1759–1767.

4. Haun, D. B., Rekers, Y., and Tomasello, M. (2014). "Children Conform to the Behavior of Peers; Other Great Apes Stick with What They Know." *Psychological Science,* 25 (12): 2160–2167.

5. Warneken, F., Gräfenhain, M., and Tomasello, M. (2012). "Collaborative Partner or Social Tool? New Evidence for Young Children's Understanding of Joint Intentions in Collaborative Activities." *Developmental Science,* 15, 54–61.

6. Rock, D. (2008). "SCARF: A Brain-based Model for Collaborating with and Influencing Others," *NeuroLeadership Journal,* 1. https://qrisnetwork.org/sites/default/files/materials/SCARF%20A%20Brain-based%20Model%20for%20Collaborating%20with%20and%20Influencing%20Others.pdf.

7. Chiu, C.-Y., Gelfand, M. J., Yamagishi, T., Shteynberg, G., and Wan, C. (2010). "Intersubjective Culture: The Role of Intersubjective Perceptions in Cross-Cultural Research." *Perspectives on Psychological Science*, 5 (4), 482–493; Gelfand, M. J., and Harrington, J. R., "The Motivational Force of Descriptive Norms: For Whom and When Are Descriptive Norms Most Predictive of Behavior?" *Journal of Cross-Cultural Psychology*, 46.

8. Rock, D., and Cox, C. (2012). "SCARF in 2012: Updating the Social Neuroscience of Collaborating with Others." *NeuroLeadership Journal*, 4: 1–14.

9. Yamagishi, T., Hashimoto, H., and Schug, J. (2008). "Preferences Versus Strategies as Explanations for Culture-Specific Behavior." *Psychological Science*, 19: 579–584.

10. Bartz, A. (2018). "This Healthcare Company Is Determined to Have the Healthiest Employees in the World." Johnson & Johnson, February 25. https://www.jnj.com/innovation/how-johnson-johnson-is-improving-workplace-wellness-for-healthiest-employees.

11. Berry, J. W., and Annis, R. C. (1974). "Acculturative Stress: The Role of Ecology, Culture and Differentiation." *Journal of Cross-Cultural Psychology*, 5: 382–406.

12. Gelfand, M., and Jackson, J. (2016). "From One Mind to Many: The emerging science of cultural norms." *Current Opinions in Psychology*, 8: 175–181.

13. Mansfield, P. (2004). "Anomie and Disaster in Corporate Culture: The Impact of Mergers and Acquisitions on the Ethical Climate of Marketing Organizations." *Marketing Management Journal*, 14 (2): 88–99.

14. Crossman, A. (2020). "The Sociological Definition of Anomie." ThoughtCo., August 29. https://www.thoughtco.com/anomie-definition-3026052.

15. Culture Amp. (n.d.). "How the Motley Fool Improved Company Culture." https://www.cultureamp.com/case-studies/the-motley-fool.

CHAPTER 6: MORE THAN MY LOVE HANDLES: CULTURE CONNECTION POINTS

1. "Guideline for the Prevention, Detection, Evaluation, and Management of High Blood Pressure in Adults." (2017). *Journal of the American College of Cardiology*, 17 (19): e130–e248.

2. https://careers.southwestair.com/. Last accessed June 6, 2022.

3. "Southwest Airlines Once Again Ranked Among Forbes' Best Employers in America," *PR Newswire*, February 18, 2022. https://www.prnewswire.com/news-releases/southwest-airlines-once-again-ranked-among-forbes-

best-employers-in-america-301485867.html#:~:text=(NYSE%3A%20 LUV)%20(%22,Southwest%20has%20made%20the%20list.

4. Sampson, H. (2019). "Southwest's Plan to Conquer the Airline Industry, One Joke at a Time." *Washington Post*, October 16. https://www.washingtonpost.com/travel/2019/10/16/southwests-plan-conquer-airline-industry-one-joke-time/.

5. http://talmundo.com/blog/how-onboarding-answers-the-employee-wellbeing-crisis.

6. https://www.saplinghr.com/top-employee-onboarding-programs#1.

7. Vesere, A. (2021). "Remote Onboarding & Mental Well-Being—Here's How We Did It." Equalture, May 4. https://www.equalture.com/blog/remote-onboarding-mental-wellbeing-heres-how-we-did-it/.

8. Frieden, T. (2010). "A Framework for Public Health Action: The Health Impact Pyramid," *American Journal of Health Promotion*, 100 (4): 590–595.

9. Allison, D., and Mattes, R. (2009). "Nutritively Sweetened Beverage Consumption and Obesity." *JAMA*, 301 (3): 318–320.

10. Thorndike, A., Sonnenberg, L., Riis, J., Barraclough, S., and Levy, D. E. (2012). "A 2-Phase Labeling and Choice Architecture Intervention to Improve Healthy Food and Beverage Choices." *American Journal of Public Health*, 102: 527–533.

11. Safeer, R., and Keenan, J. (2005). "Health Literacy: The Gap Between Physicians and Patients." *American Family Physician*, 72: 463–468.

12. Ibid.

13. Legorreta, A., Schaff, S., Leibowitz, A., and van Meijgaard, J. (2015). "Measuring the Effects of Screening Programs in Asymptomatic Employees: Detection of Hypertension Through Worksite Screenings." *JOEM*, 57 (6): 682–686.

14. "Employer Costs for Employee Compensation." (2021). News release, Bureau of Labor Statistics, U.S. Department of Labor, December. https://www.bls.gov/news.release/pdf/ecec.pdf.

15. Heath, C., and Heath, D. (2007). *Made to Stick: Why Some Ideas Survive and Others Die*. New York: Random House.

16. Mental Health at Work. (2018). "Tim's Story." YouTube, September 14. https://www.youtube.com/watch?v=Xnr83SCBOQk.

17. "A New Era of Employee Well-Being." (2021). Business Group on Health 12th Annual Employer-Sponsored Health & Well-being Survey, January.

18. Ibid., p. 33.

19. https://hbr.org/2016/03/how-to-design-a-corporate-wellness-plan-that-actually-works.

20. Ibid., p. 62.

21. Gruber, J. (2002). "Smoking's Internalities." *Regulation*, 25 (4): 52–57.

22. French, S., Hannan, P., Stat, M., Harnack, L. J., Mitchell, N. R., Toomey, T. L., and Gerlach, A. (2010). "Pricing and Availability Intervention in Vending Machines at Four Bus Garages." *Journal of Occupational and Environmental Medicine*, 52 (1): S29–S39.

23. Pink, D. (2009). *Drive*, pp. 20–22. New York: Penguin Group.

24. https://www.workstars.com/recognition-and-engagement-blog/2019/11/20/10-companies-getting-workplace-wellbeing-right/.

25. https://www.jhsph.edu/research/centers-and-institutes/institute-for-health-and-productivity-studies/_docs/promoting-healthy-workplaces/JNJ.pdf.

26. https://www-fars.nhtsa.dot.gov/Main/index.aspx.

27. Pfeffer, J. (2018). *Dying for a Paycheck*, p. 38. New York: Harper-Collins.

28. Thaler, R., and Sunstein, C. (2009). *Nudge*, pp. 7–8. New York: Penguin Books.

29. Loprinzi, P., Branscum, A., Hanks, J., and Smit, E. (2016). "Healthy Lifestyle Characteristics and Their Joint Association with Cardiovascular Disease Biomarkers in US Adults." *Mayo Clinic Proceedings*, 91 (4): 432–442.

30. https://www.workstars.com/recognition-and-engagement-blog/2019/11/20/10-companies-getting-workplace-wellbeing-right/.

31. Human Resources Institute, LLC. (2011). "Creating a Healthy Work Environment." UC Davis Human Resources. https://hr.ucdavis.edu/departments/worklife-wellness/managers/wbeing-toolkit/environs. Last accessed June 18, 2022.

32. Bassett, D., Freedson, P., and Kozey, S. (2010). "Medical Hazards of Prolonged Sitting." *Exercise and Sport Sciences Reviews,* 38 (3): 101–102.

33. https://www.workstars.com/recognition-and-engagement-blog/2019/11/20/10-companies-getting-workplace-wellbeing-right/.

34. Morris, J. N., Heady, P. A., Raffle, C. G., and Parks, J. W. (1953). "Coronary Heart-Disease and Physical Activity of Work." *Lancet,* 2: 1053–1057.

35. https://www.classicfm.com/music-news/taiwan-hospital-piano-staircase-boost-exercise/.

36. Hanson, K., Lukas, D., Merchlewitz, C., Rice, J., Robicheau, G., and Ulvestad, W. (2017). "The Effect of Coloring on Perceived Stress Levels of Hospital Nurses: A Quasi-Experimental Pilot Study." Retrieved from Sophia, the St. Catherine University repository website: https://sophie.stkate.edu/ma_hhs/13.

37. https://www.workstars.com/recognition-and-engagement-blog/2019/11/20/10-companies-getting-workplace-wellbeing-right/.

38. https://www.huffpost.com/entry/wegmans-wellness_n_3696411.

39. I. Lowensteyn, Berberian, V., Belisle, P., DaCosta, D., Joseph, L., and Grover, S. A. (2018). "The Measurable Beliefs of a Workplace Wellness Program in Canada: Results after One Year." *Journal of Occupational and Environmental Medicine*, 60: 211–216.

40. Doyle, J., Severance-Fonte, T., Morandi-Matricaria, E., Wogen, J., and Frech-Tamas, F. (2010.) "Improved Blood Pressure Control Among School Bus Drivers with Hypertension." *Population Health Management,* 13 (2): 97–103.
41. Harshman, R.S., Richerson, G., Gerald, T., et. al. (2008). "Impact of a Hypertension Management/Health Promotion Program on Commercial Driver's License Employees of a Self-Insured Utility Company." *JOEM* 50 (3): 359–365.
42. Safeer and Keenan, "Health Literacy."
43. Heath and Heath, *Made to Stick.*

CHAPTER 7: THE FRIENDS AND FAMILY PLAN: PEER SUPPORT

1. Christakis, N., and Fowler, J. (2009). *Connected: The Surprising Power of Our Social Networks and How They Shape Our Lives.* Boston: Little, Brown.
2. Ibid.
3. Wing, R. R., and Jeffery, R. W. (1999). "Benefits of Recruiting Participants with Friends and Increasing Social Support for Weight Loss and Maintenance." *Journal of Consulting and Clinical Psychology* 67: 132–138.
4. Shah, Y. (2015). "Healthier Habits Are Easier to Adopt as a Couple, Study Finds." *Huffpost,* January 21.
5. Wansink, B. (2006). *Mindless Eating: Why We Eat More Than We Think.* New York: Bantam.
6. McClure, S., Laibson, D., and Loewenstein, G. (2004). "Separate Neural Systems Value Immediate and Delayed Monetary Rewards." *Science,* 306: 503–507.
7. Lin, K. (2021) "How a New Buddy System Is Helping Health Workers Grapple with Covid's Toll." *STAT,* June 21. http://statnews.com/2021/06/21/how-a-new-buddy-system-is-helping-health-workers-grapple-with-covids-tool/.
8. http://cdc.gov/vhf/ebola/pdf/buddy-system.pdf.
9. "The Wow Company's Buddy System Provides Staff with a Human Connection." (2022). *Be the Business: Rebuild.* http://archive.bethebusiness.com/rebuild-your-business/employee-engagement-wellbeing/the-wow-companys-buddy-system-provides-staff-with-a-human-connection/.
10. https://www.capc.org/documents/download pdf.
11. https://hbr.org/2019/06/every-new-employee-needs-an-onboarding-buddy.
12. Dimlow, R. B. (2018). "A Fresh Perspective on Feedback." LinkedIn, May 1. https://www.linkedin.com/pulse/fresh-perspective-feedback-kristen-roby-dimlow/.

13. Union Pacific: Employee Safety. https://www.up.com/aboutup/community/safety/employee/.

14. https://www.up.com/cs/groups/public/@uprr/@corprel/documents/up_pdf_nativedocs/pdf_up_2020_build_america_rep.pdf.

15. Christakis, N. A., and Fowler, J. H. (2008). "The Collective Dynamics of Smoking in a Large Social Network." *New England Journal of Medicine,* 358: 2249–2258.

16. Schulz, U., Pischke, C., Weidner, G., Daubenmier, J., Elliot-Eller, M., Scherwitz, L., Bullinger, M., and Ornish, D. (2008). "Social Support Group Attendance Is Related to Blood Pressure, Health Behaviours, and Quality of Life in the Multicenter Lifestyle Demonstration Project." *Psychology, Health & Medicine,* 13 (4): 423–437.

17. https://www.cdc.gov/diabetes/prevention/about.htm.

18. "National DPP Case in Point: Three Employers. Three Approaches." (2017). American Medical Association. https://coveragetoolkit.org/wp-content/uploads/2019/06/Employer-Diabetes-Prevention-Case-Studies.pdf.

19. Note that CHIP was rebranded in 2021. For consistency with the referenced material, I will refer to the program by its original name.

20. Shurney, D. W. (2018). "Cummins' Vision: Improved Health Through Lifestyle Medicine Innovation." *American Journal of Lifestyle Medicine,* 12 (1, January–February): 46–48. https://www.ncbi.nlm.nih.gov/pmc/articles/PMC6125019/.

21. https://www.forbes.com/sites/mindsharepartners/2019/12/19/what-leading-companies-are-doing-to-change-the-culture-of-workplace-mental-health/?sh=451c94836081.

22. Allen, J. (2008). "Healthy Habits, Helpful Friends: How to Effectively Support Wellness Lifestyle Goals." Healthyculture.com, Burlington, VT.

23. Holt-Lunstad, J. (2022). "Positive Social Connection: A Key Pillar of Lifestyle Medicine." *The Journal of Family Practice,* 71 (1): S40–S42.

24. Sarkar, M., and Fletcher, D. (2014). "Ordinary Magic, Extraordinary Performance: Psychological Resilience and Thriving in High Achievers." *Sport, Exercise and Performance Psychology,* 3(1): 46–50.

25. Mann, A. (2018). "Why We Need Best Friends at Work" *Gallup Workplace,* January 15. https://www.gallup.com/workplace/236213/why-need-best-friends-work.aspx.

26. Hickman, A. (2018). "Why Friendships Among Remote Workers Are Critical." *Gallup Workplace,* March 29. https://www.gallup.com/workplace/236072/why-friendships-among-remote%20workers-crucial.aspx.

27. "Intel Announces Expanded Paid Leave Benefits." (2019). *Intel Newsroom,* December 17. http://newsroom.intel.com/news/intel-announces-expanded-paid-leave-benefits/#gs.o9m2bj.

28. "Eskenazi Health Farmer's Market." (2021). *Eskanazi Health.* https://www.eskanazihealth.edu/event/eskanazi-health-farmer's-market.

29. Pesce, N. (2018). "The In-Office Farmers Market Is the Hottest Workplace Perk Right Now." *MarketWatch,* November 29. http://marketwatch.com/story/the-in-office-farmers-market-is-the-hottest-workplace-perk-right-now-2018-11-29.

30. Main, K. (2018). "15 Coolest Emerging Company Perks to Watch for in 2019." *Fit Small Business,* November 26. http://fitsmallbusiness.com/merging-company-perks/.

31. Mahoney, B. (2016). "Celebrating Employee Wellbeing Success." Virgin Pulse, June 16. http://virginpulse.com/blog-pot/celebrating-employee-wellbeing-success/.

32. http://purdue.edu/hr/CHL/healthyboiler/program/healthy_boiler_program.php.

33. http://purdue.edu.hr/CHL/healthyboiler/pdf/Purdue_HBGuide_2022.pdf.

34. Raths, D. (2021). "Pandemic Increases Significance of Employee Wellness Programs." *Healthcare Innovation,* September 22.

35. http://westohioumc.org/conference/virgin-pulse.

36. Bandura, A. (1985). *Social Foundations of Thought & Action: A Social Cognitive Theory.* Pearson.

———

CHAPTER 8: HOW TO BE THE BEST BOSS: LEAD WITH WELL-BEING

1. https://graemecowan.com.au/3-caring-ceos-share-qualities-that-have-improved-workplace-mental-health/.

2. Abrams, K., Phelps, A., Lu, K., and Firth, V. (2021). "The Health-Savvy CEO: Health and Wellness Have Become Urgent CEO Priorities." *Deloitte Insights,* July 9. https://www2.deloitte.com/us/en/insights/topics/leadership/ceo-role-employee-health-wellness.html.

3. https://www.dell.com/en-us/dt/corporate/social-impact/reporting/2030-goals/transforming-lives-moonshot-goal-overlay.htm#:˜:text=With%20our%20technology%20and%20scale,world's%20most%20pressing%20societal%20challenges.

4. "Dell, Inc." (2022). The Health Project. http://thehealthproject.com/winner/dell-inc/#:˜:text=In%202004%2C%20Dell%20launched%20a,cost%20increases%20for%20the%20company. Last accessed June 18, 2022.

5. https://www.labcorp.com/organizations/employers/employee-wellness.

6. Goth, G. (2021). "Post-Pandemic, Should Employers Still Subsidize Fitness at Home?" SHRM, February 24. https://www.shrm.org/resourcesandtools/hr-topics/benefits/pages/post-pandemic-should-employers-still-subsidize-fitness-at-home.aspx.

7. Reynolds, S. (2022). "Mental Health Awareness Month." LinkedIn. https://www.linkedin.com/in/saralouisereynolds/recent-activity/shares/. Last accessed June 5, 2022.

8. Business Group on Health. (2020). "Business Group on Health Honors 39 Large Employers with 'Best Employers: Excellence in Health & Well-Being' Awards." *GlobeNewswire*, October 7. https://www.globenewswire.com/news-release/2020/10/07/2104980/0/en/Business-Group-on-Health-Honors-39-Large-Employers-with-Best-Employers-Excellence-in-Health-Well-Being-Awards.html.

9. https://techtalk.gfi.com/survey-81-of-u-s-employees-check-their-work-mail-outside-work-hours/.

10. "Johnson & Johnson." (2015). Institute for Health and Productivity Studies, Johns Hopkins University. https://www.jhsph.edu/research/centers-and-institutes/institute-for-health-and-productivity-studies/_docs/promoting-healthy-workplaces/JNJ.pdf.

11. Pink, D. (2009). *Drive: The Surprising Truth About What Motivates Us*. New York: Penguin.

12. Hamermesh, D., and Stancanelli, E. "Long Workweeks and Strange Hours." National Bureau of Economic Research, Working Paper No. 20449, September 2014. https://www.nber.org/system/files/working_papers/w20449/w20449.pdf.

13. Jenkins, S., and Osberg, L. (2004). "Nobody to Play with? The Implications of Leisure Coordination." *Contributions to Economic Analysis*, 271: 113–145. https://www.sciencedirect.com/science/article/abs/pii/S0573855504710056.

14. HR Daily Advisor Staff. (2017). "How Many Days of Vacation Time Are Being Left on the Table? The Number May Surprise You!" *HR Daily Advisor*, June 22. https://hrdailyadvisor.blr.com/2017/06/22/many-days-vacation-time-left-table-number-may-surprise/.

15. Sevin, B. (2018). "Three Keys to Producing Durable Organizational Change." *Aubrey Daniels International*. https://www.aubreydaniels.com/sites/default/files/3%20Keys%20to%20Producing%20Durable%20Organizational%20Change_0.pdf.

16. https://www.pennmedicine.org/news/news-releases/2018/june/1-in-4-americans-develop-insomnia-each-year.

17. Garefelt, J., Platts, L. G., Hyde, M., Hanson, L.L.M., Westerlund, H., and Åkerstedt, T. (2020). Reciprocal relations between work stress and insomnia symptoms: A prospective study. *Journal of Sleep Research*, 29: e12949.

CHAPTER 9: CULTURE KILLERS: WATCH OUT FOR THE SPEED BUMPS

1. http://9to5mac.com/guides/apple-park/.
2. https://www.vice.com/en/article/wx5nmw/amazon-introduces-tiny-zenbooths-for-stressed-out-warehouse-workershttps://www.fastcompany.com/90649089/4-reasons-why-workplace-wellness-efforts-fail.
3. Sadoski, M., and Quest, Z. (1990). "Reader Recall and Long-term Recall for Journalistic Text: The Role of Imagery, Affect, and Importance." *Reading Research Quarterly*, 25: 256–272.
4. Ydste, J. (2015). "Health Insurer Aetna Raises Wages for Lowest-Paid Workers to $16 An Hour." *NPR*, April 30. https://www.npr.org/2015/04/30/403257223/health-insurer-aetna-raises-wages-for-lowest-paid-workers-to-16-an-hour.
5. Kotter, J. (1996). *Leading Change*, pp. 35–50. Boston: Harvard Business School Press.
6. Denning, S. (2001). *The Springboard: How Storytelling Ignites Action in the Knowledge-Era Organizations*. Boston: Butterworth-Heinemann.
7. http://goodnet.org/articles/5-companies-excelling-in-employee-wellness.
8. https://gwtoday.gwu.edu/take-stairs-see-stars-0.
9. Rogers, E. (1962). *Diffusion of Innovations*. New York: Free Press of Glencoe.
10. Silverman, S. B., R. E. Johnson, N. McConnell, and A. Carr. (2012). "Arrogance: A Formula for Leadership Failure." *The Industrial-Organizational Psychologist*, 50 (1): 21–28.
11. Steiner, I. D. (1986). "Paradigms in Groups." In L. Nerkowitz (Ed.), *Advances in Experimental Social Psychology* (Vol. 19, pp. 251–289). Orlando, FL: Academic Press.
12. Cameron, K. S., Dutton, J. E., and Quinn, R. E. (2003). *Positive Organizational Scholarship: Foundations of a New Discipline*. San Francisco: Berrett-Koehler.
13. Christakis, N., and Fowler, J. (2009). *Connected: The Surprising Power of Our Social Networks and How They Shape Our Lives*. Boston: Little, Brown.
14. Heward, S., Hutchins, C., and Keleher, H. (2007). "Organizational Change — Key to Capacity Building and Effective Health Promotion." *Health Promotion International*, 22 (2): 170–178.
15. Ibid.
16. Saunders, E. G. (2019). "6 Causes of Burnout, and How to Avoid Them." *Harvard Business Review*, July 5. https://hbr.org/2019/07/6-causes-of-burnout-and-how-to-avoid-them.
17. Slemp, G. R., and Vella-Brodrick, D. A. (2014). "Optimising Employee Mental Health: The Relationship Between Intrinsic Need Satisfaction, Job

Crafting, and Employee Well-Being." *Journal of Happiness Studies*, 15 (4): 957–977.

18. Gallo, C. (2015). "How the Apple Store Creates Irresistible Customer Experiences." *Forbes*, April 10. https://www.forbes.com/sites/carmine-gallo/2015/04/10/how-the-apple-store-creates-irresistible-customer-experiences/?sh=1179259517a8.

19. Markovic, I. (n.d.). "How Apple Improved their Employee Retention Rate by 28%." eduMe. https://www.edume.com/blog/how-apple-improved-employee-retention-rate.

20. Edwards, J. R., Caplan, R. D., and Van Harrison, R. (1998). "Person-Environment Fit Theory: Conceptual Foundations, Empirical Evidence, and Directions for Future Research." In C. L. Cooper (Ed.), *Theories of Organizational Stress,* pp. 29–67. New York: Oxford University Press.

21. Csikszentmihalyi, M., and Csikszentmihalyi, I. S. (1988). *Optimal Experience: Psychological Studies of Flow in Consciousness.* Cambridge, UK: Cambridge University Press.

22. Tims, M., Bakker, A. B., and Derks, D. (2013). "The Impact of Job Crafting on Job Demands, Job Resources, and Well-Being." *Journal of Occupational Psychology,* 18 (2): 230–240.

23. Slemp and Vella-Brodrick, "Optimising Employee Mental Health."

24. National Academies of Science, Engineering, and Medicine; National Academy of Medicine; Committee on Systems Approaches to Improve Patient Care by Supporting Clinician Well-Being. (2019). "Taking Action Against Clinical Burnout: A Systems Approach to Professional Well-Being." The National Academies Press. http://nap.edu/25521.

25. Lewis, A. (2012). *Why Nobody Believes the Numbers*. Hoboken, NJ: Wiley.

26. https://www.valuer.ai/blog/50-examples-of-corporations-that-failed-to-innovate-and-missed-their-chance.

27. https://www.cnbc.com/2021/08/29/amazons-biggest-hardest-to-solve-esg-issue-may-be-its-own-workers.html.

28. Ibid.

CHAPTER 10: COUNTING CULTURE: ASSESSING YOUR PROGRESS

1. Salpini, C. (2019). "'Behind Closed Doors': The Friction between the Nike Brand and Its Corporate Culture." *Retail Dive*, September 3. https://www.retaildive.com/news/behind-closed-doors-the-friction-between-the-nike-brand-and-its-corporat/561608/.

2. http://purpose.nike.com/worker-engagement.

3. https://s1.q4cdn.com/806093406/files/doc_downloads/2021/08/ Nike10k2021.pdf.

4. Benjamins, M. R., Hummer, R. A., Eberstein, I. W., and Nam, C. B. (2004). "Self-Reported Health and Adult Mortality Risk: An Analysis of Cause-Specific Mortality." *Social Science & Medicine,* 59: 1297–1306.

5. Friedman, R. (2014). *The Best Place to Work.* New York: Penguin Group.

6. http:comparably.com/awards/rules.

7. "Best Global Company Culture 2022." (2022). Comparably, March 29. https://www.comparably.com/news/best-global-company-culture-2022/.

8. http://fortune.com/company/cisco-systems/best-companies.

9. http://forbes.com/best-employers/#3d033ee0461b.

10. https://www.businesswire.com/news/home/20220214005108/en/Forbes-Names-Philips-a-Top-Place-to-Work-in-%E2%80%9CAmerica%E2%80%99s-Best-Employers-of-2022%E2%80%9D-Ranking.

11. PennWatch Editor. (2020). "91% of Americans Make New Year's Resolution Tied to Fitness, Health and Wellness." PennWatch, December 30.https://pennwatch.org/91-of-americans-make-new-years-resolution-tied-to-fitness-health-and-wellness/.

12. https://www.workstars.com/recognition-and-engagement-blog/2019/11/20/10-companies-getting-workplace-wellbeing-right/.

13. Institute for Productivity Studies, JHI. (2015). "Extraordinary Workplace Wellness Programs." YouTube, July 18. https://www.youtube.com/watch?v=s-QbV_OstxQ&t=60s.

14. Blake, A. (2021). "Hypertension Guide | Nearly Half of Americans Have Hypertension, Many Don't Know It, and Under Half Have It Under Control." Casana, June 11. https://casanacare.com/blog-and-news/hypertension-guide-nearly-half-of-americans-have-hypertension-and-only-half-of-those-with-hypertension-have-it-under-control/.

15. Wang, G., Zhang, Z., Ayala, C., Dunet, D. O., Fang, J., and George, M. G. (2015). "Cost of Hospitalization for Stroke Patients Aged 18–64 Years in the United States." *Journal of Stroke and Cerebrovascular Diseases,* 23 (5): 861–868. https://www.ncbi.nlm.nih.gov/pmc/articles/PMC4544732/.

16. Andrews, R. M. (2008). "The National Hospital Bill: The Most Expensive Conditions by Payer, 2006. Healthcare Cost and Utilization Project, Agency for Healthcare Research and Quality, September, p 7. https://www.hcup-us.ahrq.gov/reports/statbriefs/sb59.pdf.

17. Centers for Disease Control and Prevention. (2019). *CDC Worksite Health ScoreCard: An Assessment Tool to Promote Employee Health and Well-Being.* Atlanta: US Department of Health and Human Services. https://www.cdc.gov/workplacehealthpromotion/initiatives/healthscorecard/pdf/

CDC-Worksite-Health-ScoreCard-Manual-Updated-Jan-2019-FINAL-rev-508.pdf.

18. Safeer, R., Lucik, M., and Christel, K. (2021). "Using the CDC Worksite Health ScoreCard to Promote Organizational Change." *American Journal of Health Promotion,* 35 (7): 997–1001.

19. http://news.nike.com/news/nike-inc-fy21-impact-report.

20. http://goodonyou.eco/how-ethical-is-nike/.

21. http://comparably.com/companies/nike.

CHAPTER 11: DINNER IS SERVED

1. Cision. (2022). "Cisco Tops Fortune's 25th Annual 100 Best Companies to Work For List in 2022." *PR Newswire*, April 11. https://www.prnewswire.com/news-releases/cisco-tops-fortunes-25th-annual-100-best-companies-to-work-for-list-in-2022-301522364.html.

2. https://www.cisco.com/c/m/en_us/about/corporate-social-responsibility/2019/next-level.html.

3. Ors, R. (2021). "In Practice: How Cisco's Purpose and Culture Help Drive Employee Engagement and Well-being," Thomson Reuters. https://www.thomsonreuters.com/en-us/posts/legal/in-practice-stahlkopf-cisco-purpose-culture/.

4. https://www.cisco.com/c/m/en_us/about/corporate-social-responsibility/2019/next-level.html.

5. Ibid.

6. https://www.uctoday.com/collaboration/how-are-big-brands-tackling-wellbeing-issues-in-wfh-environments-cisco/.

7. Tindillere, R. (2018). "Back to Business: How Cisco Employees Are Supporting Each Other As They Return to Work." Cisco blog, October 9. https://blogs.cisco.com/wearecisco/back-to-business-how-cisco-employees-are-supporting-each-other-as-they-return-to-work.

8. https://www.crn.com/news/networking/cisco-employs-mandatory-work-from-home-policy-due-to-coronavirus.

9. https://www.cio.com/article/189097/cisco-opts-out-of-return-to-office-in-favor-of-individuals-and-teams-choosing-how-cisco-works.html.

10. https://blogs.cisco.com/news/expanding-well-being-care-beyond-our-employees-in-response-to-covid-19.

11. https://www.reuters.com/business/cisco-ceo-says-quarter-staff-ukraine-have-left-2022-03-01/.

12. https://www.prnewswire.com/news-releases/cisco-webex-powers-personal-well-being-higher-performing-teams-and-inclusive-collaboration-301259794.html.

13. https://www.inc.com/magazine/201511/paul-keegan/does-more-pay-mean-more-growth.html.

14. https://www.simplypsychology.org/maslow.html.

15. Bialowolski, P., Weziak-Bialowolski, D., Lee, M. T., Chen, Y., VanderWeele, T. J., and McNeely, E. (2021). "The Role of Financial Conditions for Physical and Mental Health. Evidence from a Longitudinal Survey and Insurance Claims Data." *Social Science & Medicine*, 281: 1–10.

16. Stewart, C. C., Yu, L., Lamar, M., Wilson, R. S., Bennett, D. A., and Boyle, P. A. (2020). "Associations of Health and Financial Literacy with Mortality in Advanced Age." *Aging Clinical and Experimental Research*, 32: 951–57.

17. A. Molarius, Berglund, K., Eriksson, C., Lambe, M., Norström, E., Eriksson, H. G., and Feldman, I. (2007). "Socioeconomic Conditions, Lifestyle Factors, and Self-Rated Health Among Men and Women in Sweden. *European Journal of Public Health*, 17: 125–133.

18. Ferreira, M. B., de Almeida, F., Soro, J. C., Herter, M. M., Pinto, D. C., and Silva, C. S. (2021). "On the Relation Between Over-Indebtedness and Well-Being: An Analysis of the Mechanisms Influencing Health, Sleep, Life Satisfaction, and Emotional Well-Being." *Frontiers in Psychology*, 12: 591875. https://www.frontiersin.org/articles/10.3389/fpsyg.2021.591875/full.

19. Israel, S., Caspi, A., Belsky, D. W., Harrington, H., Hogan, S., Houts, R., Ramrakha, S. Sanders, S., Poulton, R., and Moffitt, T. E. (2014). "Credit Scores, Cardiovascular Disease Risk, and Human Capital." *Proceedings of the National Academies of Science USA,* 111 (48): 7087–17092.

20. Bialowolski et al., "The Role of Financial Conditions for Physical and Mental Health."

21. Meisenzahl, M. (2021). "Costco Is Raising Starting Wages to $17 an Hour." *Insider,* October 26. https://www.businessinsider.com/costco-raising-wages-to-17-an-hour-2021-10.

22. Shaw, G. (2020). "Does Having a Sense of Purpose Improve Your Health?" *WebMD*, March 31. http://webmd.com/balance/features/senes-purpose-health.

23. Britannica, The Editors of Encyclopaedia. (2022). "Viktor Frankl." Encyclopedia Britannica, March 22. https://www.britannica.com/biography/Viktor-Frankl.

24. Crumbaugh, J., and Maholick, L. "An Experimental Study of Existentialism: The Psychometric Approach to Frankl's Concept of Noongenic Neurosis." *Journal of Clinical Psychology*, 20: 200–207.

25. Bilodeau, K. (2019). "Will a Purpose-Driven Life Help You Live Longer?" Harvard Health Publishing, November 28. https://www.health.harvard.edu/blog/will-a-purpose-driven-life-help-you-live-longer-2019112818378.

26. http://gallup.com/workplace/350060/people-best-performance-start-purpose.aspx.

27. http://news.gallup.com/poll/177191/world-faces-shortage-purpose.aspx.

28. Ibid.

29. "IBM's Culture of Health." https://www.ibm.com/ibm/responsibility/employee_well_being.shtml. Last accessed April 17, 2022.

30. https://www.ccl.org. Last accessed May 3, 2022.

31. O'Neill, K. (2020). "Steps You Can Take to Build a Resilient Organization." Center for Creative Leadership, September 16. https://www.ccl.org/articles/leading-effectively-articles/steps-you-can-take-to-build-a-resilient-organization/.

32. "Healthy at Hopkins, Support in Action." (2022). YouTube, July 5. https://www.youtube.com/watch?v=NRPp16JEKxc&t=15s.

33. "Working Well: A Global Survey of Workforce Wellbeing Strategies, Executive Summary." (2016). Xerox, October. https://www.globalhealthyworkplace.org/casestudies/2016_Global_Wellbeing_Survey_Executive-Summary.pdf.

34. http://ibm.com/ibm/responsibility/employee_well_being.shtml.

35. Fisher, J., and Phillips, A. (2021). *Working Better Together, How to Cultivate Strong Relationships to Maximize Well-Being and Boost Bottom Lines*. New York: McGraw-Hill.

ABOUT THE AUTHOR

RICHARD SAFEER, MD, Earned his BS in Nutritional Biochemistry at Cornell University under the tutelage of T. Colin Campbell, author of the China Study, before attending medical school at State University of New York at Buffalo, where he graduated Magna Cum Laude. Today, Dr. Safeer is the Chief Medical Director of Employee Health and Well-Being at Johns Hopkins Medicine. He is a regular speaker at conferences on the topic of building a culture of health and well-being and has published numerous journal articles on the topic. He taught the inaugural graduate-level course, "Organizational Health," at American University.

After graduating from medical school, Dr. Safeer devoted his career to helping people achieve overall wellness and helping organizations support health and well-being. He first practiced family medicine and then joined the faculty at The George Washington University, in the department of Family Medicine, eventually serving as residency director. He left academia to become Medical Director of an occupational health center and then Wellness Director for the Mid-Atlantic region of the parent company, Concentra Medical Centers. In 2005, he joined CareFirst BlueCross BlueShield in Baltimore, Maryland, as the Medical Director of Preventive Medicine. He has been credited by some for bringing wellness into the realm of responsibilities of the managed care industry and led CareFirst BCBS to be among the first cohort of health plans to be accredited for Wellness by the National Committee for Quality Assurance.

Dr. Safeer holds faculty appointments in both the Johns Hopkins University School of Medicine and the Bloomberg School of Public Health. He is a fellow of the American Academy of Family Practice, the American College of Lifestyle Medicine (where he served on the board), and the American College of Preventive Medicine. He is on the *New England Journal of Medicine* Catalyst Insight Council.

He lives in Columbia, Maryland, with his wife and daughter. His two sons are in college. Dr. Safeer has hiked and camped in the Andes, Alaska, Australia, and across the United States. He enjoys swimming, tennis, and bicycling, and just about any activity that helps keep the love handles from coming back.

If you want to learn more about Dr. Safeer and how to shape a well-being culture in your workplace, visit him at RichardSafeer.com.

INDEX

235